ILLUSTRATED
WORLD OF
THE BIBLE
LIBRARY

ILLUSTRATED

WORLD OF

LIBRARY

McGRAW-HILL BOOK COMPANY, INC.

THE BIBLE

3. THE LATTER PROPHETS

NEW YORK · TORONTO · LONDON

First published in Jerusalem — Ramat-Gan, Israel,
under the title, VIEWS OF THE BIBLICAL WORLD: Volume 3

41169

PRINTED IN ISRAEL

IN preparing this third volume of "Illustrated World of the Bible Library", which contains the books of the Latter Prophets, the editors have again been guided by the principles on which the first two volumes were based. For a full description and explanation of these principles the reader is referred to the introductions to these earlier volumes.

The books of the Latter Prophets cover a period of about four hundred years, from the apogee of the Assyrian empire down to almost the end of Persian domination. The period opens with Judah and Israel enjoying political power and economic prosperity under Uzziah and Jeroboam II, the son of Joash; it includes the destruction first of Samaria, and then of Jerusalem, with the consequent deportations of their inhabitants; and it ends with the Return to Zion and the national revival in the early days of the Second Temple. These four hundred years saw the development of literary prophecy in Israel, from Amos and Hosea, the first of the prophets, to Haggai, Zechariah and Malachi who were the last of the inspired band. The historical record of the first part of this period is contained in the Second Book of Kings and the Second Book of Chronicles, and that of its latter stage in Ezra-Nehemiah.

These books present the events in a chronological, though incomplete, sequence, in contrast to the works of the Latter Prophets, where the various references and allusions to these same events occur in no fixed chronological order and are coloured by the personal conceptions of the individual prophet.

The greater part of the Latter Prophets is made up of disconnected sermons and oracles which were later put together and edited by the prophet or his disciples, not necessarily in their correct historical sequence. The aim of the Latter Prophets was to show their contemporaries the deeper causes of the events of the time, to castigate their iniquities, to instruct them in the Law and provide them with moral guidance, and to proclaim the vision of the Messianic age. Hence, throughout the prophetical books chapters of rebuke alternate with passages of consolation, both together embodying the prophet's view of the essential process of history underlying the derivative individual events. Each of the prophets has his own distinct, intensely personal style: there is here none of the stylistic uniformity that marks the historiographical books of the Bible.

The message of the Latter Prophets is only partly concerned with the transitory events of their own times in the fields of politics and warfare. Their preoccupation with social justice, their hatred of the rich grinding the faces of the poor, and their detestation of all types of moral laxity are features of more lasting interest, as lapses in the social and moral field are unfortunately not limited to any particular period. But the eternal value of the prophets of Israel lies undoubtedly in the field of religion. It was they who first insisted in Israel on the replacement of the vain pomp of sacrifices with the contrition of a repenting sinner, placing the individual in direct relation with his God; it was they who demanded that instead of the clannish worship of former ages there should be recognition of the universality of the one God, before whom all other deities were but empty idols; and it was they who first drew the eschatological picture of the eternal reign of justice, peace and mercy — not only for Man but for all Nature — in the Messianic era to come. These lofty ideals are stated in a language of exalted beauty, which has served as an inspiration to poets and writers in succeeding generations.

This special character of the prophetical books made the preparation of an illustrated commentary on them a peculiarly difficult undertaking. The ideological contents and highly individual style of these books, not to mention the special nature of the prophetic vision, are hardly amenable to visual presentation. Fortunately, however, some help can be obtained from the fact that, in most cases, the prophet's words are prompted by contemporary historical events the record of which has sometimes been preserved in the documents or art of the peoples of the ancient East. Thus, the remains of the cultures of Israel's closest neighbours — Edom, Moab and Ammon — and of the great empires of Egypt, Assyria and Babylon have provided us with important material illustrative of the words of the prophets. This material is particularly relevant to the explanation of the prophecies against the nations and of those passages in the prophetical books where the reader is transported to foreign lands.

The cultures of the ancient Orient are thus a rich source of illustration for the books of the earlier prophets. For parts of the Latter Prophets, they are supplemented by the newer civilizations of the Greeks and Scythians, and above all by the culture of Persia which has left its imprint on the prophets of the early days of the Second Temple — Haggai, Zechariah and Malachi.

Moreover, since the prophet's words are addressed directly to his contemporaries, he uses the forms of expressions best suited to bringing home to his hearers the essentials of his teaching. Hence the frequent occurrence in the prophetical books of symbolical acts, and also of figures of speech and proverbs rooted in the physical nature of the country and in the daily habits of the Israelite of those times, whether town-dweller or countryman, rich or poor, educated or ignorant. This has enabled us to enrich our visual commentary with pictures illustrating the Palestinian landscape and the animal and plant life of Palestine and the neighbouring countries, together with the various crafts practised at the time and the daily activities of the population. Sometimes the figure employed by the prophet goes back to an ancient literary tradition the echoes of which can also be heard in non-Israelite poetry. In such cases, parallel passages have been quoted from the literatures of the peoples of the ancient East, especially from the early Canaanite epics. In choosing our material we have been guided by the saying of the Jewish sages that "no two prophets prophesy in the same style" *(Bab. Tal. Sanhedrin, 89a)*. We have accordingly tried to bring out, as far as possible, the distinctive character of each book as it emerges from its inner spirit, its principal themes and its typical symbolism, in addition to illustrating the physical setting of the particular prophet and his time.

CREDITS

The third volume of "Illustrated World of the Bible Library" has been prepared by the same editorial team as the second volume: Prof. Michael Avi-Yonah, Dr. Abraham Malamat and Dr. Shemaryahu Talmon.

Once again the Editors are glad to acknowledge their indebtedness to the members of the Editorial Board, of the Editorial Advisory Council, and to the Assistants (whose names appear on the front page of this volume) and particularly to Dr. Menahem Haran and Dr. Haim Tadmor, two of the editors of the fourth volume, for their assistance in the editing of the commentaries on Ezekiel and The Twelve Minor Prophets.

We also wish to thank all those who have helped us in obtaining the reproductions or have given us the benefit of their comments on the text: Prof. W. F. Albright of Baltimore; Dr. R. D. Barnett of London; Prof. N. Glueck of Cincinnati; Prof. A. Parrot and Prof. C.F.A. Schaeffer of Paris; Prof. G. E. Wright of Boston; Father R. North, S.J., of the Pontifical Biblical Institute of Jerusalem; Mr. R. W. Hamilton of Oxford; Dr. M. Dothan, Prof. M. Stekelis and Mr. S. J. Schweig of Jerusalem.

We further wish to express our appreciation to all those distinguished public figures, both in Israel and abroad, who have given this project their whole-hearted support from the outset, and above all to H.E. the President of Israel, Mr. Izhak Ben-Zvi; the Prime Minister, Mr. David Ben-Gurion; the former Minister of Education and Culture, Mr. Z. Aranne; and the Minister of the Interior, Mr. M. H. Shapira.

Once again it is our pleasant duty to thank the Israel Ministry for Foreign Affairs, the Ministry of Education and Culture, the Ministry of Commerce and Industry, the Ministry of Finance, and the Ministry of Defence, as well as the Jewish Agency and "Malben" for their encouragement and ready assistance.

We also wish to thank all the museums, individuals and photographers that helped us in obtaining the plates required. Those in Israel include the staff and librarians of the Archaeology Department of the Hebrew University; the Department of Antiquities (museum and library) of the Ministry of Education, and its former director, Prof. S. Yeivin; the National and University Library, Jerusalem; the Haaretz Museum, Tel-Aviv; the James de Rothschild Expedition at Hazor; the collection of A. Reifenberg, Jerusalem; the Shrine of the Book, Jerusalem; the Tell Qasile Collection, Tel-Aviv; the Pontifical Biblical Institute, Jerusalem. Contributions from abroad have been provided by the Metropolitan Museum, New York; the Oriental Institute of the University of Chicago; the Archaeological Expedition at Samaria; the Archaeological Expedition to Dura-Europus; the Museum of Fine Arts, Boston; the University Museum, Philadelphia; the Brooklyn Museum; the Balti-

13

more Museum; the Pierpont Morgan Library, New York; the Yale University Museum; the British Museum, London; the Ashmolean Museum, Oxford; the Royal Scottish Museum, Edinburgh; the Hittite Museum, Ankara; the Museum of the Ancient Orient, Istanbul; the Staatliche Museen, Berlin; the Louvre, Paris; the Cabinet des Médailles, Paris; the Rijksmuseum von Oudheden, Leiden; the Torino Museum; the Marburg and Alinari photographic collections.

The Editorial Board also wishes to thank the following authors, editors and publishers for their kind permission to use plates published by them: W. F. Albright, W. Andrae, N. Avigad, D. Baldi, R. D. Barnett, P. Berger, A. M. Blackman, H. Bonnet, E. Douglas van Buren, M. Burrows, E. Chiera, Ch. Chipiez, F. M. Cross, G. Dalman, W. R. Dawson, N. de G. Davies, A. Deimel, J. Dossin, M. Dunand, G. R. Driver, A. Erman, C. S. Fisher, H. Frankfort, A. Furman, S. J. Gadd, K. Galling, A. H. Gardiner, P. C. Gau, A. J. Gayet, H. Gressmann, H. Grimme, L. H. Grollenberg, U. Hölscher, L. Klebs, S. N. Kramer, P. Lemaire, A. Lhote, G. Loud, D. G. Lyon, R. A. S. Macalister, M. J. L. Mallowan, Ch. McCown, B. Meissner, A. Mekhiterian, J. T. Milik, P. Montet, S. Moscati, H. H. Nelson, P. E. Newberry, J. Nougayrol, A. T. Olmstead, M. Oppenheim, M. Pallottino, R. A. Parker, A. Parrot, A. T. Peet, G. Perrot, W. M. Flinders Petrie, K. Pflüger, W. Phillips, H. Ranke, G. A. Reisner, P. Rost, A. Rowe, H. W. P. Saggs, A. H. Sayce, C. F. A. Schaeffer, H. Schmökel, O. Schröder, C. Schumacher, W. Stevenson-Smith, C. Steuernagel, E. L. Sukenik, F. Thureau-Dangin, J. Trever, O. Tufnell, N. H. Tur-Sinai, B. Ubach, C. Watzinger, R. Weill, M. Werbrouck, J. G. Wilkinson, H. E. Winlock, L. Woolley, W. Wreszinski, G. E. Wright;

American Schools of Oriental Research, E. J. Brill, Ltd., British Museum, British School of Archaeology in Iraq, F. A. Brockhaus, Constable & Co., W. de Gruyter & Co., Editions Cahiers d'Art, Editions Ides et Calendes, Egypt Exploration Fund, Egypt Exploration Society, Folkswang Verlag, Fondation égyptologique Reine Elizabeth,

M. P. Geuthner, V. Gollancz, Hachette, Harvard University Press, J. C. Hinrichs, Imprimerie nationale, G. Klipper, Marietti, Metropolitan Museum, J. C. B. Mohr-Paul Siebeck, Monestir de Montserrat, John Murray Ltd., Oriental Institute — University of Chicago, Oxford University Press, Palestine Exploration Fund, Penguin Books, Ltd., Presses universitaires de France, Routledge & Kegan Paul, Ltd., Ferdinand Schöningh, A. Skira, Society of Antiquaries, University Museum — University of Pennsylvania, The Trustees of the Late Sir Henry S. Wellcome, Yale University Press.

In addition we have availed ourselves of the comprehensive studies of A. H. Layard and P. E. Botta. The photographs in Israel were taken mainly by Z. Kluger, B. Rotenberg and A. Allon. Use has also been made of photographs taken by M. Baram, A. Volk, A. Tal and J. Lister. Finally, we express our warm appreciation to the management and workers of the Schwitter A.G., Zürich; to the A. Levin-Epstein Ltd. Press, Bat-Yam; to the Haaretz Press Ltd., Tel-Aviv; to the Hakorech Binders' Cooperative, Holon (supported by "Malben"); and to the Tel-Aviv Bindery — for their care and devotion in making the plates, setting up the text, and printing and binding this volume.

The English translation of the biblical text used in this publication is mainly that of the *Revised Standard Version of the Bible,* copyrighted 1946 and 1952 by the Division of Christian Education, National Council of Churches, and used by permission.

THE EDITORS

ISAIAH

THE vision of Isaiah the son of Amoz, which he saw concerning Judah and Jerusalem in the days of Uzziah, Jotham, Ahaz, and Hezekiah, kings of Judah.　　　　　(Isaiah 1 : 1)

The plate on the right is a reproduction of the first column of the complete scroll of Isaiah which was discovered in 1947, in one of the caves of Oumran in the Judean desert, close to the shore of the Dead Sea. The scroll was written in the second or first cent. B.C., and is thus the oldest known complete manuscript of a book of the Old Testament. It is now in "The Shrine of the Book" on the campus of the Hebrew University, Jerusalem.

I̶T shall come to pass in the latter days that the mountain of the house of the LORD shall be established as the highest of the mountains . . .

(Isaiah 2 : 2)

Isaiah the son of Amoz uttered his prophecies in the dark days when the kingdom of Judah was threatened with conquest by the armies of Assyria (see pp. 35, 63). Even in the midst of Jerusalem's political eclipse, the prophet foresaw its future greatness as God's Holy City. At the heart of his prophecy stands his vision of the nations congregating on the Temple Mount (cf. Mic. 4 : 1-5), a vision which is the starting point of the whole later prophetic conception of the millennium and a true expression of Jewish universalism. Such was the influence of this prophecy that the vision of the Temple Mount became a symbol of the everlasting peace (cf. Hos. 2 : 18; Ps. 46 : 9) for which all the nations will long.

The Temple Mount is the northern part of the more easterly of the two hills on which ancient Jerusalem was built (see Vol. II, p. 220). This part of the city-area was developed mainly in the reign of Solomon, who chose it as the site of his Temple and of the adjacent royal palace and its treasuries. The spur of the Temple Mount is bounded on three sides by deep watercourses: on the east by the Kidron Valley, on the south by the Valley of Hinnom, and on the west by the central valley that separates the spur from the western hill. Above is a photographic view of the Temple Mount as it appears to-day within the wall which surrounds the Old City of Jerusalem. In the centre of the photograph is the Dome of the Rock, built over the "Foundation-Rock". This, according to a late tradition, is the rock that formed the threshing floor of Araunah (see Vol. II, p. 198) on Mount Moriah, the site of Solomon's Temple (2 Chron. 3 : 1).

AND the people will oppress one another, every man his fellow and every man his neighbour, the youth will be insolent to the elder, and the base fellow to the honourable.

(Isaiah 3 : 5)

The religious and moral decline of Judah in the reigns of Ahaz and Hezekiah is revealed in Isaiah's descriptions of the dissolution of the bonds of society, resulting from the breakdown of the social hierarchy in which every individual had his appointed place and function. Slaves usurped authority, because "the mighty man and the soldier, the judge and the prophet" (Isa. 3 : 2) were no more; youths treated their elders with scorn, thus transgressing the commandment to "honour the face of an old man" which was one of the primary ordinances of the Mosaic Law (Lev. 19 : 32), as indeed it is still, to this day, one of the foundations of oriental society. Similar descriptions of social chaos and administrative disorganization have been found in the admonitions of Ipuwer, an Egyptian moralist, who lived in the period of anarchy between the Old and Middle Kingdoms (end of the third millennium B.C.): "Why, all the maidservants unbridle their tongues. When the ladies speak, it is burdensome to the servants . . . A thing has been done the like of which has not happened for a long time: the king has been taken away by paupers . . . Behold now, matters have come to such a pass that the land is despoiled of the kingship by a few irresponsible men . . . Behold, noble ladies glean (in the field) and noblemen are in the workhouse. But he who never even slept on a plank is now the owner of a bed . . . No palace is left standing; they are all become like a frightened flock of sheep without a shepherd . . ."

Reproduced below is a papyrus fragment of Ipuwer's admonitions in a copy from the time of the Nineteenth or Twentieth Dynasty (13th-12th cent. B.C.).

IN that day the LORD will take away the finery of the anklets, the headbands, and the crescents.

(Isaiah 3 : 18)

Isaiah upbraids the ostentatiousness of the women of Jerusalem whose passion for material comfort and magnificent personal adornment drives their fathers and husbands to amass ill-gotten wealth, pervert justice, and oppress the poor (Isa. 3 : 12-15; cf. Amos 4 : 1). Since the conduct of these women is hastening the downfall of Jerusalem, they will be the first to suffer from its destruction. The long list of jewels and ornaments given here by the prophet is the most detailed in the Old Testament and is the source of the Talmudic expression "the twenty four jewels of the bride." Its purpose is to indicate the full extent of contemporary luxury in Judah. Only a few of the ornaments listed can be accurately identified. The names of some of them are found only here in the Old Testament.

The picture on the right is a reproduction of a piece of gold jewellery from Megiddo (first part of the Late Bronze Age) which is usually identified with the "pendant" *(netifa)* of Isa. 3 : 19. On the left is a gold ornament of the type known from its shape as a "crescent" (Heb. *saharon),* from the end of the Bronze Age. This particular example, with its granulated metal-work and falcon's head in the centre, was found at Tell el-Ajjul, ancient Beth Eglayim.

INSTEAD of perfume there will be rottenness . . . and instead of well-set hair, baldness . . .

(Isaiah 3 : 24)

The destruction of Jerusalem will be followed by poverty and destitution. The pampered women of the city will be stripped of their gorgeous raiment and jewellery, either to mark their mourning and lamentation (Amos 8 : 10), or because the conquering foe will take them off into exile bare-footed and with heads shorn (Isa. 3 : 17). The Israelite woman, like other oriental women, especially those of the upper classes, paid no less careful attention to her coiffure (cf. Vol. II, p. 267) than she did to her dress and adornment (see p. 22). Just as unkempt, neglected hair was a sign of humiliation and enslavement (Isa. 47 : 2), so, conversely, an elegant, well-tended coiffure was a mark of nobility and honour. Country women were apparently in the habit of letting their locks fall down over their shoulders (Song of Sol. 4 : 1; 6 : 5), whereas the ladies of the city used to bind up their hair, curling and fixing its ends until their coiffure was "well set", *(maaseh miqsheh),* as described in our verse. This fashion was certainly imported into Israel from foreign lands, (indeed, this use of the Hebrew word *miqsheh* to describe hair-style is unique in the Old Testament). An illustration of the fashion is provided by a terra cotta bust of a woman which comes from Spain, dating to the 5th or 4th cent. B.C., the period of Phoenician expansion (left plate). The woman's hair is swept upwards in Greek style and enclosed in a mitre-shaped headdress the ends of which hang down over her shoulders. A formal hair-set is also found on the statuettes of the goddess Ashtoreth which have been discovered in Palestine (see right plate; and cf. the right plate on p. 34).

I<small>T</small> will be for a shade by day from the heat . . . (Isaiah 4 : 6)

It is in the manner of the prophet Isaiah to conclude his grim prophecies of divine retribution with words of comfort and future hope to "the tenth", the remnant of Judah which will be left after God has purged away the sinners from His people (cf. pp. 28-29). These few survivors from Judah and Jerusalem will be the seed from which will grow "the branch of the Lord", a new people, prosperous and multiplying, watched over and protected by God, as a vineyard is guarded by its owner.

Isaiah, as a native of Jerusalem, was well acquainted with the work done in the vineyards that abounded on the slopes of the Judean hills and with the habits of their owners (see p. 25). It was therefore natural for him to describe God's protection of His people by the metaphor of the booth (sukkah) which the vine-grower puts up in his vineyard to protect himself and his workers from the burning rays of the sun. When the fruit begins to ripen in the cucumber-field and in the vineyard, the farmer and vine-grower take increased precautions to guard their property from theft, and watch is kept at all hours of the day and night. To provide protection from the sun's heat, which is at its greatest at this season of the year (Song of Sol. 1 : 6), it is customary to fix poles in the ground and on them to erect a temporary structure made of interlacing branches (see the picture) or covered with mats. Such a booth is at once a shady retreat and a raised look-out post for the watchman (cf. Job 27 : 18). It also serves as a "lodge" (Isa. 1 : 8) which provides shelter from the dew at night. At the end of the grape-gathering, the booth is abandoned to be washed away piecemeal in the rainy season.

H E digged it and cleared it of stones, and planted it with choice vines . . .   (Isaiah 5 : 2)

In the song of the vineyard, the prophet Isaiah presents a parable of Israel's betrayal of its God, using metaphors that were immediately intelligible to his hearers. The picture drawn by him is that of a vine-grower who prepared a piece of land on a hill-slope ("he digged it"; see p. 26), removed the stones from it ("and cleared it of stones"), and piled them up as walls at the sides of his plot (Prov. 24 : 30-31) to protect the vineyard from damage by farm animals and wild beasts (Song of Sol. 2 : 15). The stones were also used in the building of watch-towers, and especially in the construction of walls in the steeply sloping parts of the vineyard to prevent soil-erosion. The terraces thus formed became level shelves of soil suitable for the planting of vines. After the vine-grower had cleared the ground for his vineyard, he planted there the best strain of vine (Jer. 2 : 21). However, in spite of all its owner's careful tending, the vineyard belied its promise and produced only inedible wild grapes.
Photographed here is a hill-slope in Upper Galilee, near Beth-Gan, which has been cleared for vine-planting. The stone walls fencing off the terraces stand out in a setting of rocky, uncleared terrain. Some of the terraces have already been planted with vines.

I WILL make it a waste;
it shall not be pruned or
hoed . . .   (Isaiah 5 : 6)

In his parable, Isaiah likens God, in His love for Israel, to the vine-grower who tended his vineyard in the hope of being rewarded for his pains. When Israel belied its promise God, regretting the favour He had shown His people, acted like the vine-grower who, despairing of his vineyard, breaks down its walls and abandons it to be trampled on by farm animals and wild beasts (Isa. 5 : 5). The cultivated soil thus reverts to being waste land (Heb. *batah*).

The Hebrew word *batah,* which occurs only here in the Old Testament, means barren land which produces only sparse herbage and is unsuitable for growing crops and fruit-trees. Poor soil of this kind comes into being in forest areas which have been cleared by the inhabitants, or where the trees have become stunted as a result of their branches being nibbled away by the unchecked grazing of herds of goats. The unprotected soil is then eroded away down to the substratum of rock by the action of wind and torrential rain. Only wild plants of little value to man can grow on this kind of waste land, such as the thorny burnet *(Poterium spinosum L.;* see the photograph above), the branches of which were used as fuel (Eccles. 7 : 6); and the thyme *(Thymus capitatus [L.] Lk. et Hoffm.).*

A BOVE him stood the seraphim; each had six wings: with two he covered his face, and with two he covered his feet, and with two he flew. (Isaiah 6 : 2)

It was in the year of King Uzziah's death that Isaiah had that vision of the divine throne which, in the opinion of the ancient Jewish sages and of modern scholars alike, marks the beginning of his prophetic activity. The prophet presumably received this mystic insight while standing before the Temple in Jerusalem, the interior of which seemed to him to be filled with the train of God's vestments. The whole setting of the vision, with its suggestion of a court sitting in judgment, resembles the divine revelation granted to Micaiah the son of Imlah (1 Kings 22 : 19-22; cf. Job 1 : 6). Above God's throne hover seraphim who proclaim the holiness of the Lord of Hosts (cf. Ps. 29 : 1; 103 : 20-21). This is the only place in the Old Testament where the seraphim are mentioned as part of the heavenly host. Each one is depicted as having six wings; two for flying, two to cover its feet — just as in Ezekiel's chariot-vision the living creatures (Ezek. 1 : 11) covered their bodies with two of their wings — and two to cover its face, since the glory of the Divine Presence is too terrible to behold (cf. Ex. 3 : 6; 1 Kings 19 : 13).

Figures of this kind with four wings (Ezek. 1 : 6; cf. Vol. I, p. 22), or six, are represented in the art of the ancient East. Reproduced here is a relief of the tenth or ninth cent. B.C. from Gozan (Tell Halaf) depicting a six-winged creature. The two wings with which it flies grow out of its shoulders and the other four out of its loins. It holds a staff in either hand and has a horned crown on its head.

AND though a tenth remain in it, it will be burned again, like a terebinth or an oak, whose stump remains standing when it is felled.

(Isaiah 6 : 13)

The destiny of the nation of Israel which, though again and again overrun by its foes and its people killed or exiled, always regains its former strength, is likened by Isaiah to the life-cycle of the terebinth and oak, the common forest-trees of Palestine. The application of the parable is two-fold. Though lopped by wood-cutters and its branches thrown to the ground (cf. Ezek. 19 : 12), the tree is still capable of growing new branches after a time. Again, though the tree sheds its leaves at the end of the summer, its trunk and branches remain, to clothe themselves again with fresh foliage in the next year. In just the same way will the remnant of Israel, the surviving tenth, burgeon once more when God's wrath has abated.

The terebinth (Heb. *elah)* mentioned here by Isaiah is the Palestinian terebinth *(Pistacia palaestina Boiss.),* commonly found in stony soil and scrub, which is the only deciduous variety of the various kinds of terebinth indigenous to Palestine (see the photograph of its branches on p. 29; and cf. p. 209). In the winter it is bare of foliage, but in the spring it is covered with young leaves of a reddish colour. The oak mentioned here is the oak of Tabor *(Quercus ithaburensis Boiss.),* the more common of the two kinds of deciduous oak found in Palestine (seen leafless in the photograph on p. 28; cf. Vol. I, p. 92). This sturdy, shapely tree, which is commonly found growing in scrub and woodland, sheds its leaves at the end of the summer and sprouts fresh leaves at the beginning of the spring.

BECAUSE Aram, with
Ephraim and the son of
Remaliah, has devised evil
against you, saying, "Let
us go up against Judah and
terrify it, and let us conquer it for ourselves, and
set up the son of Tabeal as
king in the midst of it."
(Isaiah 7 : 5-6)

In 734 B.C. Syria and the kingdom of Israel (Ephraim) formed a military alliance against Tiglath-Pileser III, the Assyrian monarch, and pressed Ahaz, the king of Judah, to join them (see Vol. II, p. 282). When he refused, they advanced upon Jerusalem (2 Kings 16 : 5; Isa. 7 : 1) with the intention of deposing Ahaz and placing the son of Tabeal on the throne in his stead. Who this "son of Tabeal" was and where he came from is not at all certain. It would appear that he was the head of an aristocratic family named Tobel (in Aramaic Tabel; the biblical form of the name, Tabeal = "good-for-nothing", may simply be a mocking distortion). This family, though perhaps related to the Davidic dynasty, may have opposed the pro-Assyrian policy of Ahaz and favoured an alliance with Pekah, the king of Ephraim. Further information about the name Ben Tabel and about the man's origin has now been provided by an Assyrian letter discovered at Calah (the modern Nimrud). The letter (reproduced above on the right), which was sent by a royal official to the Assyrian king, contains a reference to "the land of Tabel" on the eastern side of the Jordan, to the west of Rabbath-Ammon (see the map). The writer mentions the emissary of Aianur, the ruler of the land of Tabel, who is bringing a despatch to the king of Assyria, informing him that people from the territory of Gader have made a raid into Moab and killed the inhabitants of a Moabite city. From this it may be inferred that the ruler of the land of Tabel held a position of importance in the administration of the Assyrian province of Trans-Jordan. The son of Tabel may well have been one of the ancestors of the Tobiads who ruled beyond the Jordan in the times of the Second Temple (Neh. 13 : 7; Josephus, Antiquities xii.4).

WITH bow and arrows men will come there, for all the land will be briers and thorns.

(Isaiah 7 : 24)

Isaiah prophesies that the revolt of Syria and Ephraim will fail and that the Assyrian armies will lay the country waste. Large tracts of cultivated land will be abandoned (cf. Isa. 32 : 13; and see p. 26). While some of the fallow land will make good pasture (Isa. 7 : 25), the rest will be overgrown with briers, thorns and thickets (cf. Isa. 9 : 18; 10 : 17), which will provide lairs for beasts of prey such as the bear and lion, and thus be a constant menace to man and his domestic animals (cf. 2 Kings 2 : 24; 17 : 26). Hunters will then come to these areas to hunt the wild beasts. Although hunting is not often mentioned in the Old Testament (see Gen. 25 : 27; Lev. 17 : 13; Jer. 16 : 16; and cf. Vol. I p. 74), it is known to have been popular in antiquity, especially in aristocratic circles. Representations of the hunt, particularly of kings hunting wild animals from their chariots, are a common feature of the art of the ancient East. In hilly regions, like those of central Palestine, hunting was done on foot and the hunter's weapon was the long-range bow.

The picture above is a reproduction of a basalt Hittite relief, found in the palace-gateway at Alaça-Huyük (from the beginning of the second half of the second millennium B.C.). It shows a kneeling bowman aiming an arrow at a wild boar which is charging at him. In the lower half of the relief another bowman, the details of whose figure have been obliterated, is shooting at a stag.

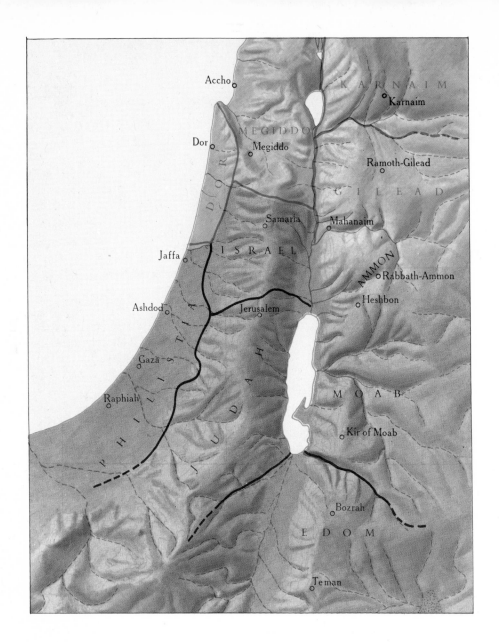

IN the former time he brought into contempt the land of Zebulun and the land of Naphtali, but in the latter time he will make glorious the way of the sea, the land beyond the Jordan, Galilee of the nations.   (Isaiah 9 : 1)

In the verse above, Isaiah is referring to the results of Tiglath-Pileser III's military campaigns against the kingdom of Israel, after the latter had joined Damascus and other neighbouring kingdoms in an attempt to throw off Assyrian overlordship (see p. 30). In 733 Tiglath-Pileser marched westwards, advanced on Damascus, capital of Aram, sacked its dependent cities and laid siege to the capital itself. It is quite possible that, on this campaign ("in the former time"), he also invaded Israel and carried off some of the population of Zebulun and Naphtali into exile.

In 732 Tiglath-Pileser completed his suppression of the revolt. The kingdom of Aram-Damascus was broken up, once and for all, into Assyrian provinces. The kingdom of Israel was also conquered by the Assyrian monarch who deposed Pekah the son of Remaliah from his throne and exiled many of the inhabitants to prevent any repetition of the revolts (see Vol. II, pp. 280-281). Tiglath-Pileser lopped off large tracts of territory from the Israelite kingdom, leaving virtually only the mountains of Ephraim under the control of the puppet-king appointed by him, Hosea the son of Elah. The districts detached from Israel were made into provinces of the Assyrian empire, following the regular Assyrian policy in such cases. The province of "Dor", named after its principal city the site of which is a tell near the village of Tantura, comprised the coastal plain which is called by Isaiah "the way of the sea", on account of the international artery of communication which ran along it. The province of "Megiddo" extended over the Valley of Jezreel and over Galilee, here and in other passages in the Old Testament called "Galilee of the nations" (see Vol. II, p. 80). Tiglath-Pileser may also at this time have conquered those areas of Trans-Jordan which were part of the kingdom of Israel (cf. 1 Chron. 5 : 6) and made them into the province of "Gilead" (see the map).

FOR the yoke of his burden,
and the staff for his shoulder,
the rod of his oppressor, thou
hast broken as on the day of
Midian.   (Isaiah 9 : 4)

The description of the captive's lot in terms of the yoke in which the farm animal labours is common in the Old Testament, especially where the reference is to the enslavement of Israel to the great powers of the ancient world, Egypt (Lev. 26 : 13), Assyria (Isa. 10 : 27) and Babylon (Jer. 27 : 1-8). The yoke was usually made of wood (Jer. 28 : 13; see p. 125). But occasionally, as may be inferred from the poetical language of the Old Testament, it was also made, wholly or in part, of metal (Jer. ibid.; Deut. 28 : 48). The prophet's words give us a reliable picture of what actually used to happen in those countries where prisoners-of-war were set to work, like animals, at back-breaking tasks, called in Hebrew *sebel* (= "heavy burden", Ex. 1 : 11; cf. Vol. I, p. 128) or *mas obed* (= forced labour, Gen. 49 : 15). This reality is frequently depicted in the art of the ancient East. For example, the Assyrian relief from Dur-Sharruken (the modern Khorsabad), reproduced here, clearly shows captives straining in the yoke, as they drag heavy burdens under the watchful eye of a taskmaster (middle of the second row from the top). The part of the yoke which rests on the shoulders was called the shoulder-bar (*matteh ha-shekhem*). Isaiah likens the liberation of Israel from its Assyrian bondage to the breaking of a yoke and the lifting of a burden from the shoulders (Isa. 10 : 27; 14 : 25).

Shall I not do to Jerusalem and her idols as I
have done to Samaria and her images?

(Isaiah 10 : 11)

The threatening utterance against Jerusalem by the king of
Assyria, whom the prophet does not explicitly name, must
have been made after the capture and destruction of Samaria by
Shalmaneser V in the year 722 B.C. (see Vol. II, p. 283), and
even after the capture of Carchemish (Isa. 10 : 9) by his successor, Sargon II, in 717. The Assyrians used to boast of the
victories of their kings over their enemies, of the capture of the
gods of the vanquished nations (see Vol. II, p. 289) and of the
destruction of their temples (cf. p. 66). As they had done to the
idol-worshipping kingdoms and also to Samaria, so they proposed to do to Jerusalem, whose God was regarded by the
Assyrian monarch as just another pagan deity.
The plates above are reproductions of clay Israelite idols found
at Samaria and dating to the 8th cent. B.C., i.e. roughly the
time of the city's destruction. They apparently represent pagan
gods.

THEY have crossed over Maabarah, at Geba they lodge for the night; Ramah trembles, Gibeah of Saul has fled. Cry aloud, O daughter of Gallim! Hearken, O Laishah! Answer her, O Anathoth! Madmenah is in flight, the inhabitants of Gebim flee for safety. This very day he will halt at Nob, he will shake his fist at the mount of the daughter of Zion, the hill of Jerusalem.

(Isaiah 10 : 29-32)

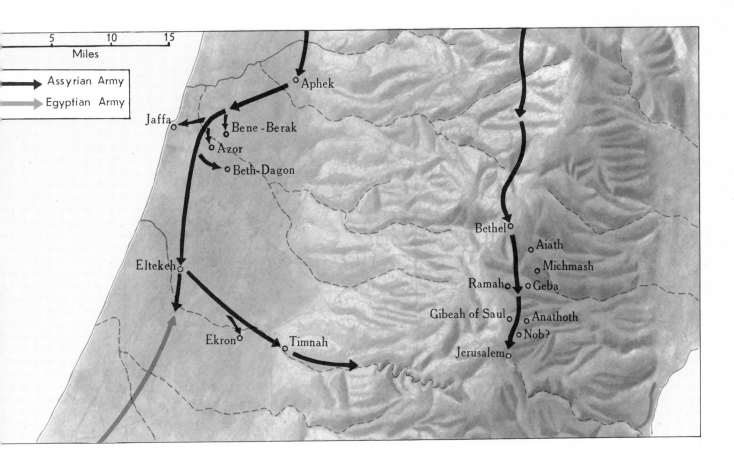

Undeterred by the warnings and threats of the Assyrians, Hezekiah, the king of Judah, allied himself with the states that had risen in revolt against the Assyrian ruler Sennacherib. As a result, the Assyrian army advanced on Jerusalem, probably in two converging columns. The annals of Sennacherib state that his army marched along the coastal plain through Benei Beraq, Azor and Beth-Dagon, and on to Eltekeh and Timnah. After defeating the Egyptian expeditionary force sent to Hezekiah's aid in the valley of Eltekeh (see p. 64) and capturing Ekron (see p. 277), Sennacherib advanced on Jerusalem. At the same time, we are informed by Isaiah that a second Assyrian column was approaching the Judean capital from another direction, by way of the mountain range running from Samaria to Jerusalem. Most of the places along this second line of advance have been identified (see the map): Michmash is to-day a tell near the village of Mukhmas, (see Vol. II, p. 129); Maabarah is situated at the crossing of the deep gorge of Wadi Suwanit; Geba is the modern Jaba, about six miles north-east of Jerusalem; Ramah is the modern er-Ram; and Gibeah of Saul is Tell el-Ful (see Vol. II, p. 134; on Anathoth see p. 95, and on Nob see Vol. II, p. 144). The Assyrians moved fast, despite the difficult mountainous terrain which made the going particularly hard for the cavalry (cf. Isa. 5 : 26-29). Before the inhabitants of the outlying cities could raise the alarm, the enemy's forces had already reached the environs of Jerusalem and the population of the neighbouring districts fled for their lives. The lower picture is a copy of a relief from Nineveh, from the reign of Sennacherib (681 - 704 B.C.), showing the Assyrian cavalry advancing through mountainous terrain.

THE cow and the bear shall feed; their young shall lie down together; and the lion shall eat straw like the ox.

(Isaiah 11 : 7)

The future reign of the Messianic king of David's line is envisaged by Isaiah as a period of just dealings between individuals (Isa. 11 : 3-4), peace between nations (Isa. 2 : 1-4; cf. Mic. 4 : 3-4) and amity in the animal world. Then will be renewed the ancient covenant made between God and His creatures in the Garden of Eden, in the days before the Flood, when corruption had not yet entered the world. There will be no more bloodshed on earth and the beasts of prey will once more eat grass, as at the creation (Gen. 1 : 30; Isa. 65 : 25), when, in the words of the Sumerian myth about paradise (Enki and Ninhursag), "the lion kills not, the wolf snatches not the lamb." The Roman poet Virgil, in his Fourth Eclogue, described the future golden age in remarkably similar terms: there will be world peace, the ox will not fear the lion and there will be no more snakes.

A scene of this kind adorns the sounding-box of a lyre from the middle of the third millennium B.C. which was found in the royal tombs at Ur (see the picture). Although the exact significance of this inlay must remain uncertain, there can at least be no doubt that it is meant to illustrate concord in the animal world. A lion and a wolf (or dog) are seen together laying a table with food (upper section). The lion is carrying a large jug in his left paw and a dish (or perhaps a lamp) in his right. The wolf, who has a knife buckled to his waist, is carrying a table with slices of meat. In the lower section an ass is plucking a lyre while a bear dances to the notes. Seated at the bear's feet is a jackal, or jerboa, who is shaking a sistrum and at the same time beating a drum. The base of the lyre is itself shaped like a bull.

THE oracle concerning
Babylon which Isaiah the
son of Amoz saw.
(Isaiah 13 : 1)

The coming destruction of Babylon, as depicted by Isaiah, is merely one striking illustration of his central prophetic conception of the working out of the God of Israel's design in human history. The punishment to be inflicted
on the sinful empire is an exact recompense for its own crimes. When the day of reckoning for the iniquity of the
wicked and the haughtiness of the ruthless (Isa. 13 : 11) comes, the would-be lords of the earth and masters of the
heavens will be annihilated (cf. p. 39). A remote nation, dwelling beyond the ken of the peoples of Mesopotamia,
will destroy them and their land and lay their king in the dust (ibid., 15-20).
In his oracle about Babylon, Isaiah makes no mention of Israel. His subject is the fate of nations and empires, and
parallels to the spirit of his prophecy can be found in Babylonian literature too, especially in the reflections of
Nabonidus, the last of the rulers of the neo-Babylonian empire. On a basalt stele (reproduced here) he explains
the assassination of Sennacherib by his sons (681 B.C.) as a consequence of the god Marduk's wrathful desire to
take revenge on Sennacherib for the destruction of Babylon by the Assyrians. The overthrow of the Assyrian
empire itself is also explained by the same reasoning. Marduk sent against Assyria a foreign and barbarous nation
which came from afar and avenged the Babylonians by plundering and destroying and by breaking down the
Assyrian temples. In the historiosophy of the Babylonian writings this explanation is limited to the specifically
political vicissitudes of nations and empires; whereas, in Isaiah's vision, the punishment of the ruthless monarch
is an integral part of the prophet's conception of a universal, all-embracing Day of the Lord "against all that is
proud and lofty" (Isa. 2 : 12).

B<small>UT</small> wild beasts will lie down there, and its houses will be full of howling creatures;
there ostriches will dwell . . .   (Isaiah 13 : 21)

The destruction of Babylon will be as complete as the overthrow of Sodom and Gomorrah. Even nomadic
shepherds will not pitch their tents in its ruins. Consequently the derelict houses and palaces will become lairs for
creatures of the desert (cf. Isa. 34 : 13; Jer. 50 : 39). One of such creatures listed here is the ostrich *(bath ha-yaanah)*,
a bird which, in the Old Testament, is associated with the jackal as a symbol of desolation (Isa. 13 : 22; 43 : 20).
The bird is usually identified with *Struthio camelus,* the largest of all winged creatures, which, until recently, was
found in the desert regions of the Middle East. Its wings are so small that it cannot fly at all, but it runs very fast
on its long, powerful legs. The ostrich's feathers were used for ornamentation, and exquisite drinking vessels
were made from the shells of its eggs. It was therefore much hunted. The ostrich-hunt and the presentation of
ostrich-feathers and ostrich-eggs as gifts feature in the art of the ancient East, in Egypt and Mesopotamia alike.
Reproduced here are sections of Assyrian cylinder-seals from the 12th-10th cent. B.C. Above — a scene depicting
the hunting of desert animals, including a lion and an ostrich. At the top left of p. 39 — an ostrich in flight with
her young.

YOU said in your heart, "I will ascend to heaven; above the stars of GOD I will set my throne on high; I will sit on the mount of assembly in the far north; I will ascend above the heights of the clouds, I will make myself like the Most High."   (Isaiah 14 : 13-14)

Isaiah describes the arrogant boasting of the king of Babylon (though, according to some scholars, the prophet is actually referring to his own contemporary, the Assyrian monarch) in terms taken from ancient Canaanite mythology, the phraseology and metaphors of which were known in Israel (cf. pp. 53, 105, 274). Philo of Byblos (first cent. A.D.) informs us that Alyon (Heb. *elyon),* the god whose equal the king of Babylon vaunts himself, was the grandfather of El, the chief deity of the Canaanite pantheon. The Babylonian monarch chose as his residence "the far corners of the north" where Baal, the son of El, had his throne. In its original sense, the expression "far corners of the north" *(yarkethei ha-zaphon)* refers to a sacred mountain on the Syrian coast, north of Ugarit, which was known in antiquity as Mount Cassius, and is the modern Jebel Aqra. Hence the god was called "Baal of the North" *(baal zaphon),* the name which was also given to one of the sites of his cult in Egypt (Ex. 14 : 2; see Vol. I, p. 141).

In the Ugaritic Epic of Baal (tablet 2, column 1, lines 25-34; see the plate at the bottom right) there is a description of an unsuccessful attempt to depose Baal from the far corners of the north and to enthrone Ashtar the Tyrant, another of the gods, in his stead:

> "Straightway Ashtar the Tyrant
> Goes up to the fastness of Zaphon
> (And) sits on Baal Puissant's throne.
> (But) his feet reach not down to the footstool,
> Nor does his head reach up' to the top.
> So Ashtar the Tyrant declares:
> 'I'll not reign in Zaphon's Fastness'."

In the religious tradition of the Old Testament the original significance of the terms *yarkethei zaphon* and *elyon* had become so blurred that they could be used of the God of Israel, and the psalmist (Ps. 48 : 2) could even describe the dwelling-place of the Lord on Mount Zion as being "in the far corners of the north".

AN oracle concerning Moab . . . because Kir is laid waste in a night, Moab is undone.
(Isaiah 15 : 1)

Isaiah's oracle concerning Moab (Isa. 15-17) is a prophetic lament in the style of an ancient ballad (cf. Nu. 21: 27-30). It describes the destruction which, still in the prophet's lifetime, will fall with appalling suddenness on the cities of Moab, and first of all upon Kir, the most important of the country's fortresses. This city is referred to as "Kir-Moab" only in this verse; elsewhere it is called Kir-Heres (Isa. 16 : 11), or Kir-Hareseth (Isa. 16 : 7; 2 Kings 3 : 25).

Kir Moab, known to the Arabs as el-Kerak, i.e. "the city", was built on a rock-pinnacle overlooking the main highway that ran from Egypt to northern Mesopotamia, along the Trans-Jordan plateau. On the site of the ancient city potsherds have been found dating back to the end of the Bronze Age and the beginning of the Iron Age, as well as the remains of a tunnel connecting the citadel with the water-source that lay outside its walls. Because of its central position and powerful fortifications, Kir Moab was a key-point in every attempt to conquer the whole country. Thus it was Kir Moab that checked the advance of Jehoshaphat, king of Judah, and Jehoram, king of Israel, when they unavailingly laid siege to it in the reign of the Moabite ruler, Mesha (2 Kings 3). In post-biblical times the city was inhabited by Nabateans, the remains of whose temples have been discovered in the neighbourhood.

In the Roman period, the city served as a posting-station and guard-fortress on the imperial road built by Trajan which passed close by it. Centuries later, the Crusaders erected on the site one of the strongest of their castles in the Middle East. The ruined walls of this castle are seen in the photograph above.

BUT now the LORD says, "In three years, like the years of a hireling, the glory of Moab will be brought into contempt . . ."

(Isaiah 16 : 14)

Isaiah states that his prophetic vision of the destruction of Moab (cf. Jer. 48; and see pp. 148-149) will come to pass in exactly three years' time (cf. Isa. 20 : 3). The prophet's phraseology here is derived from the juridical procedure customary in fixing the period of employment of a hired labourer by his master. In such cases the usual length of service was apparently three years (in Isa. 21 : 16 the complete Isaiah text of the Dead Sea Scrolls reads "three years, according to the years of a hireling" for the "one year" of the Massoretic text). A three-year term of hired service would also seem to be implied by the injunction of the Mosaic Law that a slave is to be set free after six years, seeing that he will then have completed double the service of a hired labourer: "for at half the cost of a hired servant he has served you six years" (Deut. 15 : 18). The period of "three years" in the relations between master and servant is also found in the Code of Hammurabi (sect. 117), in the collection of laws relating to persons who have sold themselves into slavery because they were unable to pay their debts: "If an obligation came due against a seignior and he sold (the services of) his wife, his son, or his daughter, or he has been bound over to service, they shall work in the house of their purchaser or obligee for three years, with their freedom re-established in the fourth year". A contract concerning hired labour from the time of the First Dynasty in Babylon (18th cent. B.C.) speaks of two women who bought "Asir-Adad the son of Lipit-Irra for a period of one year . . . he shall commence his service on the fourth day of the month Asin-Adad, and in the month Mamitum he shall end (his period of service)" (see the reproduction on the right).

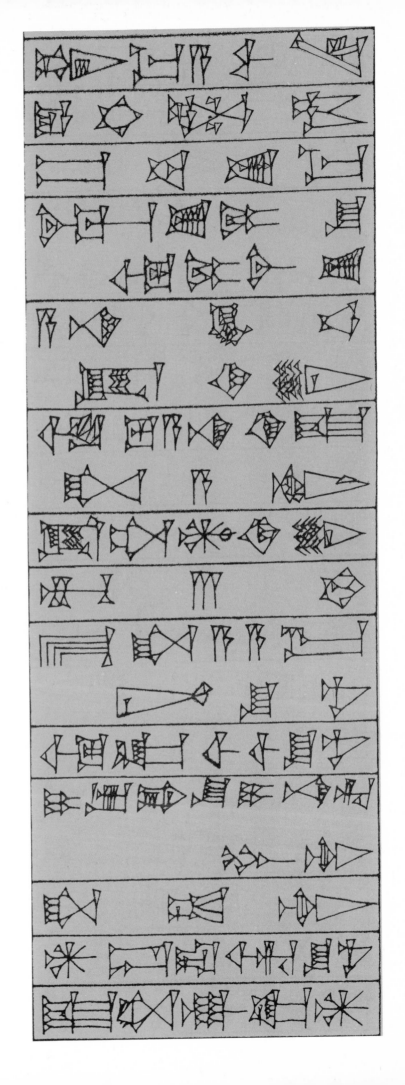

THE nations roar like the roaring of many waters, but he will rebuke them, and they will flee far away . . .

(Isaiah 17 : 13)

The army of the nations advancing upon Jerusalem with great tumult is compared by the prophet to the roaring waters of a great torrent (cf. Isa. 8 : 7). Though loud, this tumult will be of short duration, just like the roar of the floodwaters that sweep past and are gone. The simile is taken from the flash floods which are a well known seasonal phenomenon in the southern parts of Palestine, especially in the Negev. In this region, on the rare occasions in the course of the year when it does rain, there is such a violent downpour in such a short space of time that an enormous volume of water, far more than the soil is capable of absorbing, collects in the beds of the watercourses and runs off down them to the sea. The swirling torrents thus formed sweep away everything in their path, even rolling large boulders along with them. The roar of the waters approaching down the valley serves as a warning signal to man and beast to save themselves from being drowned by getting out of the channel with all speed. Vast quantities of water, converging from a wide drainage-basin, continue to pour in spate down the valley for several hours. Then the flow suddenly stops and the channel once more dries up — till the next flooding.

In the photograph above the Brook Besor (Wadi Shellal), in the central Negev, is seen in flood (see Vol. II, p. 156).

CHASED like chaff on the mountains before the wind and whirling dust before the storm.

(Isaiah 17 : 13)

The hostile armies that come to harrass Israel are doomed to vanish like the winter torrents in the watercourses of the Negev (see the previous page), or to be whirled away by the wind like wild plants that have shrivelled up and become detached from their roots. Isaiah compares the fleeing foe to tumbleweed driven before the storm (cf. Ps. 83 : 13). He is referring to a composite prickly plant known to botanists as *Gundelia Tourne-fortii L.*, which is common in all parts of Palestine, including the northern Negev. After the fruits of the tumbleweed have ripened, its stem dries up during the summer until it breaks off at its base, or until the whole plant comes out of the ground roots and all. The tumbleweed (Heb. *galgal*) is then driven whirling *(mithgalgel)* by the wind across the flat expanses of the Negev and the Arabah. Sometimes hundreds of tumbleweeds collect in valleys and in folds in the ground, until they are sent flying again by the wind.

In the photograph below tumbleweed plants are seen before their withering.

Egypt's main source of life and livelihood was the Nile which provided the inhabitants with fish in abundance and water for the irrigation of their fields (see Vol. I, p. 136). The punishment in store for Egypt is portrayed by Isaiah in a series of vivid vignettes which illustrate in detail the realities of life in the land of the Nile. To the terrors of the enemy without the gates and of social anarchy within (Isa. 19 : 2-4), there will be added all the horrors of the Nile's failure (cf. Ezek. 30 : 12; 32 : 13). The level of its waters will fall till the irrigation canals running off it dry up and all the cultivated fields are parched. Finally, the reeds along the river's banks will wither and even the fish will die, thus depriving the fishermen of their subsistence.

The various methods of fishing mentioned by the prophet are frequently depicted in the art of ancient Egypt. In the wall-painting reproduced above, which is from the tomb of Khnumhotep at Beni Hasan (19th cent. B.C.), two Egyptians are seen casting fish-hooks into the river; one of them is using a kind of rod to which is tied a line with a hook at its end, while the other's tackle consists of only a line and hook (cf. p. 112). Other methods are illustrated in the relief, reproduced below, which was found in the tomb of Mereruka at Sakkarah (time of the Sixth Dynasty, second half of the third millennium B.C.). In the bottom row a large number of fishermen, working in two teams, are hauling nets full of fish out of the river, under the watchful eye of an overseer (in the middle). At the right of the upper row the fishing is being done with a hand-net manipulated by a single fisherman. In the middle of this row fish are being caught in fixed nets spread under the surface of the water. The fish enter the net by its wide, open end, while the other narrower end is kept closed by a rope held by the fishermen. At the left of the same row — fishing with line and hook.

THE workers in combed flax will be in despair, and the weavers of white cotton.

(Isaiah 19 : 9)

The drying-up of the Nile will ruin both the flax-growers and the spinners and weavers who earned their livelihood by processing the flax. The growing (Ex. 9 : 31) and processing of flax played an important part in the economy of ancient Egypt. Indeed, the exquisite and valuable Egyptian cloths were famed for their quality throughout the ancient East (see Ezek. 27 : 7; Prov. 7 : 16), and the remnants of them discovered by modern archaeologists testify to the high technical standard achieved by the Egyptians in the crafts of spinning and weaving (see Vol. I, pp. 172-173). That Isaiah was well acquainted with the methods of flax-processing is proved by his precisely worded description of the craftsmen as "the workers in combed flax and the weavers of white cotton". Another proof can be found in his connecting this detail of his prophecy with the drying up of the Nile, since large quantities of water were required for the processing of flax, as described by Pliny in his *Natural History* (19 : 1); after the harvest the bundles of flax are soaked in water until the twine which binds them is dissolved, which is a sign that the plants are ready for processing. After this, the flax is cut and dried in the sun, beaten out and carded by being drawn through the teeth of wooden or metal combs placed on an inclined plank (see the reproduction above of a wall-painting from the tomb of Menna at Sheikh Abd el-Gurnah, time of the Eighteenth Dynasty, 14th cent. B.C.). After the strands had been separated out in this way, they were ready to be spun for twining into ropes or weaving into cloth.

The various stages in the processing of flax are frequently portrayed in Egyptian art. A design from the tomb of Amenemhet at Beni Hasan (time of the Twelfth Dynasty, 19th cent. B.C.), reproduced below, illustrates (from left to right) the growing of flax, the soaking and pounding of the sheaves, the spinning of the threads and the manufacture of cloth.

45

In his oracle concerning the overthrow of Egypt and Ethiopia Isaiah mentions a historical event that took place in his lifetime, thereby providing us with a reference point for the chronology of his period. From the inscriptions of Sargon II (721-705 B.C.) we know that, in his reign, there were two Assyrian campaigns against Ashdod. The first of these, which appears to have taken place in the early part of 713 B.C., resulted from the refusal of Aziru, the king of Ashdod, to pay tribute to Sargon and his attempt to suborn the rulers of the other cities in his region to revolt against Assyria. Aziru was defeated and deposed, being replaced on the throne by his brother. But the new king did not reign for long. He was deposed by the people of Ashdod who chose one Iamani as their king and made preparations to withstand a siege, at the same time despatching emissaries to Philistia, Edom, Moab, Judah, the Aegean islands, and even to Egypt to request military aid against Assyria. Sargon sent his army to Ashdod under the command of the general who was the king's viceroy (Heb. *tartan*; Akkadian *tardinnu* = "second"; cf. 2 Kings 18 : 17). The city was conquered and sacked and its territory became an Assyrian province (712-711 B.C.). This is the event that is referred to above in the opening verse of Isaiah's prophecy against Egypt. The prophet was commanded to go unclothed and barefoot for three years (Isa. 20 : 3), as a warning to the king of Judah not to send help to Ashdod nor to join the revolt against Assyria which was destined to end in the surrender and deportation of the rebels.

Reproduced above is a relief from Dur-Sharruken (the modern Khorsabad), showing, on the right, an Assyrian general (the "field marshal"?) standing before Sargon II with his hand raised in greeting.

IN the year that the commander in chief, who was sent by Sargon the king of Assyria, came to Ashdod and fought against it and took it.

(Isaiah 20 : 1)

THE oracle concerning Arabia . . . For they have fled from the swords, from the drawn sword, from the bent bow, and from the press of battle. (Isaiah 21 : 13, 15)

Isaiah's oracle concerning Arabia follows immediately after his oracle about Seir, perhaps because of the geographical proximity of the two regions. Of the Arab tribes, he singles out for special mention Dedan and Tema which inhabited the northern part of the Arabian desert (Isa. 21 : 11-15; cf. Jer. 49 : 8). Even these desert-dwellers will feel the heavy hand of Assyria. The beduin, whose principal weapon was the simple bow, will be powerless to withstand the onslaught of a trained army equipped with long swords, composite bows(see Vol. I, p. 64), javelins and shields. In war the Arab tribes trusted to the advantage given them over foot-soldiers by the speed of their camels. But these fast camels were of no avail against the heavily armed cavalry corps developed by the Assyrians from the beginning of the first millennium B.C. onwards, and their riders were forced to give up the unequal battle. Abandoning their unfortified places of habitation, they scattered all over the desert.

The relief reproduced here — one of many from the palace of Ashurbanipal at Nineveh (from the 7th cent. B.C.) — faithfully portrays the character of the Assyrian engagements with the Arab nomads. The Assyrian infantry and cavalry are seen in hot pursuit of pairs of Arab warriors who are fleeing on their camels. Each pair of fighters consists of a camel-driver, who controls the animal with a stick held in his hand, and an archer armed with a simple bow.

THUS says the LORD GOD of hosts, "Come, go to this steward, to Shebna, who is over the household, and say to him: What have you to do here and whom have you here, that you have hewn here a tomb for yourself, you who hew a tomb on the height, and carve a habitation for yourself in the rock?"

(Isaiah 22 : 15-16)

Shebna was one of the chief ministers in the kingdom of Judah during the reign of Hezekiah. At one time he held the office of "the steward who is over the household", and at another time that of the king's secretary (2 Kings 18 : 26, 37; Isa. 36 : 3, 22). He was evidently one of the ministers who sought to persuade Hezekiah to revolt against his Assyrian overlord, relying on Egypt for military support (see p. 58). He thereby incurred the wrath of the prophet who was demanding a policy of non-involvement (Isa. 7 : 4). Shebna had a special tomb hewn for himself out of the rock on a height, since, after the manner of the aristocracy, he did not wish to be buried in an ordinary grave (2 Kings 23 : 6; Jer. 26 : 23). The prophet's words imply that Shebna's tomb was conspicuously cut out of the rock-face, and not a subterranean burial-niche of the kind customary in ancient Israel. In the village of Shiloah, at the foot of the Mount of Olives to the east of the Kidron Valley, an epitaph has been discovered, in the ancient Hebrew script (see the reproduction below), engraved in stone above the entrance to just such a prominent rock-hewn structure (see photograph above). The wording of the inscription runs as follows: "This is [the sepulchre of . . .]yahu who is over the household. There is no silver and no gold here, but [his bones] and the bones of his slave-wife with him. Cursed be the man who opens this." Since the name Shebna is apparently an abbreviation of "Shebnayahu", and there is no mention in the Old Testament of another royal official "over the household" with a name ending in -yahu who was buried in Jerusalem, and since the style of the lettering fits the period of Hezekiah, scholars are inclined to assign this epitaph to the Shebna - Shebnayahu who was one of Hezekiah's ministers. The form and situation of the rock-hewn tomb lend some support to the proposed identification.

THE oracle concerning Tyre. Wail, O ships of Tarshish . . .

(Isaiah 23 : 1)

Tyre "the bestower of crowns" (Isa. 23 : 8), one of the most important ancient cities of the eastern Mediterranean seaboard, was built on an island about one third of a mile off the coast. From this island base the Tyrians conducted a flourishing overseas trade, venturing forth to establish their colonies in distant parts of the Mediterranean littoral. Wherever they went, the Tyrian traders carried with them the Canaanite culture of their mother-city which thus spread as far afield as Greece, North Africa and Spain (cf. Ezek. 27; and see p. 183). From the time of David and Solomon, when Hiram was king of Tyre, the Tyrians and Israelites were allies (see Vol. II, pp. 212; 219; 222-223). The reciprocal economic and cultural relations which had existed between Tyre and Sidon, on the one hand, and Israel, on the other, throughout the rule of Omri's dynasty apparently took a turn for the worse after the assassination of Jezebel the daughter of Ethbaal, king of Sidon (1 Kings 16 : 31; see Vol. II, p. 267). In the Book of Amos (1 : 9) Tyre is accused of breaking the "covenant of brotherhood"; and it is probable that in Isaiah's time too relations between Tyre and Judah were not amicable. This was the situation that induced the prophet to predict the destruction of Tyre.

Since Tyre was entirely surrounded by sea, it was virtually unconquerable from the mainland. The armies of both Assyria and Babylon laid siege to it, but could not reduce it for lack of powerful sea-forces (Ezek. 29 : 18; see p. 123). The first conqueror of Tyre was Alexander the Great who, in the year 322 B.C., besieged it for seven months. His troops finally gained access to the island along a causeway which he ordered to be thrown up in the sea. In the course of time, this causeway gradually grew wider and higher until it turned the island of Tyre into a peninsula, as shown in the above aerial photograph which was taken from the north.

Hᴇʀ merchandise and her hire will be dedicated
to the ʟᴏʀᴅ; it will not be stored or hoarded . . .

(Isaiah 23 : 18)

The commerce and wealth of Tyre were famous throughout the ancient East. As early as the eleventh cent. B.C.
Tyre had become the metropolis of Phoenicia, a commercial and industrial centre and a base for overseas colo-
nization. Anchored in its two natural harbours, one on the north and the other on the south side of the island,
were large fleets of vessels which sailed all over the Mediterranean. The political and economic rise of Tyre began
in the time of Hiram's father, Abibaal, who reigned in the first half of the 10th cent. B.C. Under his rule the
manufacturers and merchants (Isa. 23 : 8; Prov. 31 : 24) formed themselves into large guilds which gained a
monopoly of the city's trade and sea-traffic, established new Phoenician colonies, developed metal industries in
Tyre and its colonies, and turned the city into "the merchant of the peoples" (Ezek. 27 : 3), "the city renowned that
was mighty on the sea" (Ezek. 26 : 17). The Israelite prophets, Jeremiah and Ezekiel, have left us vivid pictures
of the flourishing trade done by Tyre in ornaments and luxury goods, a trade which extended over the whole of
the ancient East (see pp. 183-184). All this merchandise was stored in warehouses and depots in the harbour; and
it is these stores that are the target of Isaiah's wrathful words. They are to be expropriated from the Tyrians and
given to Israel to fill the treasury of the Lord's Temple.
The picture above is a photograph of a store of close on eighty oil-and wine-jars, no doubt similar to those which
also existed at Tyre. This particular store was discovered in the harbour-area of the city of Ugarit, on the Mediterranean coast north of Tyre. The jars shown are from the 15th or 14th cent. B.C., i.e. the golden age of Ugarit.

THE earth is utterly broken, the earth is rent asunder, the earth is violently shaken.

(Isaiah 24 : 19)

Devastating earthquakes were such a common occurrence in Old Testament times, that the prophets and poets of Israel frequently drew their parables from this dreaded manifestation of nature's powers (2 Sam. 22 : 8; Jer. 4 : 24). Particularly famous was the earthquake in Uzziah's reign which became the starting-point of a system of chronological reckoning (Amos 1 : 1 ; and see p. 231). It is probable that Isaiah had this same earthquake in mind in chapter 24 of his prophecies (verses 1, 3, 18, 19).

Earthquakes are part of the natural processes by which the features of the earth, especially its deep depressions, are formed. Hence the Jordan rift was a highly seismic area where tremors are still frequently felt even to-day. In the past, the earthquakes were more violent and caused serious damage to the settlements all along the rift. The photograph above is an aerial view of the deeply fissured, chaotic landscape south of the Dead Sea. This scene of veritable barrenness and desolation was regarded by the ancients as a mute testimony to the earthquakes that had shaken and shattered the whole region.

AND the high fortification of his walls he will bring down, lay low, and cast to the ground, even to the dust.

(Isaiah 25 : 12)

The fate of the nations hostile to Israel, who are to meet their doom at God's hands, is typified for the prophet by the downfall of Moab and the total destruction of its fortresses and strongholds (cf. p. 40) which had been thought powerful enough to defy any foe (cf. Jer. 48 : 1-11).

The cities of Moab, and indeed of the ancient Middle East as a whole, were so built and fortified as to give the impression of impregnable strength. The city itself, which stood on a hill or mound, was surrounded by a strong outer wall with, in its centre, a heavily fortified gateway flanked by protecting towers (see pp. 146-147). In the heart of the city, usually at its highest point, towered the royal citadel which was also encircled by a wall. The prophet's words here are inspired by the striking contrast between the spectacle of a flourishing city standing proudly on its mound and the desolate appearance of the same city, after it has been reduced to ruins by a victorious enemy, — a contrast that was familiar enough in the countries of the ancient East with their constant wars. Such scenes of destruction were also frequently portrayed in oriental art, as, for example, on the relief from the Bronze Gates at Balawat, from the reign of Shalmaneser III (858-824 B.C.), which is reproduced here. Assyrian soldiers are shown attacking the city of Parga in the country of Hamath and tearing down its walls. While the bowmen harrass the city's defenders with their arrows, the team of a battering-ram is forcing a way through the wall close to one of its protective towers. The wall is gradually disintegrating into heaps of rubble.

IN that day the LORD with his hard and great and strong sword will punish Leviathan the fleeing serpent, Leviathan the twisting serpent, and he will slay the dragon that is in the sea.

(Isaiah 27 : 1)

In his description of the coming war of the Lord against the enemies of His people, Isaiah makes metaphorical use of expressions borrowed from the mythology of the ancient East. One of the myths current in that region, echoes of which have also been preserved in the Old Testament (Job 41 : 1-5), related how, when the world was first formed, its divine creator fought a life-and-death battle against the forces of darkness. In Israel these mythical monsters had become purely symbolical names, but in other cultures they were real enough. Thus, in the Babylonian myth, Marduk overcomes Tiamat (= Heb. *tehom)*, the goddess of the waters under the earth, and her minions; and the Hittite storm-god masters the dragon Illuyankas who has revolted against him. This primeval struggle found expression both in poetry and in visionary descriptions. Reproduced below is a relief from Malatya, belonging to the 8th cent. B.C., which shows two Hittite gods, armed with spears, swords and clubs, fighting against the dragon Illuyankas. However, the closest resemblance to Isaiah's words occurs in the ancient Canaanite myth which was found in the Ugaritic epics. There the monsters mentioned by the prophet appear amongst the supporters of the sea-god who is the rival of Baal, the god of the heavens and of fertility. Anath, Baal's sister, deals the monsters a stunning blow, as described in the epic of *Aliyan Baal,* on the obverse side of tablet A :
> "For she smites Lotan (= Leviathan), the fleeing serpent,
> And destroys the twisting serpent."

After performing her heroic deeds, Anath boasts of her victory :
> "I have caught the dragon, caught him;
> I have smitten the twisting serpent,
> The tyrant with the seven heads."

DOES he who ploughs for sowing plough continually? does he continually open and harrow his
ground when he has levelled its surface . . .
(Isaiah 28 : 24-25)

God's control of the world is here illustrated by the allegory of the wise farmer who works his land properly and
suits all his actions to the requirements of the particular season and place. First, he ploughs his field and breaks up
("opens") the hard clods of earth, so that he can level ("harrow") the ground before sowing it with seed. The
harrowing of the ground, terrace by terrace, was particularly important in sloping terrain like that in the Jerusalem
hills, to check the run-off of rain-water and thus prevent soil-erosion (cf. p. 25). After levelling the surface of the
soil, the farmer sows his crops at the proper season and in the most suitable areas of ground. This orderly func-
tioning of the universe is the work of God who "is wonderful in counsel, and excellent in wisdom" (Isa. 28 : 2).
Just as He has taught the farmer his craft, so He will instruct His people in justice and righteousness, making
"justice the line and righteousness the plummet" (ibid. 17) in Zion.
In the photograph above a peasant is seen ploughing his land in the environs of Jerusalem. On the hill-slope there
is a checkerwork of plots that have been harrowed, levelled, and fenced in.

ND the vision of all this has become to you like the words
of a book that is sealed. When men give it to one who can
read, saying, "Read this," he says, "I cannot, for it is sealed."

(Isaiah 29 : 11)

God's words to the people are like a sealed "book" (Heb. *sefer*) which cannot be read. This comparison is to be understood in the light of the forms of writing customary in antiquity. The word *sefer* in the Old Testament usually means a despatch or letter. "Books" of this kind were employed for internal communication by kings and officials (2 Sam. 11 : 14; 2 Kings 10 : 1, 6), and also passed between different kingdoms in the course of political negotiations (2 Kings 5 : 5; 20 : 12; Isa. 39 : 1). In Egypt, important letters were usually written on papyrus, while in Mesopotamia and Anatolia they were inscribed on clay tablets. In Israel, in the period of the First Temple, ordinary letters were also written on relatively worthless potsherds. To keep the contents secret, the rolled-up papyrus letter was fastened with a seal, and an official despatch written on a clay tablet was placed in a clay envelope (see p. 130). In either case, therefore, the communication could not be read without first breaking the seal.

The plate above is a photograph of the obverse side of one of the ostraca (No. 3) which were excavated in a chamber beside the city-gate of Lachish and are from the last days of the kingdom of Judah. This particular letter was sent by Hoshayahu, the commander of a small fortress on the road from Lachish to Jerusalem, to Yaosh, who was apparently the commander of Lachish. In it, Hoshayahu seeks to clear himself of the suspicion — levelled against him by Yaosh in other letters — of having read a secret letter from the king which he, Hoshayahu, had forwarded to Yaosh: "As the Lord lives, no one has ever tried to read to me a letter! And also whatever letter may have come to me, I have not read it . . ." (lines 9-13).

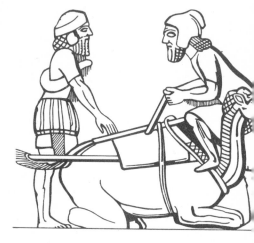

A N oracle on the beasts of the Negeb . . . they carry their riches on the backs of asses, and their treasures on the humps of camels . . . (Isaiah 30 : 6)

Isaiah had no faith in any political alliance, least of all in one with Egypt which he regarded as "a broken reed" (Isa. 30 : 2-5; 31 : 1-3; and see p. 58). He therefore opposed the sending of a mission by the king of Judah, Hezekiah, to the king of Egypt, to request military aid from the latter. Nevertheless, the mission set out on its long and arduous journey, taking with it a baggage train of camels and asses laden with gifts for the Egyptian monarch. The verse above is the only reference in the Old Testament to asses being used as beasts of burden instead of being ridden on, as was the usual custom (Judges 10 : 4; 12 : 14; Zech. 9 : 9). The camel, on the contrary, and likewise the donkey, had been the beasts of burden par excellence in the Orient from time immemorial, especially for communication between oases or between countries separated by stretches of desert, such as Egypt and Canaan (cf. Vol. I, pp. 56, 97).

The procedure of loading the camel was as follows. First, the camel was made to kneel and a saddle (or, for riding on, a cushion; see Vol. I, p. 85) was placed on its hump, and over this, or under it, two parallel poles running the whole length of the camel's back. The burden was then fastened to these poles, having, in most cases, been first put into sacks (Heb. qantel) so that its weight might be disposed equally on either side of the camel.

The picture at the top right is a copy of a scene on an Assyrian relief from Nineveh, showing two men fastening a saddle on to the back of a kneeling camel. On the left there is a photograph of a modern camel-caravan resting at a halt.

AND the oxen and the asses that till the ground will eat salted provender,which has been winnowed with shovel and fork.

(Isaiah 30 : 24)

The withdrawal of Sennacherib's army from Jerusalem (see p. 64) inspired the prophet with new hope for his people's future. When the Israelites turn back from their evil ways and renounce idol-worship, the Lord will have mercy on them and will set them free from the yoke of Assyria and pour out His blessings on their land. Then the rains will fall at their proper time and there will be an abundance of rich food for man and beast. Even work-animals will eat "salted provender", a delicacy usually reserved for stalled cattle which were being fattened for human consumption. This mixed fodder which is to be fed to the oxen (Job 6 : 5) and the asses will not now consist almost entirely of the usual straw and chaff, but will contain winnowed grain with an additional tasty and appetizing seasoning.

The fattening of livestock is frequently mentioned in the Old Testament (1 Sam. 28 : 24; Amos 6 : 4) and also features in the art of the ancient East, especially that of Egypt. Reproduced here is a relief from the tomb of Mereruka at Sakkarah, from the time of the Sixth Dynasty (second half of the third millennium B.C.), showing, in the bottom row, a train of fattened oxen, and, at the top, the fattening of rams.

WOE to those who go down to Egypt for help and rely on horses, who trust in chariots because they are many and in horsemen because they are very strong . . .　　　(Isaiah 31 : 1)

Isaiah opposed the pro-Egyptian policy of Hezekiah, king of Judah (Isa. 30-31; and see p. 56), just as he had opposed the pro-Assyrian policy of Hezekiah's father, Ahaz (Isa. 7 : 4; 10 : 20; cf. Vol. II p. 282). Labouring under the delusion that he was pursuing a "realistic" policy, Hezekiah put his trust in the military support of "a people that cannot profit them" (Isa. 30 : 5), on the assumption that the small army of Judah, which consisted mainly of foot-soldiers, would be no match for the cavalry and chariotry that formed the main force of the Assyrian army.

The considerable technical knowledge required for the manufacture and maintenance of chariots was developed primarily in the great empires of antiquity (see Vol. II, p. 122). The high cost of horses and the heavy expense of their upkeep made it impossible for the small states, including Judah, to vie with Egypt and Assyria in the maintenance of highly trained and extremely manoeuvrable cavalry forces. The relief from the palace of Ramses II at Thebes (13th cent. B.C.), reproduced here, gives a good idea of the power of the Egyptian chariot corps as it advances into battle.

EACH will be like a hiding-place from the wind, a covert from the tempest, like streams of water in a dry place, like the shade of a great rock in a weary land.   (Isaiah 32 : 2)

In the Old Testament, the rock which offers protection from the wind, the rain and the burning heat of the sun became a symbol of refuge and security. The true worth of such a rock is well known to the inhabitants of the hot lands of the East, especially to those living in the arid or desert areas, who require shade from the sun's parching rays in the summer months and shelter from torrential downpours in the rainy season (Isa. 4 : 6). Hence, the Lord, the Rock and Fortress of Israel, is described as "a shelter from the storm and a shade from the heat" (Isa. 25 : 4); and, similarly, the king that rules his people justly is a protection and a shelter to the heavily burdened and oppressed. In the wide expanses of southern Palestine vegetation is sparse. In the Judean desert and the Negev, only a few, isolated trees grow, mainly in the beds of watercourses; by far the greater part of the region is completely bare. Human beings can, therefore, find shelter from sun and wind, rain and cold, only in caves or in the lee of heavy rocks, like the crag known as "the Frog" or "the Lion" beside the Scorpions' Ascent (see the photograph). This rock is so named on account of its peculiar shape which, to passing wayfarers, looked like the head of an animal. Many such boulders and crags, which seem to have been architecturally designed or bear a striking resemblance to animal forms, are found in the wastes of the Negev and the Arabah. These remarkable shapes are the result of the constant wearing away of the rock by the action of rain and wind.

YOUR tackle hangs loose; It cannot hold the mast firm in its place, or keep the sail spread out . . .

(Isaiah 33 : 23)

Isaiah employs a variety of similes to describe the future might of Israel and the Lord's protection of His people. Like a tent the pegs of which are so firmly fixed in the ground that no wind can blow it down, so will Israel stand fast against its foes (Isa. 33 : 20). Again, the Zion of the future will be encircled by rivers, as a symbol of its blessedness, and also for its defence against the enemy in place of wall and rampart (Isa. 26 : 1; 33 : 21). The hostile hosts, unable to penetrate the wide protective ring of water, will be like a ship caught by a storm in mid-ocean, its tackle hanging loose and its mast snapped off from its base so that the crew cannot run up a sail.

From the earliest times, the peoples of the Middle East have travelled along rivers and crossed the open sea in sailing vessels. The most expert sailors were the Egyptians and the Sidonians from whom the Israelites learnt the craft of seamanship (see p. 184). The picture above is of an Egyptian luxury vessel, with a central mast to which are attached numerous halyards for the raising of the square sail. At the stern can be seen the long oar which served as a rudder. The picture is a wall-painting from the tomb of Rekhmire at Thebes (15th cent. B.C.).

BUT the hawk and the porcupine shall possess it, the owl and the raven shall dwell in it . . .   (Isaiah 34 : 11)

The complete destruction of Edom is depicted by Isaiah in terms which have already been used in his prophecies concerning the overthrow of other nations (cf. p. 38), but which were particularly appropriate to the landscape and natural conditions of Edom. The soil of the whole country will become like the pitchy and sulphurous region around the Dead Sea (Isa. 34 : 9-10) with which the inhabitants of Edom were well acquainted. The fertile soil will be ruined and become the abode of desert fowl — another picture that must have been familiar enough to the Edomites, since part of their own country was arid. The owl *(Asio;* Heb. *yanshuf)* is a nocturnal bird of prey, about 14 in. in height and weighing approximately 13 oz. (see the photograph). It is found nearly everywhere in the world. Like other nocturnal birds mentioned in the Old Testament *(tinshemeth; kos; qipoz)* the owl was, in folklore, considered the symbol of desolation, as also were the raven *(oreb)* (see Vol. I, p. 188) and the hawk *(qaath)* which are again mentioned together with the owl in other passages of the Old Testament.

THE wilderness and the dry land shall be glad, the desert shall rejoice and blossom, like the crocus.   (Isaiah 35 : 1)

The prophet combines his prophecy of the retribution that is to be meted out to the nations, Israel's foes, with a vision of consolation for his oppressed compatriots, languishing far from their land. Singing and rejoicing they will return home along a well-made highway, with no fear of wild beasts (Isa. 35 : 8-9; cf. 40 : 3-4). The whole creation will be renewed at Israel's rebirth: the desert and the waste land will be redeemed from their barrenness and be filled with flowers and blossoms as far as the eye can see (cf. p. 71).

In particularly dry years, the annual plants of the desert do not flower at all and the only living hues to be seen are those of the perennial vegetation, such as the broom (Heb. *rotem)* which, with its lovely blossom, is one of the most beautiful of the plants flourishing in Palestine (see Vol. II, p. 242), or the acacia. In years of more than average rainfall, on the contrary, the valley-beds and low-lying parts of the desert are carpeted with both annual and perennial flowers. Moreover, the flowers of the desert bloom about two months before the flowers in cultivated areas. Hence the prophets' allegorical use of the flowering of the desert as a symbol of national revival, as in the verse above and also in Isa. 41 : 19: "I will put in the wilderness the cedar, the acacia, the myrtle, and the olive; I will set in the desert the cypress, the plane and the pine together."

Below is a photograph, taken in the rainy season, of flowers blooming and trees blossoming amid the stony scrub of Nahal Arugoth in the wilderness of En-Gedi.

IN the fourteenth year of King Hezekiah, Sennacherib king of Assyria came up against all the fortified cities of Judah and took them.

(Isaiah 36 : 1)

The Assyrian king Sennacherib (704-681 B.C.), the son and successor of Sargon, advanced upon Judah with his army and conquered parts of the country (cf. 2 Kings 18 : 13; 2 Chron. 32 : 1). When he ascended the throne, revolts broke out in various parts of the Assyrian empire which he only succeeded in finally suppressing after years of warfare. Among the many military campaigns that he conducted during these years were those against the kings of Babylon, Elam and Egypt. From his annals it transpires that he conquered Judah on his third campaign, i.e. in 701 B.C., in the course of his war against Hezekiah and his allies in Philistia and Trans-Jordan who had together risen in concerted revolt against Assyria, on the death of Sennacherib's father, Sargon (705 B.C.). The rebellious kings stopped paying tribute to the Assyrian monarch and even seized Padi, the king of Ekron, who had remained loyal to Sennacherib, and carried him off prisoner to Jerusalem. Sennacherib directed his attack, first of all, against Tyre and Sidon, whereupon all the kings who had revolted, with the exception of Hezekiah and Zidqa, the ruler of Ashkelon, surrendered to him. Continuing his advance, the Assyrian king penetrated into Judah and captured its fortified cities. The battle for Lachish was particularly fierce (see Vol. II, pp. 286-287). According to the Assyrian annals, Sennacherib captured forty-six fortified Judean cities and also many unwalled towns. He then laid siege to Jerusalem, shutting Hezekiah up in it, to quote his own words, "like a bird in a cage."

The picture at the top right is a reproduction of a damaged relief, from the palace of Sennacherib at Nineveh, in which the king is portrayed sitting on the royal throne with a footstool beneath his feet. The details of the monarch's figure have been reconstructed in the drawing on the left.

Now the king heard concerning Tirhaka of Ethiopia, "He has set out to fight against you ..."

(Isaiah 37 : 9)

Tirhaka, the commander of the Egyptian army who ascended the throne of the pharaohs in 689 B.C. (cf. Vol. II, p. 288), had, even before that, encouraged the kings of southern Syria and Palestine to revolt against the Assyrian ruler and promised them military aid, should the Assyrians attack them. When Sennacherib's army approached the region in 701, all the rebels surrendered to him, with the exception of Hezekiah, king of Judah, and Zidqa, king of Ashkelon. Sennacherib therefore set out on a punitive campaign against these two rulers (see p. 63). One of his columns advanced along the coast into the territory of Zidqa, while the other followed the ridge of the mountain range running from Samaria to Jerusalem (see p. 35). In his annals, Sennacherib relates that the expeditionary force sent by the king of Egypt and the king of Ethiopia tried to bar his way: "Bowmen, chariots and horsemen of the king of Ethiopia, a host of countless multitudes. In the Valley of Eltekeh they drew up their battle-lines against me and sharpened their weapons. With the aid of my lord the god Ashur, I fought them and inflicted defeat upon them." However, although the Egyptian army failed in its main objective, it did at least gain Hezekiah time to strengthen the defences of Jerusalem and prepare it for a siege.

Reproduced above is a partially gilded bronze statue of Tirhaka seen presenting a thank-offering to the god Hemen of Upper Egypt, who is represented in the form of a bird. The occasion of the offering was, apparently, the ending of the severe drought that afflicted Egypt in 685 B.C.

"BEHOLD, you have heard what the kings of Assyria have done to all lands, destroying them utterly. And shall you be delivered? ... Where are the king of Hamath, the king of Arad ..."

(Isaiah 37 : 11, 13)

The wars referred to by Sennacherib, in the warning which was conveyed to Hezekiah by Rabshakeh, were all fought in the years when the Assyrian empire was expanding westwards into the Mediterranean coastlands, in the ninth and eighth cent. B.C. One after another, the Aramean kingdoms in northern Mesopotamia and Syria were conquered by successive Assyrian monarchs, until at last came the turn of the Hittite kingdom of Hamath in central Syria. In 853 B.C. Shalmaneser III fought a battle at Karkara, in the kingdom of Hamath, against the allied armies of the Syrian kings, one of whom was Irhuleni the king of Hamath (see Vol. II, p. 248). The results of this battle were indecisive. But in 848 Shalmaneser once again attacked the territory of Hamath and this time captured many of its cities. This victory is depicted on a fragment of a bronze relief from Balawat (reproduced above). In the upper row, the aged ruler of the city is seen being carried out of it on his litter, his hands held up in supplication as a sign of surrender to the Assyrian forces arrayed in front of the city-walls. Below, Assyrian soldiers are leading off captives from Hamath into exile.

Hamath repeatedly revolted against Assyria. In the years 743-740, the king of Hamath was forced to surrender to Tiglath-Pileser III, who detached nineteen districts from his kingdom. In the same period, Arpad also fell to the Assyrian monarch. In 720, Hamath led a confederacy of allied nations against Sargon II. After its defeat, Sargon deported many of its inhabitants to the cities of Samaria (2 Kings 17 : 24). Hence, Rabshakeh now recalls the fate of this city, and of others like it, to Hezekiah and the inhabitants of Jerusalem, in order to deter them from the revolt that they were plotting.

O<small>F</small> a truth, O <small>LORD</small>, the kings of Assyria have laid waste all the nations and their lands, and have cast their gods into the fire . . .

(Isaiah 37 : 18-19)

The fate in store for Jerusalem, should it fall to the Assyrian army, is vividly illustrated by the artistic representation of what happened to another city, Muzazir, on a relief from Dur-Sharruken, the modern Khorsabad (see the reproduction), from the time of Sargon II (721-705 B.C.), i.e. the period referred to by Isaiah. Muzazir, one of the most important cities in the land of Ararat, has been conquered by the Assyrian forces who are seen destroying one of its temples. The soldiers climb up on to the roof (on the right of the building), and from there force their way inside. At either side of the entrance to the temple a spear is fixed upright in the ground and the walls are hung with shields which had perhaps been brought there as war-trophies by the people of Muzazir, as was customary in the ancient East (see Vol. II, pp. 158-159). These weapons are now being seized by the victorious Assyrians (cf. 2 Chron. 12 : 9).

"BEHOLD, I will make the shadow cast by the declining sun on the dial of Ahaz turn back ten steps." So the sun turned back on the dial the ten steps·by which it had declined.　(Isaiah 38 : 8)

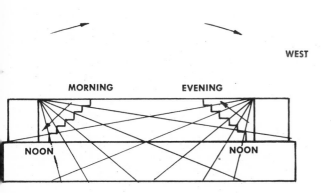

For the proper understanding of the sign given by the prophet to king Hezekiah "on the steps of Ahaz" (cf. 2 Kings 20 : 8-11), we must assume that the degrees (Heb. *maaloth*) in question were actual steps. The details of the story make it possible to reconstruct Ahaz's chronometrical device. This consisted of two sets of steps, each faced by a wall the shadow of which was cast on to the steps. At sunrise, the eastern set was entirely in the shadow which gradually grew shorter, leaving more and more steps in sunlight, as the sun rose higher towards noon. From midday to sunset, conversely, the shadow gradually lengthened on the opposite, western set, rising up the steps until they were all darkened. These processes are illustrated in the accompanying diagrams which are based on the model of an actual sun-dial found in Egypt and also on detailed drawings.

The steps of Ahaz were evidently adjacent to the royal palace, as is clearly implied by the text of our verse found in the complete Dead Sea Scroll of Isaiah: "by which it had declined *on the steps of Ahaz's upper chamber*" (which is also the reading of the Greek translation and the explanation given by Josephus). At the time when Isaiah was speaking to King Hezekiah, the shadow had already descended ten of the steps on the eastern set and, in the natural course of events, should next have begun to ascend the western set. However, at the prophet's command a miracle occurred and, instead, the shadow withdrew again up the eastern set of steps down which it had just descended.

H<small>E</small> will feed his flock like a shepherd, he will gather the lambs in his arms, he will carry them in his bosom, and gently lead those that are with young.

(Isaiah 40 : 11)

The collection of consolatory prophecies in the Book of Isaiah opens with the prophet's proclamation that the iniquity of the people of Israel has been pardoned and that its term of slavery is at an end. Now God will once again deal graciously with it, restoring it to its land and leading it as a shepherd guides his flock over safe paths, caring for the sick and feeble (cf. Ezek. 34 : 16). The description of the God of Israel as a faithful shepherd, with Israel for his flock, is a common prophetic metaphor. Unlike the political leaders through whose neglect the people had become scattered and lost (Jer. 23 : 1-2), and in contrast to the days of God's wrath when He cast out rebellious Israel from before Him and gave them into the hands of their foes, God will now gather His flock from the distant lands to which they have been dispersed and bring them back to their homeland. They will wend their way homewards at a slow pace, so that no harm should come to the suckling ewes (cf. Gen. 33 : 13-14). The tender lambs, which are not yet strong enough to cover such a great distance on their own legs, will be carried in the shepherd's arms.

The shepherd's thoughtful and devoted care of his young sheep is illustrated here by the statue of a man who has a lamb enfolded in his left arm, while his right arm is extended protectively in front of it. The statue was excavated in the temple of the Elamite god Shushinak, in the Persian city of Susa.

I STIRRED up one from the north, and he has come, from the rising of the sun, and he shall call on my name; he shall trample on rulers as on mortar, as the potter treads clay.

(Isaiah 41 : 25)

The meteoric rise of Cyrus (557-529 B.C.) to dominion over Babylon and its vassal states inspired the people of Israel with fresh hope. The prophet regarded Cyrus as the God of Israel's emissary who, advancing from the north-east, had overthrown the king of Babylon and trampled down his prefects (Heb. *seganim,* from the Akkadian *shakenu* = "governor") as the potter treads clay. Clay was one of the commonest of the materials used by man from the earliest times for making domestic utensils or for building, especially in Mesopotamia where there is no stone (cf. Vol. I, p. 44). The method by which clay was prepared for use was as follows. For making pottery, the clay was first cleansed of all impurities and then kneaded in a pit into which water was poured until the material was plastic enough to be worked. In the manufacture of bricks, the clay was reinforced by the addition of straw (Ex. 5 : 7; cf. Vol. I, p. 128). The kneading was done by treading out the clay with the feet (Nahum 3 : 14). This treading process is portrayed in a painting from a tomb at Thebes (reproduced here), from the middle of the second millennium B.C., in which potters are seen at work. In the foreground one of the workmen is standing knee-deep in the clay and kneading it with his feet. At the left two potters are fashioning a jar on a potter's wheel (see p. 114), with other completed utensils standing on either side of them. At the right there is a kiln made of bricks for the firing of the vessels.

I AM the LORD, I have called you in righteousness,
I have taken you by the hand . . .   (Isaiah 42 : 6)

The description of God as holding the hand of His emissary or supporting his right hand — a metaphor of which the prophet was particularly fond — would seem to have been taken from the common sight of the weak being supported by the strong. However, this picture gains further significance from the fact that the Babylonian monarchs used to represent themselves as handing the god Marduk on to his throne, and this tradition was followed by Nabonidus and Cyrus (see p. 75), the contemporaries of the author of the consolatory prophecies. Cyrus relates, on his prism, that "Marduk scanned and looked through all the countries searching for a righteous ruler willing to lead him in the annual procession." In the prophet's words, by contrast, a similar expression is used of God's support for His servant who is going forth to spread His teaching amongst the nations (Isa. 41 : 9-10, 13; 42 : 1). The Lord holds the hand of Cyrus in order to give him dominion over many peoples by wars and heroic deeds (Isa. 45 : 1). Illustrations of this conception of a god holding the king's hand are found in the art of the ancient East, especially amongst the Hittites. This is how, for example, the Hittite king Tudhaliyas IV (1250-1220 B.C.) is portrayed on his seal, an impression of which was brought to light at Ugarit (see the reproduction above). The god Mutawali is seen with his arm round the king's shoulder and his hand supporting the king's right hand which holds a club, perhaps belonging to the god. A similar motif is also found on other seals.

THE wild beasts will honour me, the jackals and the ostriches; for I give water in the wilderness, rivers in the desert, to give drink to my chosen people.   (Isaiah 43 : 20)

The prophet's vision of Israel's redemption spreads out beyond the narrow confines of a historical hope of national revival until it embraces the renewal of the whole universe. The Lord "is making a new thing" (Isa. 43 : 19) the like of which has never been known, a different world from His first creation (ibid. 18). Once again, when Israel goes forth from Babylon, it will cross wide expanses of desert, as it did after the exodus from Egypt. But this time the whole appearance of the desert will change. Where there was formerly nothing but deathly barrenness and shrivelling heat, the once arid earth will now yield an abundance of water and burst into bloom. The returning exiles will cross the desert without fear or danger, "for He who has pity on them will lead them, and by springs of water will guide them" (Isa. 49 : 10). The wild life of the wilderness, too, will no longer be forced to wander far and wide in search of water. Normally, these animals slake their thirst from rock-pools in the beds of water-courses, where, even in summer, water still remains from the winter rains. This craving of wild beasts for fresh, life-giving water is a common metaphor in the works of Old Testament poets and prophets (Ps. 42 : 2; Jer. 14 : 5-6). In the new world-order there will be water in plenty for the beasts too, and they will join mankind in giving thanks to God.
The picture is a photograph of a pool of water in the Yeraqam Valley, in the vicinity of the Scorpions' Ascent.

THE ironsmith fashions it and works it over the coals; he shapes it with hammers, and forges it with his strong arm . . .

(Isaiah 44 : 12)

In order to hold up to ridicule the idolaters who bow down in worship to the works of human hands, the prophet gives a vivid and detailed description of the way in which an idol was made by an "ironsmith" (a term which is here meant to include any kind of metal-worker; cf. Deut. 27 : 15). In this description, a clear distinction is drawn between idols of wood (see p. 73) and those of metal. The latter were usually made by casting bronze, or some other metal, into a mould (cf. Vol. I, p. 290). The statue thus formed was then embellished with engravings or overlays in gold and silver (cf. Isa. 40 : 19). Detailed representations of the manufacture of idols are found in the pictorial art of ancient Egypt, as, for example, in the wall-painting from the tomb of the two sculptors of the time of Amenhotep II (first half of the 14th cent. B.C.) which was excavated at Thebes (see the reproduction below). In the bottom row, a sculptor is putting the finishing touches to the statue of a sphinx; another craftsman is painting ornaments on a vase. In the top row, gold rings are being weighed and carpenters are working on ebony vessels.

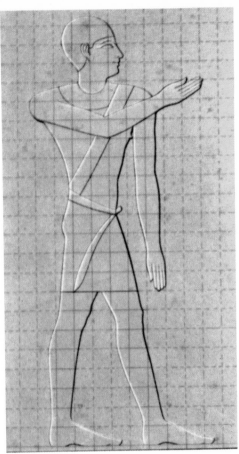

THE carpenter stretches a line, he marks it out with a pencil; he fashions it with planes, and marks it with a compass; he shapes it into the figure of a man . . .   (Isaiah 44 : 13)

Wooden statues were carved from durable, hard-wood tree-trunks (Isa. 40 : 20). The craftsman first of all selected a suitable log of wood and then drew a series of squares on it to facilitate the precise delineation of the figure required, as illustrated in a painting from the Twenty-Sixth Dynasty in Egypt (7th-6th cent. B.C.) which is reproduced at the top right. This squaring was done with a compass and a "pencil" (Heb. *sered).* The exact meaning of this latter word, which occurs only here in the Old Testament, is uncertain. One view, adopted in the translation above, is that it denotes a pointed metal instrument; another that it is the name of a colour (red). The next stage in the process was planing the wood and cutting away the superfluous parts of it until the idol itself, which was usually in human form (see the painting from Thebes at the top left), began to take shape. Sometimes the idol was made in separate sections which, when completed, were fastened together by nails. In the reproduction on p. 72, at the right of the lower register, an Egyptian craftsman is seen modelling part of a statue with a chisel (cf. Jer. 10 : 3).

HALF of it he burns in the fire; over the half he eats flesh, he roasts meat and is satisfied; also he warms himself and says, "Aha, I am warm, I have seen the fire!"   (Isaiah 44 : 16)

The contemptuous derision felt by the prophets of Israel for the worshippers of idols is depicted in a series of realistic vignettes taken from everyday experience. Here the prophet is describing the nothingness and complete impotence of man-made idols. It is as if he were appealing to the idolaters to examine their own actions with open eyes and to learn a lesson from what they see. For how can a man place his trust in a statue made from the self-same tree-trunk whose branches he has used for roasting meat and baking bread, and even for lighting a fire to warm himself with? The prophet's amazed contempt is provoked by the cries of delight uttered by the idol-worshipper as he warms himself in the glow of those very same logs from which he previously made the gods to whom he does obeisance.

Reproduced below is an Egyptian stone statue, from the time of the Fifth Dynasty (middle of the third millennium B.C.), representing a woman sitting beside an oven made of stones and baking bread. She is raking out the ashes and fanning the flame with her left hand, while her right is held to her temple, as if to feel the heat.

THUS says the LORD to His anointed, to Cyrus, whose right hand I have grasped, to subdue nations before him and ungird the loins of kings, to open doors before him that gates may not be closed.   (Isaiah 45 : 1)

The hope of redemption cherished by the prophet of consolation finds its political expression in the glorification of Cyrus, the founder of the Persian empire. For the prophet, Cyrus is much more than one of the kings of the nations: he is the emissary of God who will set Israel free from the yoke.

Cyrus was originally king of Anshan, a city in Elam (557-529 B.C.). In 553 he revolted against his overlord Astyages the king of Media, and in 550 defeated him in battle and captured his capital Ecbatana. Only a few years later (547), his armies overcame Croesus, the king of Lydia in Asia Minor. This victory gave Cyrus the world-famous treasures of Croesus; and it is perhaps to this event that the prophet is referring when he says: "I will give you the treasures of darkness and the hoards in secret places" (Isa. 45 : 3). In 539 Cyrus advanced on Babylon, the capital of the Babylonian empire, which opened its gates to him without offering any resistance. The Babylonian king, Nabonidus (555-539 B.C.) was taken captive, while his son, Belshazzar, apparently fell in battle. These events are perhaps alluded to by the prophet in the verse at the top of this page. A similar description of Cyrus as the subduer of nations is found in "the political story" about Nabonidus (see the copy of the inscription at the bottom left): "Cyrus is the king of the world whose victories are true victories and whose yoke all the kings of the lands wear." After his conquest of Babylon, Cyrus restored all the captives from the various nations conquered by the Babylonians to their homelands and rebuilt their temples. It is clear from the Old Testament that the deportees from Judah received the same treatment (see Ezra 1 : 1-11; 6 : 3-5).

Photographed above is the traditional tomb of Cyrus at Pasargadae in Persia (about 40 miles north of Persepolis). Built at the top of seven tiers of steps, the tomb towers high above the surrounding countryside.

When Cyrus destroys Babylon, he will treat its idols as the Babylonians, in the days of their victories, had treated the idols of the nations conquered by them. Even the two chief Babylonian gods, Bel and Nebo, will be powerless to save themselves from being hacked down from their pedestals and carried off by their captors.

Bel (an Akkadian word meaning "lord") was the title of Marduk, the chief deity of the Babylonian pantheon. The Babylonian story of the creation (Enuma-elish) relates that Marduk, the son of Ea, was first one of the young gods, but then rose to be their leader by conquering Tiamat, the goddess of the deeps, who tried to annihilate the gods. From her corpse Bel created the heavens and the earth. The New Year of Marduk was celebrated at Babylon with great solemnity, as the day on which, in Babylonian tradition, the fate of the world was decided for the coming year. On a boundary-stone (reproduced below) of the Kassite period, from the reign of Melishuhi (12th cent. B.C.), the god Marduk is seen wearing a crown, with a horned mythical creature crouching at his feet. At the right edge of the stone are the emblems of other gods.

Nebo, the son of Marduk, was the god of wisdom and writing. In the Babylonian New Year ceremonies statues of Nebo were first carried in procession to the temple of Marduk, and then statues of Marduk accompanied the statues of his son in the return procession back to the latter's shrine. It is possible that, in our verse here, the prophet had such a procession in mind. The statue of Nebo, reproduced above, was excavated at Calah (the modern Nimrud) and is from the time of Adadnirari III (810-782 B.C.). Engraved on the statue is the following inscription: "Trust in Nebo; do not trust in any other god."

Bᴇʟ bows down, Nebo stoops, their idols are on beasts and cattle . . .   (Isaiah 46 : 1)

THEY lift it upon their shoulders, they carry it, they set it in its place, and it stands there; it cannot move from its place . . .

(Isaiah 46 : 7)

The prophet turns the barbs of his polemic against the nations who place their faith in idols that are incapable of saving themselves, let alone anyone else. Instead of refuting the basic tenets of idolatry, he concentrates his attack upon the emblems of the idolatrous cults, those lifeless objects which are regarded by their worshippers as gods. His denunciation lays bare the nothingness of idols as being made from materials used by man in his daily life (see p. 74). Although they have a human form, they are even more helpless than a human being. The idol is powerless to move from its place (cf. Ps. 115 : 7) unless its worshippers carry it on their shoulders. In the ancient East it was the custom to carry the images of the gods in cultic processions (see p. 76) and in triumphal parades (cf. Vol. II, p. 289). A relic of this custom is perhaps also to be found in Amos' admonition to the Israelites: "You shall take up Sakkuth your king and Kaiwan your star-god, your images, which you made for yourselves" (5 : 26). The picture is a reproduction of a relief from the palace of Tiglath-Pileser III (744-727 B.C.) at Calah. Four statues of gods are seen being borne away from a conquered city on the shoulders of the Assyrian monarch's troops. The horned god on the left is holding an axe and a bundle of forked lightning, the symbols of the deity Adad. It is difficult to identify the figure of the god (or goddess) in front of him, since the greater part of it is hidden by a curtain. At the right there are two seated goddesses. Each of them is wearing a crown topped by an astral disc and flanked by horns, the symbol of divine power.

COME down and sit in the dust, O virgin daughter of Babylon; sit on the ground without a throne, O daughter of the Chaldeans! For you shall no more be called tender and delicate. Take the millstones and grind meal . . .

(Isaiah 47 : 1-2)

The rise of the Persian empire sealed the doom of mighty Babylon. Instead of the wealth and comfort to which they had grown used, the inhabitants of the great metropolis were now reduced to humiliating slavery. The prophet compares the city of Babylon to a fine lady who, by a turn of fortune's wheel, suddenly finds herself a serving-woman. The rich men and the notables of those days, and especially their wives, lived lives of magnificent luxury. Only members of the highest class and of the aristocracy used to sit on chairs or recline on couches, which were sometimes of the most ornate workmanship (Amos 3 : 12; 6 : 4), while the simple citizens and slaves sat on the ground. Hence, not sitting on a chair was regarded by the upper classes as a sign of social degradation (Jer. 13 : 18). The daughters and wives of the rich did not demean themselves to do the hard work of grinding flour (see Vol. I, p. 281) which was usually done by serving-women (Ex. 11 : 5), or by male or female captives taken from the conquered and exiled nations (Judg. 16 : 21; Lam. 5 : 13). Grinding was particularly heavy work for just those delicate and pampered high-class ladies who were usually the first to be carried off into captivity (Amos 4 : 2-3).

Reproduced above is a section of an Assyrian relief from Nineveh in which a group of captives from Elam is shown being led away into exile by their Assyrian captors. At a halt on the march, the deportees are sitting on stones and eating a meal prepared for them by their wives.

THUS says the LORD GOD: "Behold, I will lift up my hand to the nations, and raise my signal to the peoples; and they shall bring your sons in their bosom, and your daughters shall be carried on their shoulders."

(Isaiah 49 : 22)

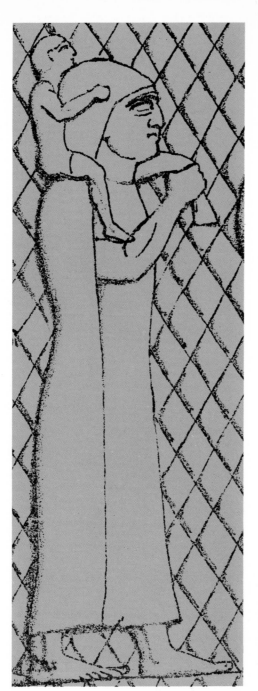

Zion in its desolation is likened to a mother bereaved of all her children (Isa. 49 : 21; 51 : 18). Conversely, Zion redeemed will be like a bereaved mother whose children have miraculously been restored to her. The same foes that had deported Zion's children with brutal ferocity will, in the days that are to come, be compelled by the Lord to restore them with all due care for their well-being and comfort. The kings and tyrants of the nations will conduct the people of Israel on their hazardous journey, as a nurse bears an infant in her bosom (Nu. 11 : 12) or as a mother carries her young child on her shoulders.

In antiquity, oriental women, like their sisters to-day, were in the habit of carrying their children on their hip (Isa. 60 : 4; 66 : 12) or back, wrapped in a large kerchief or in the ample folds of their garment and fastened to their body, so as to leave their hands and arms free for the performance of their domestic tasks. The reproduction at the top right — a wooden statue of a non-Egyptian woman from the tomb of Useri at Beni Hasan (Twelfth Dynasty, 19th cent. B.C.) — illustrates the carrying of a child on the mother's back in the folds of her garment. The other method of carrying the child — on the shoulders — was particularly common on long journeys. This is illustrated by those works of art from the ancient East which depict captives being marched off into exile, as in the detail (at the top left) from one of the reliefs of Sennacherib at Nineveh showing the capture of Lachish in 701 B.C. and the deportation of its inhabitants (for the whole relief see Vol. II, p. 287 bottom). It was probably some such scene that the prophet had in mind when he painted his picture of the return to Zion, with the difference that this time, on the march of redemption, there will be "the oil of gladness instead of mourning, the mantle of praise instead of a faint spirit" (Isa. 61 : 3).

MORNING by morning he wakens, he wakens my ear to hear as those who are taught.

(Isaiah 50 : 4)

The Servant of the Lord, who, according to one interpretation, is to be identified with the prophet himself, hearkens to God's words as a pupil listens, morning after morning, to his master's teaching. This simile implies the existence of established methods of instruction by which no doubt the "sons of the prophets", amongst others, were trained. In the lands of the East, the temples usually also served as schools.and the priests were teachers (cf. Mal. 2 : 7). The principal subject taught was writing, for the training of future generations of "scribes". Writing exercises, such as the copying out of various texts on clay tablets and on papyrus, have been unearthed by archaeologists all over the Middle East. Evidence of the antiquity of systematic study in those lands is provided by a Sumerian tablet from the first part of the second millennium B.C. which is reproduced at the bottom left. The tablet was written by a teacher and sets out a pupil's daily school time-table. Before going to bed the pupil says to his mother: "Wake me up early in the morning, for I must not be late (or) my teacher will cane me". When he gets to school his teacher checks his homework. If he is not satisfied with the writing or finds some other fault, he thrashes the pupil. The outstanding pupil, on the contrary, is praised by the teacher who foretells a distinguished future for him.

Some idea of the appearance of an ancient institute of learning may be obtained from the remains of a school from the beginning of the second millennium B.C. which were brought to light in the excavation of the royal palace at Mari on the Euphrates (see the plate at the bottom right). On and beside the rows of benches there are round clay vessels in which the various writing implements were kept.

How beautiful upon the mountains are the feet of him who brings good tidings, who publishes peace, who brings good tidings of good, who publishes salvation, who says to Zion, "Your God reigns."

(Isaiah 52 : 7)

The prophet of consolation opens his prophecy of Israel's revival with a vision of the redemption of Jerusalem. In his mind's eye, he sees the watchmen announcing to the remnants of the population left in the devastated city the glad tidings of the returning exiles' approach. The description of them as coming down from the mountains is thoroughly realistic, since "round about Jerusalem there are mountains" (Ps. 125 : 2) which rise above the Temple Mount (see p. 20), so that anyone approaching the city must descend into it. The ancient roads leading to Jerusalem, such as the highway from Shechem via Bethel to the Mount of Olives or the approach from the west through Chephirah and Kiryath-Yearim, all ran along the mountain-ridges. When, from these ravine-girt peaks, the returning exiles catch their first glimpses of the city in all its glory, they know that their long journey is almost ended. This is the moment to which the prophet refers in his exhortation: "Get you up to a high mountain, O herald of good tidings to Zion; lift up your voice with strength, O herald of good tidings to Jerusalem" (Isa. 40 : 9; cf. Nah. 1 : 15).

The photograph above is a view of Jerusalem from the west, from the neighbourhood of the new settlement of Mevassereth Yerushalayim ("the bringer of good tidings to Jerusalem") which stands not far from the site of the ancient city of Kiryath-Yearim. The houses on the ridge in the background are those of the capital, while those at the right, in the valley, belong to the village of En Kerem.

B<small>EHOLD</small>, I have created the smith who blows the fire of coals, and produces a weapon for its purpose . . .

(Isaiah 54 : 16)

When the redemption comes, no enemy will be able to harm Israel any more. No ravaging army will be permitted to spread havoc in its land, nor will any weapon made by a smith avail against Israel. For the Lord, who created all creatures including the smith, will be His people's shield.

The metals in common use in the ancient East in the time of the First Temple were copper and pig iron. The use of these metals in the manufacture of weapons depended on a knowledge of the processes whereby a sufficiently high temperature could be generated to soften the metal before it was worked. From the very earliest times the peoples of the East knew how to increase the heat of a fire by blowing on the flame and thus giving it more oxygen. In manufacturing processes this was done, at first, by means of a hollow reed, and later, with bellows (see p. 101) and in furnaces so constructed as to give the fire a forced draught (see p. 178), as in the smelter built by Solomon at Ezion-Geber.

The illustration is a wall-painting from Beni Hasan (reconstructed in detail at the top), from the 19th cent. B.C., showing two craftsmen blowing on to a fire through long pipes with bulbous ends, in order to fan it to the temperature required for their work.

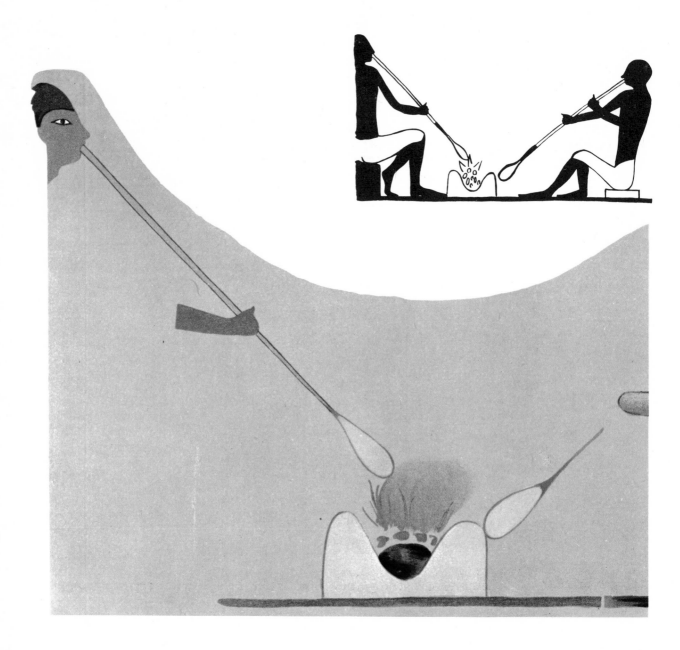

INSTEAD of the thorn shall come up the cypress; instead of the brier shall come up the myrtle; and it shall be to the LORD for a memorial, for an everlasting sign which shall not be cut off.   (Isaiah 55 : 13)

In the prophet's inspired imagination, Israel's deliverance from its Babylonian captivity is envisaged as a renewal and transformation of the whole creation, the miracle described in the words, "the uneven ground shall become level, and the rough places a plain" (Isa. 40 : 4). The desert and the steppe will burst into bloom and in the arid waste water will well up from the ground (cf. pp. 62; 71). The abandoned and neglected fields, which had become overgrown with briers and thorns for want of hands to tend them (Isa. 7 : 23-25), will once more be brought under cultivation and fruit-bearing and other goodly trees will again grow there. The thorn (Heb. *naazuz,* a word which is found in the Old Testament only here and in Isa. 7 : 19), with its spines that stick into the flesh of anyone who touches it, and the painfully stinging nettle, both of which symbolize dereliction and desolation, will be replaced by the symbols of joy and gladness — the evergreen cypress, refreshing to behold (Hos. 14 : 8), and the sweet-scented myrtle (Isa. 41 : 19; Neh. 8 : 15).
The nettle (Heb. *sarpad,* a word found nowhere else in the Old Testament) referred to here is either the stinging nettle *(Urtica urens L.;* see the photograph at the top left) or the ball-nettle *(Urtica pilulifera L.;* top right). Since nettles grow on waste land and around derelict buildings, they have become symbols of desolation.

THEY are greedy dogs; they never have enough... (Isaiah 56 : 11)

The leaders of the people of Israel betrayed their sacred trust: instead of devoting themselves to the general good, they went their own way "each to his own gain" (Isa. 56 : 11). They are compared to sheep-dogs that not only failed to bark or give warning of the danger threatening the flock (Isa. 56 : 10), but actually joined the wild beast in rending their charges. The dog, man's companion from the dawn of history, was known in the ancient East in the Stone Age. Figurines of dogs have been found on the most ancient sites of human settlement in Palestine. The dog was used in antiquity for two main purposes: guarding and hunting. In Egypt dogs were employed, as early as the third millennium B.C., in the hunting of gazelles. The dogs must have been bold enough to take on even powerful wild animals, to judge from the representations of them as fighting with lions, or guarding a flock or a human settlement from the attacks of a beast of prey (cf. Ps. 22 : 16). In Mesopotamia, too, the dog was known from the earliest times, though its use in hunting is first illustrated in reliefs (see p. 93) and mentioned in documents from the Assyrian period. Below is a reproduction of a relief from Nineveh, belonging to the 7th cent. B.C., showing a hunting-dog straining at the leash held by the hunter. The dog's eagerness is emphasized by the exaggerated prominence given by the artist to its ribs.

YOU journeyed to Molech with oil and multiplied your perfumes; you sent your envoys far off, and sent down even to Sheol.   (Isaiah 57 : 9)

The prophet's wrathful indignation at Israel's obstinate clinging to strange gods vents itself, first and foremost, on the cult of the god Molech which was widespread in Canaan. Essential features of this cult were its orgiastic rites (Isa. 57 : 7-8) and its sacred mysteries, culminating in child-sacrifice (Isa. 57 : 5; Ezek. 16 : 20-21). The dedication of oil and spices to the god was a regular part of Molech worship, as it was in every cult of the ancient East (cf. Vol. I, p. 176). Indeed, various kinds of spices and oils were used even in the worship of the God of Israel (Ex. 30 : 34). Here the prophet denounces the people for giving to idols the offerings that should have been presented to the God of Israel (cf. Ezek. 16 : 18-19). Some of the aromatic plants from which perfumes and medicines were made grew in Palestine, especially in Gilead (cf. Gen. 37 : 25; 43 : 11), and some were imported from outside the country, particularly from the Arabian peninsula (1 Kings 10 : 10; Ezek. 27 : 22). The mixing of oils and the preparation of spices are depicted in ancient Egyptian art. Above, for example, is a wall-painting from Beni Hasan (beginning of the second millennium B.C.) in which women are seen at work distilling perfume from lotus-flowers, one of the main sources of cosmetics (cf. Vol. II, p. 123). The women are bringing baskets of flowers to the press which consists of a kind of sack with sticks attached to its ends. When these sticks are twisted in opposite directions, the oil is gradually squeezed out of the flowers and drips through the porous material of the sack into a container placed underneath it. A similar method was sometimes also employed in the production of must (cf. Vol. I, p. 133).

IS such the fast that I choose, a day for a man to humble himself? Is it to bow down his head like a rush, and to spread sackcloth and ashes under him . . .

(Isaiah 58 : 5)

The prophets make allegorical use of the characteristics of the water-reed in order to paint a vivid picture of national or individual character. Thus, Egypt is frequently likened to a broken reed (2 Kings 18 : 21 ; Ezek. 29 : 6), "which will pierce the hand of any man who leans on it" (Isa. 36 : 6). The dull-spirited man is also compared to a broken reed (Isa. 42 : 3). In our verse here, the simile refers to those members of the people who, though they are not sincere observers of God's law, yet put on an outward show of repentance by fasting and mourning (cf. Esther 4 : 3) and lowering their heads like the well-known marsh-plant, the bulrush (Heb. *agmon*). As this Hebrew word appears to be used in the Old Testament of various water-plants, precise identification is difficult. One view is that it is a reed of the kind known to botanists as *Phragmites* (see Vol. II, p. 231), or of the kind known as *Arundo*. However, the reed that corresponds most closely to the descriptions given in the Old Testament is the *Scirpus*, a small plant which usually has a slightly bowed inflorescence very much as depicted in our verse (cf. Isa. 9 : 14 ; 19 : 15).

Photographed here is the rush *(Scirpus maritimus)*, which grows in marshes and at the edges of watercourses in the plains of Israel and in the mountains of Judah.

THEY hatch adders' eggs, they weave the spider's web; he who eats their eggs dies, and from one which is crushed a viper is hatched.   (Isaiah 59 : 5)

Those members of the nation who sin against God by their idolatry also transgress the laws of social morality by perverting justice and swearing false oaths (Isa. 59 : 4; cf. Amos 2 : 6-8). Their promises are worthless, like fine-spun insubstantial spiders' webs, and their deeds are false, like those fair-seeming eggs from which deadly snakes are hatched. The snake was the symbol of deceitfulness. The primeval serpent in the story of the Garden of Eden, for instance, was more subtle than any other wild creature (Gen. 3 : 1), and its name became a synonym for evil scheming and vicious machinations (Ps. 140 : 3). Of the few indigenous Palestinian snakes that are poisonous, the Old Testament mentions the viper (Heb. *zepha, ziphoni, shephiphon),* the adder *(epheh)* and the asp *(peten).*

The photograph on the left is of an adder *(Echis colorata),* a relatively rare Palestinian snake. Its habitat is the arid desert area in the southern part of the country. On the right is the Palestinian viper *(Vipera palaestina)* which is found in the proximity of populated areas of the country, especially in the coastal plain and in the valleys, and whose bite is frequently fatal to man.

Who are these that fly like a cloud, and like doves to their windows?   (Isaiah 60 : 8)

In reward for Israel's return to its God, the prophet promises the people that God will gather them in from all the places to which they have been dispersed. To make the picture of the ingathering more vivid, he employs an ornithological metaphor that would have been immediately appreciated by his hearers. Just as pigeons, whether wild or domesticated, which have wandered far from their nest nearly always fly straight back to it, so will the scattered Israelites return to their land by the straightest and shortest route. The rock-pigeon *(Columba livia)*, which is common in Palestine, nests in the crannies of rocks in the mountains and wadis (Jer. 48 : 28; Ezek. 7 : 16; Song of Sol. 2 : 14). Occasionally it also builds its nest inside caves which it enters through fissures or openings in the rock (Heb. *arubah),* here translated window. The pigeon was apparently one of the first birds to be domesticated (cf. Vol. I, p. 184), to judge from the fact that the sending off and return of a pigeon is mentioned in the story of the flood, both in the Israelite (Gen. 8 : 8-12) and in the Babylonian versions.
Below are two domesticated pigeons photographed in the Arab village of Dehi on the Hill of Moreh. The "windows" of the cote are built into the top of the mud-hut.

WHY is thy apparel red, and thy garments like his that treads in the wine press?
(Isaiah 63 : 2)

The blood-stained apparel of the soldier returning victorious from the battle-field is the same red colour as the juice-splashed garments of the grape-treader in the wine-press (Isa. 63 : 3). In eastern countries wine is still produced in this way. After the grapes have been gathered, they are brought in clusters to the wine-press (Heb. *gath* or *yeqev*, Isa. 16 : 10; Joel 3 : 13) which is usually in the vineyard itself (Judg. 9 : 27; Isa. 5 : 2) or close to it. Detailed information about the ways in which grapes were trodden out to produce wine is provided by wall-paintings and other artistic representations from ancient Egypt, a land famed for the quality of its vines. The method most commonly employed in Upper Egypt and in Palestine was treading in the press (Amos 9 : 13) consisting of a trough with an aperture in its bottom through which the new wine flowed into jars. The treading was done barefoot, to prevent the grape-pips from being crushed and spoiling the flavour of the wine.
A typical ancient wine-press is seen in the illustration above, which is a reproduction of a wall-painting found in the tomb of Api at Deir el-Medineh (Nineteenth Dynasty, 13th cent. B.C.). Above the press, supported on posts, there is a high wooden cross-bar with ropes dangling from it. These ropes are for the treaders to hold on to, so that they should not slip on the smooth grape-skins. The press is standing in a vineyard where the grapes are still being gathered. At the right of the press there are jars full of new wine.

As one whom his mother comforts, so will I comfort you; you shall be comforted in Jerusalem. (Isaiah 66 : 13)

God's special closeness to Israel is described by the prophets in similes taken from family relationships. Sometimes God is represented as the husband, and the congregation of Israel as the wife (Isa. 50 : 1; Jer. 2 : 2) that has forgotten her youthful love (Jer. 3 : 20; Hos. 2 : 15); or God is the father of Israel (Deut. 32 : 6; Isa. 63 : 16) who pardons his children (Jer. 31 : 9) in spite of their delinquencies (Isa. 1 : 4). In our verse here God is likened to a mother who compassionately comforts her children. The covenant between the Lord and Israel will be renewed and Israel will once more be like the darling child that is dandled on its mother's lap (cf. Jer. 31 : 20).

It is not only in the Old Testament that the relations between gods and mortals are thus depicted. The same allegorical descriptions are also found in the literature and art of the ancient East as a whole. But, in contrast to the Old Testament, there the allegories are concerned with the graciousness shown by the god or goddess to the ruling monarch, and not with the divine love of a whole people. One of the Ugaritic epics refers to a ruler as feeding at the breasts of a goddess; while Egyptian reliefs and statues represent the Pharaoh as sitting on the knees of the god or goddess.

Reproduced above is the statue of Queen Ankhnesmerire holding in her lap her son, the Pharaoh Pepi II of the Sixth Dynasty in Egypt (second half of the third millennium B.C.).

A ND they shall bring all your breth-
ren from all the nations as an offering
to the IORD, upon horses, and in
chariots, and in litters, and upon mules,
and upon dromedaries, to my holy
mountain Jerusalem . . . (Isaiah 66 : 20)

At the end of his message of consolation the prophet
returns to his opening theme. All the nations will
praise the God of Israel (Isa. 42 : 11-12; 66 : 19), and
will do homage to His chosen people whose scattered
sons they will reverently restore to Jerusalem with all
due pomp, borne on the backs of horses and mules or
transported in carriages. Our verse mentions vehicles
designed for comfort, such as the "litters" (Heb.
zabbim, from Akkadian *sumbu (= subbu)* which were
covered carriages for long-distance travelling. Such
carriages were in use from the beginning of the third
millennium B.C. onwards. They were also common
in the Assyrian period, as is evident from a relief from
Carchemish (reproduced below) belonging to the 9th
or 8th cent. B.C. Besides the litter there was also an
uncovered carriage, sometimes drawn by oxen, like
the one in a relief from the palace of Ashurbanipal at
Nineveh (7th cent. B.C.; see above). Carriages of
this kind were used in the deportation of captives
from Lachish (see Vol. II, p. 287, bottom).
The exact meaning of the word here translated
"dromedaries" (Heb. *kirkaroth*) is uncertain. Some
hold that it denotes swift-footed riding-camels, while
others see in them light carriages, so named because
they bounced up and down when moving and therefore seemed to be dancing along *(mekarkeroth)* (Nah.
3 : 2).

JEREMIAH

THE words of Jeremiah, the son of Hilkiah, of the priests who were in Anathoth in the land of Benjamin.

(Jeremiah 1 : 1)

Jeremiah tells us that he came of a priestly family at Anathoth. On the basis of this statement it is conjectured that he was related to the family of Abiathar, the priest who was expelled from Jerusalem by King Solomon (1 Kings 2 : 26-27). The site of Anathoth is within the confines of the modern Arab village of Anata (photographed here), about four miles north-east of Jerusalem; to be more precise, it is the tell of Ras el-Kharubeh, where archaeological remains have been found dating to the period of the kingdom of Judah. This dual proximity to the capital of Judah, on one side, and to the pasturing grounds of the Judean wilderness, on the other, left a lasting impression on the spirit of the prophet Jeremiah. He is familiar with the sights of nature and with the lives of shepherds and farmers, while at the same time he is fully conversant with the political developments in Judah and with the lives of the various strata of Jerusalem society (cf. Jer. 1 : 18). The language of his prophecies is deeply influenced by the conditions of life in the city of his birth, Anathoth, which, situated as it was on the edge of the desert, waited anxiously every year for adequate rainfall and dew, knowing full well what suffering drought could cause. Even when Jeremiah had taken up residence in Jerusalem, he still felt a strong emotional attachment to his birthplace and to his family estate in the territory of Benjamin (chap. 32).

THEY did not say, "Where is the LORD who brought us up from the land of Egypt, who led us in the wilderness, in a land of deserts and pits, in a land of drought and deep darkness, in a land that none passes through, where no man dwells?"
(Jeremiah 2 : 6)

Jeremiah yearningly reminds the daughter of Jerusalem of the devotion of her youth when she followed the God of Israel through the wilderness, in an unsown land, sustained by her fidelity to the covenant that He had made with her (Jer. 2 : 2). This description of the period of the wanderings in the wilderness as a golden age of youth is also found in the Song of Moses (Deut. 32 : 10-13), and in the utterances of the prophet Hosea (2 : 15; 9 : 10; 11 : 1). The origin of Hosea's and Jeremiah's conception is to be found in their idealization of the distant past, in contrast to the more recent sinful days that came upon the nation after its occupation of Canaan: "But when you came in you defiled my land, and made my heritage an abomination" (Jer. 2 : 7).

The "wilderness" described here with such a wealth of epithets is the arid region of the Sinai desert and the Negev where no grass grows, either in summer or winter, and which is most aptly delineated by the word "waste-land" (Heb. *yeshimon*). The features common to all these desert areas are the wide expanses bare of all vegetation and scored with large and small wadis (the "pits" of our verse). The descriptive expression "a land of drought and deep darkness" refers no doubt to the most desolate recesses of Sinai, "the howling waste of a wilderness" of Deut. 32 : 10.

The view above is a landscape in the Wilderness of Zin.

K<small>NOW</small> what you have done — a restive young camel interlacing her tracks. (Jeremiah 2 : 23)

In its brazen apostasy, the sinful people of Israel is likened by Jeremiah to a wanton woman who sins on every high hill and under every green tree (Jer. 2 : 20), or to an animal in the mating season. In her frivolity and restless inconstancy the daughter of Zion is like a restive young she-camel that frisks wantonly to and fro.

The Hebrew word here translated "young she-camel" *(bikhrah)* is found only in this verse of the Old Testament, but its meaning is clear from the corresponding words in two other Semitic languages, Akkadian and Arabic. The male form, *bekher,* also occurs (Isa. 60 : 6). According to the precise etymology of the word, *bikhrah* denotes a full-grown she-camel that has not yet given birth for the first time. Thus the point of the simile would lie in the intemperate lust of the she-camel in its first mating season.

The photograph below was taken in the Mishmar Valley near the Dead Sea south of En-Gedi. It shows young camels trailing close to their dams.

A wild ass used to the wilderness . . .   (Jeremiah 2 : 24)

The wild ass (Heb. *pere* or *arod*) is a freedom-loving, intractable creature of the wilderness that roams at will over its desert wastes: "He scorns the tumult of the city; he hears not the shouts of the driver" (Job 39 : 7; cf. Isa. 32 : 14; Jer. 14 : 6; Job 24 : 5). Its name was therefore applied symbolically to any uncivilized man of violent, lawless conduct (see Vol. I, p. 56). The Hebrew word *pere* can denote both the male and the female. Here, as in the simile of the young she-camel (see p. 97), Jeremiah compares Judah to a rampant wild she-ass on heat: "Who can restrain her lust?" The prophet Hosea describes Ephraim's soliciting of Assyria in similar terms: "For they have gone up to Assyria, a wild-ass wandering alone; Ephraim has hired lovers" (Hos. 8 : 9).

In antiquity wild-asses were hunted in the Syrian desert and in the plains of Mesopotamia. A chase of this kind is portrayed in a series of reliefs from the reign of Ashurbanipal, the Assyrian king (7th cent. B.C.), which were excavated at Nineveh. On one of these reliefs, reproduced here, wild-asses are seen in flight, hotly pursued by hunting-dogs. Some of the hunted creatures have been pierced by arrows.

AT the noise of horseman and archer every city takes to flight . . .   (Jeremiah 4 : 29)

The main theme of Jeremiah's first prophecies is a repeated warning about a nation from the north which is advancing upon Judah to lay it waste (Jer. 4 : 6; cf. 1 : 14-15; 6 : 1). The prophet again and again powerfully describes the dreadful might of the destroyer and the terror with which his coming fills the land of Judah (Jer. 4 : 13-16, 19-22; 5 : 15-17; 6 : 1-5, 22-26). Our verse here depicts the utter panic of the population at the foreign conqueror's approach and their headlong flight at the mere sound of his cavalry's hoof-beats. Scholars are divided in their opinions about the identity of this northern nation. One view is that the prophet did not have any particular people in mind and it was only later, when Nebuchadnezzar became king, that his grim vision of the future was realized in the form of Babylon. Other scholars, on the contrary, maintain that Babylon was meant all the time, since elsewhere Jeremiah explicitly prophesies that Judah will be destroyed by the Babylonians. Still others hold that the reference is to the Scythians whose predatory raids in the 7th cent. B.C., according to Herodotus, took them from their home in the region of the Black Sea as far south as Ashkelon and the borders of Egypt (see p. 147). Some of the details in Jeremiah's description of the unknown enemy, such as their strangeness, their remoteness and their weapons, would well fit the Scythians, though not only them. Particularly appropriate to the Scythians, who were famed as fearless riders, is Jeremiah's combination of "horseman and archer."

The statue reproduced above is attached to the lid of a copper jar from the 5th cent. B.C. which was found in Etruria. It portrays a Scythian horseman in the distinctive dress of his race: long trousers, a short tunic and a pointed cap. From the position of his arms, it is evident that the horseman is shooting arrows from his bow as he rides, a very difficult feat that can only be mastered by long training. The steed is seen at full gallop, as in the prophet's description: "his horses are swifter than eagles" (Jer. 4 : 13).

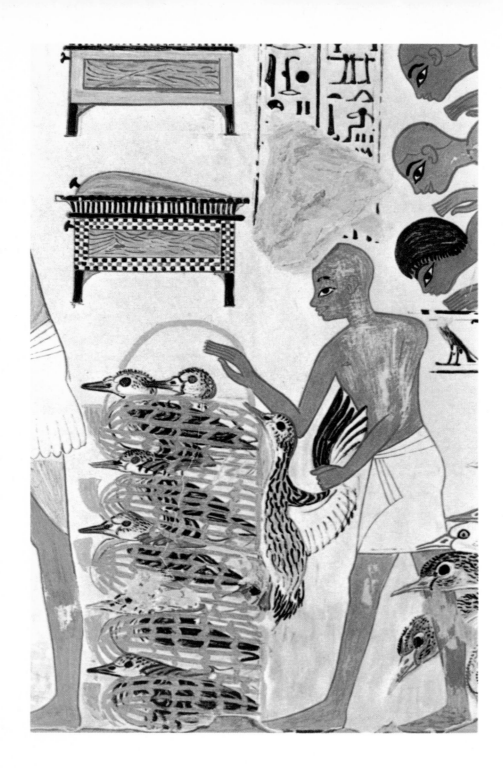

LIKE a basket full of birds, their houses are full of treachery; therefore they have become great and rich.

(Jeremiah 5 : 27)

Jeremiah, like other prophets, regards wealth and luxurious living as a cause of injustice and sin: "They have grown fat and sleek. They know no bounds in deeds of wickedness" (Jer. 5 : 28). Particularly was this the case with riches and power which had been gained, in the first place, by extortion and dishonesty. The upper classes enlarge their possessions at the expense of the poor whom they trick like hunters ensnaring their prey: "For wicked men are found among my people; they lurk like fowlers lying in wait. They set a trap; they catch men" (Jer. 5 : 26). This simile from fowling leads, by association, to another connected with the bird-cage. The houses of the wicked are as full of wealth extorted from the poor as the fowler's cage is of trapped birds. The "cage" of antiquity (Heb. *kluv*) was a wicker basket used for keeping birds, or sometimes fruit (as in "a basket [*kluv*] of summer fruit", Amos 8 : 1-2).

Reproduced above is a section of a wall-painting from the tomb of Amenemhet at Sheikh Abd el-Gurnah (reign of Thutmose III, 15th cent. B.C.) showing "bird cages" such as were common in those ancient times. In each of the wicker baskets there are two ducks. An Egyptian peasant, wearing only a loin-cloth, is putting the birds into the cage.

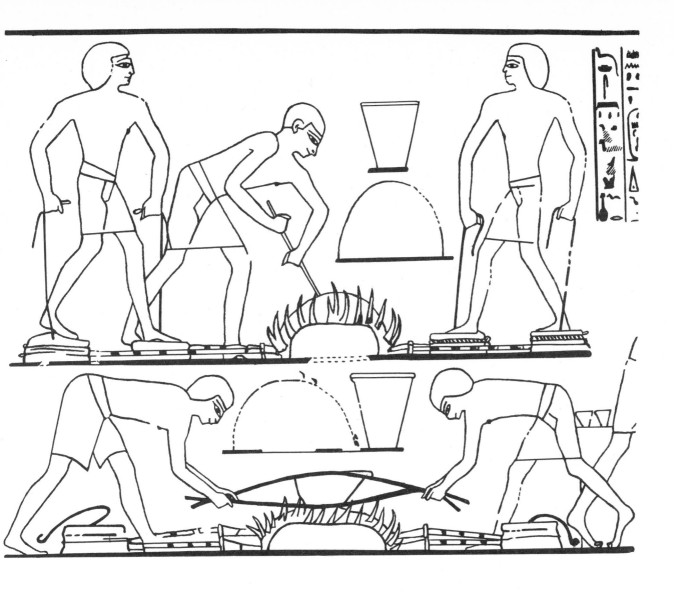

THE bellows blow fiercely, the lead is consumed by the fire; in vain the refining goes on, for the wicked are not removed.

(Jeremiah 6 : 29)

To bring home to the people their almost irredeemable sinfulness, the prophet makes use of a metaphor taken from the process of silver-extraction (cf. p. 178). In the ancient East pure silver was obtained from lead sulphide *(galena)* by subjecting the different compounds to successive processes of heating, smelting and refining. There were various grades of silver, classified according to their degree of purity. Jeremiah, in this metaphor, has in mind an inferior grade of the metal — "refuse silver" (Jer. 6 : 30) — which had been imperfectly refined (perhaps as a result of the use of an excessively hot flame) and therefore still contained a large admixture of lead that had coagulated in the process of extraction.

The refining was done in crucibles (see p. 178), and the high temperature required was obtained by fanning the fire with a bellows or with blow-pipes. The bellows mentioned in this verse were, apparently, of the type made of leather or sacking which developed out of the smiths' tube (see p. 82) and were in widespread use as early as the second millennium B.C. With this sack-bellows it was possible to increase the draught of the fire quickly and with varying degrees of intensity. The pipes through which the air was blown had clay mouthpieces at the end nearer the flame.

The use of bellows is illustrated in the above section of the wall-paintings from the tomb of Rekhmire (15th cent. B.C.). Even in those early days, the instrument had been brought to a high degree of technical perfection in Egypt. One of the metal-workers is shown raking out the fire, while his two comrades, one on either side of him, are standing on the bellows (upper register). They activate the bellows by transferring the weight of their body from one sack to the other, in a rhythmical, see-saw motion. The ropes held by the men are for raising the weights which are placed on the sack of the bellows when they are not in use. The bellows are seen in this condition in the lower register. There the two metal-workers are using a pair of bars to lift the container in which the metal has been smelted out of the fire, preparatory to pouring it out into moulds.

AND the women knead dough, to make cakes for the queen of heaven . . .

(Jeremiah 7 : 18)

In the cult of the "queen of heaven", which gained great popularity "in the cities of Judah and in the streets of Jerusalem" (Jer. 7 : 17), the main offices, such as the burning of incense and the pouring out of libations to the goddess, were performed by women (Jer. 44 : 15-20). The "queen of heaven", or "the queen of the heavens and the stars", was the title of the Mesopotamian goddess Ishtar (Astarte) whose cult apparently became widespread in Judah in the reign of Manasseh, in consequence of the growth of Assyrian influence in the country, and was not completely eradicated even after the religious reforms of Josiah. Jeremiah's words indicate that this particular form of idolatry had taken such deep root amongst the population that the Judean exiles in Egypt continued to be zealous devotees of the goddess even on foreign soil (Jer. 44 : 15-20). Further evidence of the existence of her cult in Egypt is provided by an Aramaic papyrus dating from the 5th cent. B.C. found at Hermopolis, in which the temple of the "queen of heaven" is explicitly mentioned (cf. p. 142). The women used to bake and offer to Ishtar sweetmeats (Heb. *kawwanim*, from Assyrian *kawanu-kamanu*) made, apparently, either in the likeness of the goddess herself ("cakes bearing her image", Jer. 44 : 19) or in the shape of the stars which were her symbols (see Vol. I, p. 153). Together with these pastries they also presented liquid refreshment.

The plate above is a reconstruction of an ivory carving, discovered at Calah (the modern Nimrud) on the banks of the Tigris (8th cent. B.C.), illustrating a ritual ceremony in honour of a goddess. The goddess is seen seated on a throne with two priestesses in attendance before her. The one in front is standing on a footstool (a common cultic appurtenance) and presenting an offering of foodstuffs to her divine mistress. Behind the goddess there is a line of women who are playing on various musical instruments — flutes, tambourines and what appear to be lyres. The remarkable feature of the whole representation is that the ceremony is being performed entirely by women. This would seem to indicate that the goddess is Ishtar, the "queen of heaven"

Even the stork in the heavens knows her times; and the turtledove, swallow, and crane keep the time of their coming but my people know not the ordinance of the LORD.

(Jeremiah 8 : 7)

The religious inconstancy of the people of Judah is unfavourably contrasted with the clockwork regularity with which, by natural instinct alone, certain birds migrate from continent to continent. Jeremiah, who was much given to using metaphors from bird-life, here lists a number of migrant fowl that regularly pass over Palestine at the same season every year. This mysterious phenomenon has, from the earliest times, been regarded as one of the marvels of the creation and a proof of divine providence.

The turtle-dove (Heb. *tor; Streptopilia turtur*) visits Palestine in April. The swallow (Heb. *sis*) meant here is apparently the house-swallow *(Apus apus),* large flocks of which descend upon the country at the end of February and the beginning of March. Its song is the harbinger of spring. The crane (Heb. *agur; Grus grus*) appears in Palestinian skies in spring and winter, coming in orderly formations at regular intervals. In ancient Egypt, where cranes were considered a delicacy, they were fattened up for eating, like the birds in the upper picture from the tomb of a feudal lord named Tiy at Sakkarah (Fifth Dynasty; second half of the third millennium B.C.).

The stork (Heb. *hasidah; Ciconia ciconia*) also visits the Holy Land twice a year in successive waves (see the lower picture); in spring it appears in all parts of the country, while in autumn it is seen only in the Jordan valley and in Trans-Jordan. This bird, which rears its young with almost human care, faithfully returning to its old nest year after year from distant lands, was greatly admired by the ancients. The Jews, Egyptians, Greeks and Romans alike attributed various virtues to the stork and united in singing its praises.

THUS says the LORD of hosts: "Consider, and call for the mourning women to come; send for the skilful women to come; let them make haste and raise a wailing over us..." (Jeremiah 9 : 17-18)

In his prophecies about the coming destruction of Judah, Jeremiah frequently paints powerful, sombre pictures of mourning and misery (Jer. 4 : 23-28, 31; 7 : 29; 8 : 18-22; 9 : 10-11). Sometimes the prophet himself sets an example of solitary grief (see p. 111); elsewhere he calls on the whole people to mourn as for an only son and to make bitter lamentation (Jer. 6 : 26). When the terrible blow falls, Jerusalem will have great need of skilled mourners. Hence Jeremiah's exhortation to its womenfolk: "teach to your daughters a lament, and each to her neighbour a dirge" (Jer. 9 : 20). From this we learn that there was a special art of lamentation and keening which had to be studied. Our verse here mentions professional mourning-women (Amos 5 : 16; 2 Chron. 35 : 25) who were expert at evoking tears and inducing the right funereal state of mind (Jer. 9 : 18). Such rites were traditional in the ancient East (cf. p. 191), as can be seen in both the literature and art of the time. Amongst the Arabs, even to this day, women who beat their faces and tear their flesh with their nails take part in the ceremonial mourning for the dead.

In Egyptian wall-paintings, mourning-women are sometimes depicted accompanying their lamentation with such characteristic gestures and actions as placing their hands on their heads, clapping their palms together, covering their heads with earth, baring their breasts and beating their thighs (cf. Vol. I, p. 124; Vol. II, p. 181). Reproduced above is a section of a wall-painting from the tomb of the priest Userhet at Thebes (from the reign of Seti I, c. 1300 B.C.). In it four mourning-women, dressed in white, are seen sitting on the ground holding their heads in their hands. Two of them seem to be picking up earth with their right hands in order to sprinkle it on their heads. All four are evidently professional mourners. Tears are rolling down their cheeks and their whole expression is one of grief. Above them is seen the hand of a priest who is pouring out a libation and kindling incense in memory of the dead.

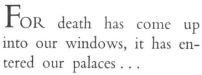

F<small>OR</small> death has come up into our windows, it has entered our palaces . . .

(Jeremiah 9 : 21)

In the dirge that will be uttered amidst the ruins of Jerusalem, the victorious enemy is compared to death that comes in by the windows, like the thief who, finding the doors of the house bolted and barred against him, forces his way in through other apertures. A similar word-picture is found in Joel's description of the locust-like foe: "They enter through the windows like a thief" (Joel 2 : 9). It is also possible that the origin of this metaphor is to be found in the ancients' fear that epidemic diseases might be carried through open windows.

Death is also described as entering by the window in the Ugaritic epic of Baal. There it is related that the god Baal gave orders that no window was to be made in his palace until he had beaten his rival Moth, who, as his name shows, was none other than the god of death (Heb. *maveth*). The left-hand plate is a reproduction of a Ugaritic cuneiform tablet containing Baal's words to the craftsman-god Kothar wa-Khasis: "Make not a window in the house, a casement within the palace". However, after overcoming Moth, Baal cancels his first order and instructs the craftsman-god to "open a casement in the house, a window within the palace." Apparently, then, the entrance of death by the windows eventually became a common figure of speech in the Canaanite and Hebrew languages. Reproduced on the right is a broken stele from a Ugaritic temple of the 18th cent. B.C. which is the only known plastic representation of the god Moth. He is shown with horns on his head, a sword fastened to a girdle round his waist, and sandals on his feet. In his right hand he holds a weapon and in his left a sceptre. Above the sceptre can be seen the Egyptian symbol of life.

CURSED be the man who does not heed the words of this covenant.   (Jeremiah 11 : 3)

The pristine covenant that had been made between the Lord and His people at the time of the exodus from Egypt (Jer. 11 : 4) was renewed in the reign of Josiah, after the discovery of the Book of the Law during the restoration of the Temple (2 Kings 22 : 8-13; 23 : 1-4). Jeremiah here warns the people to keep "the words of this covenant", at the same time pronouncing on all who should violate it a malediction ("cursed be the man") worded in the style of the Mosaic Law (cf. Deut. 27 : 15-26; and for detailed curses and admonitions, Lev. chap. 26; Deut. chap. 28). At the same time, in his inspired imagination the prophet foresees a new covenant, more enduring and more sublime than the first, which will be established in the Messianic age (Jer. 31 : 31-34; 32 : 40-41).

The covenant between the Lord and His people is an application to the sphere of Israelite religious belief of an originally juridical and political conception which was widely held in the ancient East. Specimens of treaties, especially treaties of vassalage, which have been found in the countries of the Near East, throw a clearer light on the formal structure and legal phraseology of the biblical covenant. One of the main features of treaties between nations, exactly as in the biblical covenant, is the curse which follows the detailed exposition of the terms of the treaty. For this reason the covenant itself is, in the Old Testament, sometimes called "a curse" (Heb. *alah*; Gen. 26 : 28; Ezek. 17 : 13; and elsewhere).

Such a formula of mutual obligation undertaken under penalty of a curse is illustrated, to take one example, by the treaty made in 672 B.C. between Esarhaddon, the ruler of Assyria, and Ramataia, one of his Median vassal kings. The two sides of the clay tablet discovered at Calah, on which the treaty was written, are reproduced above. It is signed with the seals of the god Ashur and those of Esarhaddon's predecessors on the Assyrian throne (see upper part of right plate). The formulation of the treaty ends with a long sequence of curses (some of which resemble those threatened by Moses for apostasy) to be brought down on the heads of all who violate its terms by the gods who are witnesses to it.

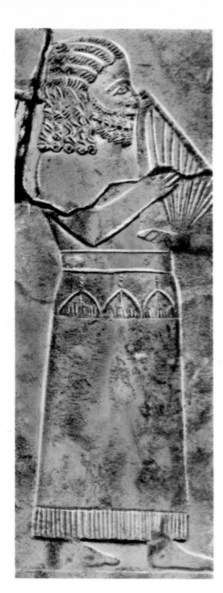

FOR as the waistcloth clings to the loins of a man, so I made the whole house of Israel and the whole house of Judah cling to me, says the LORD . . .

(Jeremiah 13 : 11)

In the true prophetic manner, Jeremiah performs symbolical acts in order to bring home to the simple masses the full meaning of his words. Here, the detailed history of the flaxen loin-cloth — its purchase, the way it fits tight round the waist, the hiding of it in the rock-cleft on the Perath brook, (now called Wadi Farah, in the neighbourhood of Anathoth), and its destruction — all this is intended to demonstrate both God's closeness to Israel and the nation's inescapable doom now that it has proved unfaithful to its God. Even as the prophet's loin-cloth was irreparably ruined, so shall Israel be destroyed "and shall be like this waistcloth, which is good for nothing" (Jer. 13 : 10).

The loin-cloth (Heb. *ezor*) or girdle *(hagurah)* was a common article of clothing in the ancient East. Its special importance as part of the warrior's accoutrement (Isa. 5 : 27) gave rise to such biblical figures of speech as "to gird on strength", "to gird up the loins" and the like. The prophets, too, were accustomed to wear a loin-cloth, as is shown by the case of Elijah whose leather girdle was one of his distinctive features (2 Kings 1 : 8). In the picture on the left — part of the series of reliefs in the palace at Shamal (the modern Zinjirli) from the 8th cent. B.C. — a lyre-player is seen wearing a tight-fitting tunic with a girdle fastened by a clasp. The girdle has tassels dangling from it in groups of three.

Possibly a distinction should be made between the girdle and the loin-cloth, the latter being merely a strip of cloth or leather wound several times around the waist with its ends hanging down over the thigh. A cloth of this kind is seen in the reproduction on the right which shows an inhabitant of Lachish from the year 701 B.C. (detail from the reliefs of Sennacherib at Nineveh). Whether the loin-cloth was worn as portrayed here, or whether it was simply a band like the girdle, it certainly fitted tight round the waist of the wearer and was therefore an appropriate object to illustrate Jeremiah's words about the former close harmonious union between God and His people.

CAN the Ethiopian change his skin or the leopard his spots? . . .   (Jeremiah 13 : 23)

The prophet's dearest desire is to bring Judah back to its God. Yet at times, in moments of bitter anger, the sins of Jerusalem seem to him so heinous that he despairs of being able to reform its inhabitants. "Woe to you, O Jerusalem. How long will it be before you are made clean?" (Jer. 13 : 27). His people's sinfulness has become so much a part of their nature that the citizens of Judah, "accustomed to do evil", can no more mend their ways than the negro can change the colour of his skin or the leopard its markings.

The leopard (Heb. *namer; Panthera pardus*) was common in ancient Palestine and is more than once mentioned by the prophets (Isa. 11 : 6; Jer. 5 : 6; Hos. 13 : 7; Hab. 1 : 8). As recently as the beginning of the present century there were still leopards in the mountains of Galilee, on the Carmel and in the Jerusalem hills, and also in the Jordan Valley and the Arabah. To-day there are only a few surviving specimens left in the Galilean mountains, like the leopard in the photograph above which was caught in the neighbourhood of Safed. Each of its ring-like markings consists of five black spots on a brownish-red background. Below is a reproduction of an Egyptian wall-painting from the tomb of Rekhmire (15th cent. B.C.) in which a negroid Nubian notable, bare-footed and wearing only a loin-cloth, is shown presenting the Pharaoh Thutmose III with a rare and precious gift — a hunting leopard.

I will appoint over them four kinds of destroyers, says the LORD: the sword to slay, the dogs to tear, and the birds of the air and the beasts of the earth to devour and destroy.

(Jeremiah 15 : 3)

In one of the harshest of his prophecies Jeremiah describes the plight of the nation as being so desperate that it could no more be saved even if Moses and Samuel were to intercede on its behalf (Jer. 15 : 1; cf. Ps. 99 : 6). The prophet then specifies the various disasters which will come upon Judah: pestilence, sword, famine and captivity (Jer. 15 : 2). Moreover, those of its population who are to be killed will be still further dishonoured after their death, when their corpses are left as unburied carrion for bird and beast: "I will make them a horror to all the kingdoms of the earth" (Jer. 15 : 4). This grim picture of devastation, which is several times repeated by Jeremiah (16 : 4; 19 : 7; 34 : 20) and also occurs in other books of the Old Testament (2 Kings 9 : 36-37; cf. Vol. II, p. 195), was apparently a standard description faithfully drawn from the cruel realities of life in the ancient world.

A vivid illustration of Jeremiah's words is provided by the palette of the "two gazelles" (reproduced above) which was found in Egypt (from the beginning of the third millennium B.C.) and was apparently used for cosmetic purposes. Portrayed on the palette are the scourges of war. At the top, naked captives, perhaps from Canaan, are being led away with their hands bound behind their backs. Below, a lion, representing the victorious king of Egypt, is seen sinking his fangs into one of the corpses of the vanquished enemy, while carrion birds are swooping down upon other dead bodies "to devour and destroy."

No one shall break bread for the mourner, to comfort him for the dead; nor shall any one give him the cup of consolation to drink for his father or his mother. (Jeremiah 16 : 7)

Jeremiah's own life is symbolical of the great disaster that is to come upon Jerusalem. He does not marry, nor does he beget children (Jer. 16 : 2). He is likewise commanded to abstain from mourning rites: he is forbidden to eulogize the dead, and to comfort the mourners or give them food, since such customs will soon have lost all meaning: "both great and small shall die in this land; they shall not be buried, and no one shall lament for them or cut himself or make himself bald for them" (Jer. 16 : 6; cf. Ezek. 24 : 16-24). It was apparently the custom, on the day of the burial, for the mourners to fast until the evening (2 Sam. 1 : 12; 3 : 35; 12 : 20, 23). After the fast, their friends used to make them a meal ("break bread with them" Jer. 16 : 7) and offer them a cup of wine, the "cup of consolation" of our verse. In ancient Egypt, where special importance was attached to the cult of the dead, this funeral meal was served not only to the mourners, but to the deceased as well (see Vol. I, p. 287). This symbolical participation of the deceased in the funeral meal is often depicted in the paintings on the walls of Egyptian tombs. The reproduction above is from such a painting in the tomb of the royal prince Sarenput (time of the Twelfth Dynasty; beginning of the second millennium B.C.) which was discovered near Aswan. The dead man is shown seated on a lion-footed chair and stretching out his left hand towards a table loaded with offerings of food which have been brought to him. His young son is standing before him with a lotus-flower in his right hand.

BEHOLD, I am sending for many fishers, says the LORD, and they shall catch them . . . (Jeremiah 16 : 16)

The prophet repeats his warning that the doom of exile is fast approaching. Like fishermen from whose nets the fish cannot escape or like hunters whose keen eye tracks down their prey, so will the enemy hunt out the Israelites, in order to deport them to a strange land (Jer. 16 : 13); "they shall hunt them from every mountain and every hill and out of the clefts of the rocks" (ibid. 16).

Fishing was much practised by all those nations of the ancient East who lived on the banks of rivers or in regions of lakes and marshes, particularly by the inhabitants of Mesopotamia and Egypt (cf. p. 44). Consequently, the fisherman's craft is frequently depicted in the art of these two peoples. For example, the picture reproduced below, which is from the tomb of Api at Thebes (time of the New Kingdom), shows two fishermen standing on the bank of a river and drawing up their net out of the water. The illustration above is a drawing made from a relief from Nineveh, dating to the 7th cent. B.C., in which a fisherman is seen standing in a tree-girt pool and holding a line by which a fish has been caught. On his shoulders he is carrying a wicker basket which is already full of fish.

HE is like a shrub in the desert . . .   (Jeremiah 17 : 6)

The contrast between the man that trusts in man and the man that trusts in God (Jer. 17 : 5-10) is found in the "wisdom literature" of both Israel and the other nations of antiquity (e.g., in the sayings of Amenemopet the Egyptian; cf. Ps. 1). Jeremiah here works this literary motif into a prophecy of retribution ("Thus says the Lord : Cursed is the man . . . Blessed is the man," Jer. 17 : 5, 7), in order to illustrate the doom in store for his contemporaries. He that trusts in the Lord will stand firm like a tree growing by streams of water; while he that places his trust in man is compared to the juniper bush which grows in stony and saline soil where it has no natural protection : "he shall not see any good come" (Jer. 17 : 6).

The juniper (Heb. *arar*) is a low, bushy tree of the conifer family. Two kinds are found in Palestine and the neighbouring countries : *Juniperus oxycedrus L.* (photographed above) which grows mainly in the mountains of Lebanon and down as far as the hills of Upper Galilee; and the red juniper (*Juniperus phoenicea L.*) which grows in Sinai and the mountains of Edom. Jeremiah is apparently referring here to the red juniper to which the description "a shrub in the desert" is most appropriate, seeing that it is the only tree capable of enduring the harsh natural conditions of the wilderness south of Petra.

So I went down to the potter's house, and ther[e] he was working at his wheel.   (Jeremiah 18 : 3[)]

For Jeremiah, the Lord symbolically stands in the same rela[-]
tionship to His people as the potter to his material: "Behold[,]
like the clay in the potter's hand, so are you in my hand, [O]
house of Israel" (Jer. 18 : 6). This simile was evidently a popula[r]
figure of speech (Isa. 29 : 16; 45 : 9) to express the Creator['s]
absolute control of His material and His complete freedom t[o]
shape it as He chose.

Archaeological finds from the countries of the ancient Eas[t,]
including Palestine, can give us an idea of how the potter di[d]
his work in antiquity. The picture at the top left is of a limeston[e]
statue, from the beginning of the Fifth Dynasty in Egy[pt]
(middle of the third millennium B.C.), representing a potte[r]
turning his wheel with one hand, while he shapes the lump [of]
clay on it into a bowl with the other. The illustration at th[e]
bottom of the page is a reproduction of a section of the wall[-]
paintings from the tomb of Amenemhet at Beni Hasan (tim[e]
of the Twelfth Dynasty; beginning of the second millenniu[m]
B.C.), showing the various departments of a large potter['s]
workshop. At the right three workmen are seen engaged i[n]
making vessels on the potter's wheel. With their left hand the[y]
turn the upper section which consists of a kind of round tab[le]
with an elongated, protruding base fitting into a recess in th[e]
lower half. The third man from the right is separating th[e]
fully fashioned article from what remains of the original lum[p]
of clay, by means of a piece of thread. Two other workme[n]
then place the vessels in the kiln. Rows of completed produc[ts]
are painted above. The basalt potter's wheel seen in the middl[e]
plate was characteristic of ancient Palestine. It consisted [of]
an upper half (with a cone-shaped boss) and a lower half (wit[h]
a corresponding recess). The wheel illustrated here was exca[-]
vated at Megiddo and belongs to the Middle Bronze Age (firs[t]
half of the second millennium B.C.). Wheels of this type wer[e]
still in use in later periods.

THUS said the LORD, "Go, buy a potter's earthen flask . . ."
(Jeremiah 19 : 1)

After his visit to the potter's workshop (see p. 114), where he was merely a spectator, Jeremiah now himself performs a symbolical act with a clay vessel before the elders of the people and the senior priests. He buys a flask, breaks it publicly and then utters a harsh prophecy against Judah and Jerusalem. Just as the flask is broken beyond repair, so are Jerusalem and its inhabitants lost beyond all hope of redemption: "So will I break this people and this city, as one breaks a potter's vessel, so that it can never be mended" (Jer. 19 : 11). Jeremiah's action, besides being symbolical of the fast-approaching destruction, was also intended to frighten his audience into a change of heart. The place chosen by the prophet for this act of symbolism was also appropriate: the Potsherd Gate, which led out into the Valley of Ben-Hinnom (Jer. 19 : 2), was apparently the same as the Dung Gate (Neh. 3 : 14) where objects of no more use or value, such as broken pieces of pottery, were dumped. Another explanation of the name Potsherd Gate is that there were potter's workshops nearby.

The exact shape of the flask (Heb. *baqbuq*) cannot be deduced from the only two passages of the Old Testament in which it is mentioned (here, and in 1 Kings 14 : 3 [AV]). However, the onomatopoeic quality of the Hebrew word, with its suggestion of the slow gurgling sound made by liquid as it is poured out, indicates that the vessel so named had a narrow, elongated neck. The elegant vessel reproduced here (from the 8th cent. B.C.) was found in the Israelite citadel at Hazor.

THEREFORE, behold, days are coming, says the LORD, when this place shall no more be called Topheth, or the valley of Ben-Hinnom, but the valley of Slaughter.   (Jeremiah 19 : 6)

In the Valley of Ben-Hinnom Jeremiah utters a dire prophecy against Jerusalem and denounces the kings of Judah and the populace of the capital for the most heinous of all their sins — the offering up of their sons and daughters by fire to Baal on the high places of Topheth (Jer. 19 : 5; cf. 7 : 31; 32 : 35). Jeremiah solemnly proclaims that their punishment will be commensurate with their crime: the place where children were burnt alive will become "a valley of slaughter" for the inhabitants on the day of Jerusalem's overthrow (Jer. 19 : 11-13). The worship of Molech on the fire-altar (Heb. *topheth*) in the Valley of Ben-Hinnom appears to have taken root in Judah as early as the reign of Ahaz. Encouraged by Manasseh, the cult was enthusiastically practised by the people until the reforms of Josiah (2 Kings 16 : 3; 21 : 6; 23 : 10), and may have been revived after Josiah's death. As a result of the ghastly scenes enacted in the Valley of Hinnom, its Hebrew name, "*Gehinnom*", i.e. Gehenna, eventually came to signify the place of torment reserved for the wicked in the next world.

The Valley of Ben-Hinnom, or more simply the Valley of Hinnom, perhaps so-called after its original possessor (Josh. 15 : 8; 18 : 16; Neh. 11 : 30), is known to the modern Arabs as Wadi er-Rababah. It runs southwards from the Jaffa Gate through the Serpents' Pool (Birket es-Sultan) and then turns eastwards into the Kidron valley. In ancient times it marked off the western and southern limits of Jerusalem and formed the border between the tribes of Judah and Benjamin (see Vol. II, p. 57). Above is a view of this valley of ill fame, flanked on the left by the spur of Mount Zion, the western hill of the Old City, and on the right by the houses of the Givath Hananiah quarter. In the middle distance the valley runs into the Brook Kidron, on the far side of which the houses of the village of Silwan are visible on the lower slopes of the Mount of Olives (see p. 294).

N OW Pashhur the priest, the son of Immer, who was
chief officer in the house of the LORD, heard . . .

(Jeremiah 20 : 1)

Pashhur the priest apparently came of the well-known family of the sons of Immer (cf. Ezra 2 : 37; Neh. 7 : 40;
11 : 12-13). The name Pashhur was common in Jeremiah's day (cf. Jer. 21 : 1; 38 : 1) and it also occurs on a
seal from the 6th cent. B.C. which was, apparently, found in the environs of Jerusalem. Engraved on the seal
(reproduced at the top left) there is the following inscription in two rows of letters: "Belonging to Pashhur
the son of Adaiahu." If this Adaiahu is the same as the Adaiah mentioned in the genealogical table of the priestly
family of Immer (Neh. 11 : 12; 1 Chron. 9 : 12), then the owner of the seal would also have been a member
of the priesthood and a descendant of Pashhur. This same Pashhur was an important Temple dignitary in Jeremiah's time. The biblical expression "chief officer in the house of the Lord" denotes one of the senior functionaries
in the priesthood and the Temple administration, whose task it was to supervise all the arrangements in the
sacred precincts. Several other priests who bore this title are known (cf. Neh. 11 : 11; 1 Chron. 9 : 11; 2 Chron.
31 : 13; 35 : 8).
The administration of temples was always a complex affair in antiquity, above all in Egypt where the priestly
hierarchy was very highly developed. Egyptian influence can probably be detected in the organization of Israelite
shrines, including the Temple at Jerusalem. The reproduction above — a wall-painting from a tomb at Thebes
dating to the Nineteenth Dynasty (13th cent. B.C.) — shows two Egyptian temple dignitaries: Reya "the
fourth prophet" of Amon, and his wife Mutemuia who was a temple-singer.

THEREFORE thus says the LORD concerning Jehoiakim the son of Josiah, king of Judah:
"They shall not lament for him, saying, 'Ah my brother!' or 'Ah sister!' They shall not
lament for him, saying, 'Ah lord!' or 'Ah his majesty!' "   (Jeremiah 22 : 18)

Jeremiah concludes his castigation of Jehoiakim's evil deeds (Jer. 22 : 13-17) with a stark prophecy of the king's
humiliating end. "With the burial of an ass he shall be buried, dragged and cast forth beyond the gates of Jerusalem" (Jer. 22 : 19; cf. 36 : 30). Possibly, however, Jeremiah's words here are not to be taken literally, but only
as implying that the Babylonian assault on Jerusalem would follow so swiftly upon Jehoiakim's death that there
would be no time for a royal burial. It was customary in Judah, as in all the other countries of the ancient Orient,
for ministers and nobles to be interred with regal pomp and even to have special dirges recited over their graves
(see 2 Chron. 35 : 25). "Ah my brother!" or "Ah sister!" was no doubt a lament commonly uttered by relatives
and friends of the deceased (1 Kings 13 : 30), while the cry "Ah lord!" or "Ah his majesty!" was presumably an
expression of grief reserved for the death of a king (cf. Jer. 34 : 5).
The burial rites of nobles and high dignitaries are portrayed on many Egyptian paintings (cf. Vol. I, p. 124;
Vol. II, p. 168). The one reproduced above — a section of a wall-painting from the tomb of an Egyptian noble
named Ramose at Thebes (reign of Amenhotep III, 14th cent. B.C.) — shows the funeral procession. The four
men at the rear are carrying caskets which contain the effects of the deceased. They are preceded by other servants
who are also carrying various of their late master's possessions — a chair, writing instruments, spices and sandals —
to his last resting-place.

BEHOLD, the days are coming, says the LORD, when I will raise up for David a righteous Branch, and he shall reign as king and deal wisely, and shall execute justice and righteousness in the land.

(Jeremiah 23 : 5)

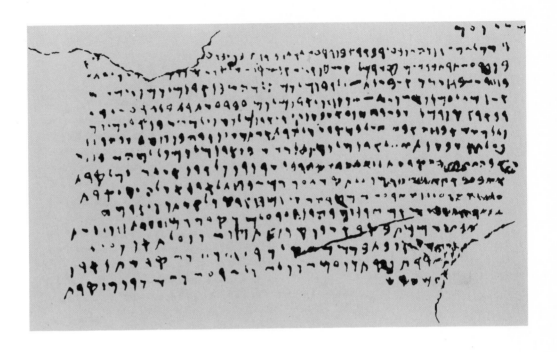

Like other prophets, Jeremiah too foretells the coming of a Messianic king of David's dynasty. But his prophecy of redemption, which was uttered on the eve of the Temple's destruction, is not of universal import, like Isaiah's, nor does it contain any mention of apocalyptical reversals of nature's order (as in Isa. 2 : 1-5; 11 : 1-10). Jeremiah's vision is confined to the ingathering of the exiles and to the restoration of the kingdoms of Israel and Judah (Jer. 23 : 6-8; cf. 30 : 10; 33 : 14-17). The appellative given by him to the Messianic king, "The Lord is our righteousness" (in the Septuagint version *Jehozedek*, Jer. 23 : 6), is used, in the first place, as a symbolical title in a prophetic vision, but at the same time it intentionally calls to mind the name of Zedekiah, the last Davidic king. Indeed, it may have been as a result of this very prophecy that his name was changed from Mattaniah to Zedekiah (2 Kings 24 : 17). However that may be, Jeremiah was certainly well disposed towards Zedekiah and, even in the darkest days of the besieged city's agony, prophesied that he would end his days in peace (Jer. 34 : 4-5).

The Hebrew word for "branch" *(zemah)*, the title given to the king that is to come, may well have established itself as a term of Messianic significance (cf. Jer. 33 : 15). Thus, Zechariah, whose prophetic activity belonged to the later period of the return from the Babylonian exile, connects his vision of the rebuilding of the Temple and the harmonious relations between king and priest with "the man whose name is the Branch" (Zech. 6 : 12-13; cf. 3 : 8). Interestingly enough, the use of this combination "branch of righteousness" has also been found outside ancient Israel, in a Phoenician inscription (see reproduction) excavated at Lapithos on the island of Cyprus (from the 4th cent. B.C.). There the ruler Yiten Baal, "the mighty one of the earth", lists the offerings dedicated by himself to the temple of Melkart "for my own life, and for the life of my descendants every day, and for a branch of righteousness for (my) womenfolk and for my menfolk" (line 11).

Extract from cylinder B of Ashurbanipal (col. V, lines 46–76)

The goddess Ishtar heard my anxious sighs and "Fear not" she said, and filled my heart with confidence. "Inasmuch as you have lifted your hands in prayer (and) your eyes are filled with tears, I have mercy." During the night in which I appeared before her, a seer reclined and saw a dream. When he awoke Ishtar showed him a night vision. He reported to me as follows: "Ishtar who dwells in Arbela came in. Right and left quivers were hanging from her. She held the bow in her hand (and) a sharp sword was drawn to do battle. You were standing in front of her and she spoke to you like the mother who bore you. Ishtar called unto you, she who is exalted among the gods, giving you the following instructions: 'You will contemplate fulfilling my orders. Whither your face is turned, I shall go forth. You told me: Wherever you go, let me go with you, O Lady of Ladies!' She informed you as follows: 'You shall stay here, where the dwelling of Nabu is. Eat food, drink wine, supply music, praise my divinity, while I go and do that work in order that you attain your heart's desire. Your face (need) not become pale, nor your feet become exhausted, nor your strength come to nought in the onslaught of battle.' In her loving bosom she embraced you and protected your whole figure. Before her a fire was then burning. To the conquest of [your] enemies [she will march forth] at (your) side Against Teumman, king of Elam, with whom she is wroth, she has set her face."

LET the prophet who has a dream tell the dream, but let him who has my word speak my word faithfully . . .

(Jeremiah 23 : 28)

God's messages and warnings to His people were made known to the prophets of the Old Testament in a manner that was clear and intelligible to everyone, in the form of "a burden" (Jer. 23 : 33-40) or "a word": "Is not my word like fire, says the Lord, and like a hammer which breaks the rock in pieces?" (Jer. 23 : 29). These prophets regarded the predictions of mere visionaries as impostures, an attitude to which Jeremiah gives forceful expression in his caustic attack on the false prophets who deluded the people by their dreams, some of which were of their own invention: "Behold, I am against those who prophesy lying dreams . . . and lead my people astray by their lies and their recklessness, when I did not send them or charge them" (Jer. 23 : 32). In contrast to this, the ancestors of the nation, judges like Gideon, kings like Solomon and wise men like the friends of Job, considered that God's will might properly be revealed in dreams. Indeed, in Deuteronomy the dreamer of dreams is placed on an equal footing with the prophet (Deut. 13 : 2). In the other lands of the ancient East, likewise, particularly in Mesopotamia, it was widely believed that a god revealed himself in dreams to his chosen ones, first and foremost amongst whom was the king, in order to vouchsafe his counsel to them, especially in times of crisis. Sometimes the gods appeared to the kings in person, and sometimes their message was delivered to professional soothsayers who were specially trained in the interpretation of dreams. One such "prophet of dreams" is mentioned in the annals of Ashurbanipal, the Assyrian monarch (668-630 B.C, not long before the time of Jeremiah). When the fate of his campaign against Elam hung in the balance, the king appealed for help to the goddess Ishtar. She graciously answered his appeal and made her message and her commands known to him through the mouth of a soothsayer. Above is a photograph of one part of these annals with a translation alongside it.

ONE basket had very good figs, like first-ripe figs, but the
other basket had very bad figs, so bad they could not be eaten.
(Jeremiah 24 : 2)

The purpose of the allegory of the fig-baskets is to extol the Judeans deported to Babylon, together with
Jehoiakin, above those who were allowed to remain in Judah and Jerusalem. The good figs are the former, while
the bad figs are the latter (Jer. 24 : 4-10). Exile will act on the deportees as a smelting crucible acts upon metal:
their suffering and remoteness from home will purify their hearts: "I will give them a heart to know that I am
the Lord" (Jer. 24 : 7). Those left in Jerusalem, on the contrary, though topographically close to God, are far
removed from Him in their conduct (cf. Jer. 29 : 17-20).
In Old Testament times, the fig *(Ficus carica L.)*, one of the seven kinds of natural produce with which Palestine
is blessed, was a staple national food. Hence its use, together with the vine, as a symbol of secure and peaceful
existence (cf. 1 Kings 4 : 25; Zech. 3 : 10). Here, Jeremiah's allegory is taken from a well-known phenomenon
in the tree's annual life-cycle, its purpose being to bring home the full meaning of God's message to the prophet's
audience. Together with the first leaves that burgeon in early spring there also appear the first small figs which,
after ripening, were called "first-ripe figs" (Heb. *bakkuroth*). These were considered delicacies, "like a first-ripe
fig before the summer" (Isa. 28 : 4; cf. Hos. 9 : 10; Mic. 7 : 1). Since the flowering of the fig-tree and the ripening of its fruit is not confined to a particular season, small figs also appear later in the year. Indeed, fruit grows
continuously on the tree as long as it is green; that is to say, until its leaves begin to fall at the end of the summer.
The fully grown fruits which develop from the late small figs are elsewhere described by Jeremiah as "vile figs"
(Jer. 29 : 17), and are the "bad figs" of his allegory here (24 : 2).
Above is a photograph of a fig-branch. Among the upper leaves are unripe small figs, while those below them
have already ripened out into "first-ripe figs."

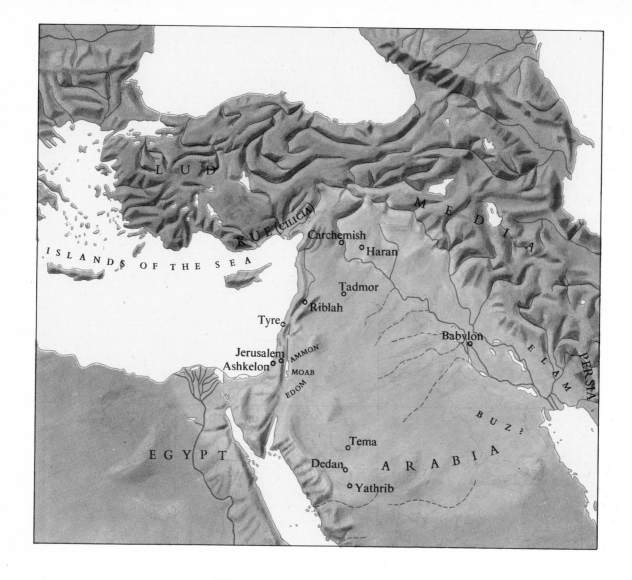

B<small>EHOLD</small>, I will send for all the tribes of the north, says the L<small>ORD</small>, and for Nebuchadrezzar the king of Babylon, my servant, and I will bring them against this land and its inhabitants, and against all these nations round about . . .

(Jeremiah 25 : 9)

Jeremiah lived at a time of profound changes in the balance of power in the Near East. As the Assyrian empire waned, its place in the political firmament was taken by the rising star of Babylon which reached the zenith of its greatness in the reign of Nebuchadnezzar. For the prophet, these epoch-making events were a sign of divine providence and Nebuchadnezzar was the Lord's servant and instrument of His purpose. In a prophecy uttered in "the first year of Nebuchadrezzar" (Jer. 25 : 1), i.e. 605-604 B.C., Jeremiah proclaimed the grandeur of Babylon and its future imperial might; to his inspired vision, this was the fateful historical moment at which slavery and slaughter were meted out by divine decree to all the nations, including Judah (Jer. 25 : 11).

Presumably, this prophecy was uttered under the impact of Nebuchadnezzar's first campaign, after the battle of Carchemish (see p. 145), when the Babylonian conqueror was on the point of subduing all the lands to the west of the Euphrates. This assumption is strengthened by a Babylonian chronicle (see the reproduction in Vol. II, p. 297) which gives a consecutive list of Nebuchadnezzar's victories over various peoples and lands, amongst them the nations whom Jeremiah was commanded to make drink from "this cup of the wine of wrath" (Jer. 25 : 15 ff.) : Judah and Philistia (see p. 147), the Arabian tribes and Elam (see p. 150). The Babylonian army penetrated as far as the borders of Egypt, but was unable to conquer that country (cf. 2 Kings 24 : 7). From other sources we learn that the Babylonians laid siege to Tyre (see p. 123), sent a force against the country of Qwe in Asia Minor (perhaps these are the distant "kings of the north" mentioned by Jeremiah here in verse 26) and extended their dominion over Tema and Yathrib (el-Medineh) in the Arabian peninsula (the region of Dedan).

The map shows the Babylonian empire at its greatest extent.

Aʟʟ the kings of Tyre, all the kings of Sidon, and the kings of the coastland across the sea.   (Jeremiah 25 : 22)

Included amongst the nations and monarchs doomed, according to Jeremiah's prophecy, to be conquered by Nebuchadnezzar, the Babylonian king, are the cities of the Phoenician coast and the Aegean islands and their rulers (cf. p. 122). The prophet Ezekiel also gives a detailed description of Nebuchadnezzar's assault on Tyre and the besieged city's ordeal (see p. 182). In the Babylonian sources there is no explicit mention of the capture of Tyre and Sidon, or of the conquest of the Aegean islands by Nebuchadnezzar. However, from documents excavated in the royal palace at Babylon (see p. 155) it is clear that there were in the city political prisoners from the cities of the Phoenician coast, including Tyre. Josephus relates that the Babylonians besieged Tyre for thirteen years without being able to reduce it (Antiquities x.11.1). Evidently, then, Nebuchadnezzar's forces did reach the Mediterranean coast, and they may have brought the mercantile centres of Canaan and also the Aegean islands and their rulers under their control or protection.
Portrayed here are a typical Phoenician king and a typical Aegean ruler. At the left — the sarcophagus of Eshmunazar, king of Sidon (4th or 3rd cent. B.C.), on which there is a Phoenician inscription extolling the monarch's greatness and listing the lands granted him in the districts of Dor and the Sharon. Above right — the head of a terra-cotta statue from the end of the sixth, or beginning of the fifth, cent. B.C., found at Mersinaki in the north-west of the island of Cyprus. The oval face, with its beard and moustache, is that of a local king. His large eyes have been given still greater prominence by lines painted in black, his hair is curled and there is an ivy-wreath on his head.

THERE was another man who prophesied in the name of the LORD, Uriah the son of Shemaiah from Kiryath-Yearim. He prophesied against this city and against this land words like those of Jeremiah.

(Jeremiah 26 : 20)

The prophet Uriah from Kiryath-Yearim (Jer. 26 : 20-24) was put to death by Jehoiakim, after he had fled to Egypt and been brought back by force. Jeremiah tells his story in order to emphasize the danger to which he was exposing himself in daring to take the rulers of Jerusalem to task. These verses also indicate, incidentally, that Jeremiah was not the only prophet of the Lord in Judah in those times, a fact which is further confirmed by the letters excavated at Lachish. These letters were written in ink on potsherds (ostraca). Their language is Hebrew and the date of their composition is shortly before the destruction of the kingdom of Judah (see pp. 55, 131). In ostracon No. 6 (see the reproduction and transliteration) it is stated that the king and his ministers were enraged against a certain prophet, of whose name only the final letters ". . . yahu" are legible (see line 10), for "weakening the hands" of the populace (the same expression, almost word for word, as in Jer. 38 : 4), and that they were therefore taking measures to silence him. The writer of the letter, Hoshayahu, requests the man to whom it is addressed, Yaosh, to do what he can to save the prophet. In another letter (ostracon No. 3, see p. 55) we read about the mission of a senior army officer, Coniah the son of Elnathan, and his men to Egypt, perhaps for the purpose of bringing back the prophet, and about a warning sent to the prophet to keep out of their way.

The story related in these letters from Lachish bears such a remarkably close resemblance to what we are told in the Old Testament about Uriah the son of Shemaiah from Kiryath-Yearim, that some scholars propose that the fragmentary name on the ostracon should be read as Uriyahu. But the Old Testament places the story of Uriah in the reign of Jehoiakim, whereas the Lachish letters belong to the later reign of Zedekiah. It is quite possible, therefore, that there were actually two different prophets, one in the time of Jehoiakim and the other in the time of Zedekiah, who, like Jeremiah, incurred the murderous displeasure of the king and his ministers.

THUS the LORD said to me: "Make yourself thongs and yokebars, and put them on your neck."

(Jeremiah 27 : 2)

Jeremiah, like other prophets, took an active part in the political life of Judah and tried to influence the course of events by admonitory utterances and symbolical actions. He believed that any attempt at revolt against Babylon was utterly pointless. For had not nations and kingdoms been commanded by God meekly to place their necks in the yoke of the Babylonian emperor? To give greater force to his contention, the prophet illustrated the necessity of subservience to Nebuchadnezzar by an act of symbolical significance. After first tying thongs and bars — the components of the yoke — on to his own neck, he then sent them to the kings of Edom, Moab, Ammon, Tyre and Sidon with their envoys who had convened in Jerusalem at the beginning of Zedekiah's reign, for the purpose of planning a revolt against Babylon (Jer. 27 : 3). To the king of Judah Jeremiah addressed the following imperative demand: "Bring your necks under the yoke of the king of Babylon and serve him and his people, and live" (Jer. 27 : 12).

However, there was more to Jeremiah's action than a purely abstract symbolism taken from the working conditions of farm animals. It is known that captives in antiquity were sometimes really placed in a yoke, partly as a sign of their abject surrender, as portrayed in a bronze relief from the gates of the palace of Shalmaneser III at Balawat (9th cent. B.C., cf. p. 33). Here the male captives are shown naked, with their necks tightly fastened in a yoke consisting of two wooden bars to which their right hands also appear to be bound.

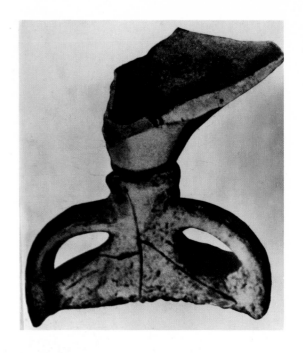

IN that same year . . . Hananiah the son of Azzur, the prophet from Gibeon, spoke to me in the house of the LORD, in the presence of the priests and all the people, saying, "Thus says the LORD of hosts, the GOD of Israel: I have broken the yoke of the king of Babylon."

(Jeremiah 28 : 1-2)

Hananiah the son of Azzur, the contemporary of Jeremiah who prophesied that the yoke of Babylon would be broken and that Jehoiachin and the other exiles from Judah would return to Jerusalem (Jer. 28 : 2-3), came from Gibeon (see Vol. II, p. 37). In the excavations carried out on the site, the names Hananiah and Azariah (a fuller form of Azzur) were found inscribed on jar-handles from the 7th cent. B.C. Evidently, then, the names of the prophet and his father were common in Gibeon. The picture on the right is a fragment of a jar found in the water-pool of Gibeon (see Vol. II, p. 164) bearing an inscription in which the name Hananiah occurs.

In the course of his refutation of the false prophet Hananiah, Jeremiah tells his hearers how to distinguish true prophets from false. Any prophet who foretells "war, famine and pestilence" can be regarded as a true prophet at once, while as for one who predicts peace, "when the word of that prophet comes to pass, then it will be known that the Lord has truly sent the prophet" (Jer. 28 : 8-9). In flattering the rulers with illusions of peace the false prophets' only concern is with their own advancement (cf. Mic. 3 : 5, 8; and p. 241).

Ecstatic visionaries — both male and female — abounded in the reigns of the last Assyrian kings (7th cent. B.C., just before Jeremiah's time). These ecstatics used to answer the king's queries with brief prophetic utterances which usually began with the words "Fear not", or sometimes with the greeting "Peace be with you." In the document reproduced here (see on the left), a woman named Belit-abisha informs King Esarhaddon that Ishtar of Arbela, the goddess of prophecy and divination (see p. 120 and Vol. I, p. 269), promises to march out before him to battle and to lay his enemies low.

BUILD houses and live in them; plant gardens and eat their produce.　　(Jeremiah 29 : 5)

True to his faith in God and to the political vision derived from it, Jeremiah warns those Judeans who had already been deported to Babylon against harbouring the illusion that they would return to Jerusalem in the near future; instead, he advises them to take root in the land of their exile and to make themselves an integral part of its economic life (Jer. 29 : 4-9, 28) which was largely based on fruit orchards. This counsel was given after the deportation in the time of Jeconiah, when the royal family and the nobility, the craftsmen and the smiths (Jer. 29 : 2; cf. 2 Kings 24 : 14 ff.) and other artisans were all carried off into exile, as is confirmed by documents excavated at Babylon. Among the people mentioned in these documents there is an exile by the name of Shelemiah, a gardener by profession (see p. 155). The gardens of Assyria and Babylon were famous throughout the ancient world; of special renown were the "hanging" gardens of Babylon which are mentioned by Greek authors as one of the wonders of the world. The archaeological evidence from the excavations carried out on the sites of Babylon and Ur of the Chaldees also indicates that royal gardens were planted in Nebuchadnezzar's reign. It may be presumed, therefore, that Jeremiah's advice was based on a knowledge of the conditions in which the exiles from Judah had to live and work, and of the economic needs of the Babylonian empire.

A series of reliefs found at Nineveh gives us a vivid picture of the garden of king Ashurbanipal (7th cent. B.C.), showing such details as its vegetation (conifers, millet, bushes), its keepers and the royal family banqueting in its grounds. A section of this royal garden is seen in the relief reproduced here. In the upper register — two keepers standing amongst the trees of the garden with its fence behind them. Below — a wild-boar in a tangled undergrowth of water-reeds or millet-clumps.

LAMENTATION
and bitter weeping...
(Jeremiah 31 : 15)

Jeremiah, with his greater personal experience of the horrors of war than the other prophets, was well qualified to describe the different degrees of lamentation and weeping, sorrow and fear. Whether the simile employed is the anguish of one bearing her first child (Jer. 4 : 31), the cry as of a woman in labour, mourning for an only son, or a most bitter wailing (Jer. 6 : 24, 26; cf. p. 104), under every guise the mourner is always one and the same — the daughter of Zion whose spirit faints at the wholesale slaughter of the vanquished city's inhabitants (Jer. 4 : 31). Jeremiah's poetical powers reach their height in his impassioned picture of the mother who rises from her grave to weep bitterly over the sufferings of her children: "Rachel is weeping for her children; she refuses to be comforted for her children" (Jer. 31 : 15). Rachel's lamentation took on a symbolical meaning for later generations of Jews and served as a source of inspiration for religious poetry and legend.

A mother's grief is illustrated by the above picture of a woman weeping in a funeral scene which is reproduced from a tomb at Sakkarah in Egypt (13th cent. B.C.). The woman's head is drooping forwards, her half-closed eyes are turned downwards, and her mouth is contorted with sobbing. The expression on her face is one of open, but restrained weeping, as becomes a silent grief.

Sᴇᴛ up waymarks for yourself, make yourself guideposts ...   (Jeremiah 31 : 21)

In Jeremiah's inspired vision of the return of the Israelite and Judean exiles from Babylon, the virgin of Israel has only to set up signposts for her guidance and she will be able to make her way back safely to Zion: "Return, O virgin Israel, return to these your cities" (Jer. 31 : 21). Judah was separated from Babylon by the wide expanse of the Syro-Arabian desert in whose pathless wastes travellers could easily lose their way. It was therefore customary to set up conspicuous marks, such as cairns of stones, along the established caravan routes. The Hebrew word in this verse for "waymarks" *(ziyyun =* "sign") is used in the Old Testament of both a monument and a sign (2 Kings 23 : 17; Ezek. 39 : 15). The exact meaning of the parallel term here translated "guideposts" (Heb. *tamrur,* which is used in this sense only here in the Old Testament) is uncertain: it may be derived from the Arabic root *mrr* meaning "to pass", in which case it may also denote a signpost.

The ancients were in the habit of setting up cairns or individual stones in conspicuous places to mark a route, especially a track through the desert. This custom is still followed by the beduin to-day. The cairn of stones seen in the photograph below stands on an ancient desert road running from the valley of Avdat down to Eilat.

TAKE these deeds, both this sealed
deed of purchase and this open
deed . . .   (Jeremiah 32 : 14)

Jeremiah purchased the field at Anathoth from Hanamel, the son of his uncle Shallum, at the height of the siege
of Jerusalem (Jer. 32 : 7-14) as a symbolical demonstration of his confidence in the restoration of Judah after its
political destruction: "Fields shall be bought for money and deeds shall be sealed and signed and witnessed"
(Jer. 32 : 44). The purchase was transacted in accordance with the legal procedure of the time, down to the smallest
detail: it was recorded in a deed (i.e. on a clay tablet or on a sheet of papyrus, see pp. 55, 133), it was witnessed,
the money was weighed out on scales, and the deeds were then stored in earthenware jars "that they may last
for a long time" (Jer. 32 : 10-15).
The above procedure originated in the legal formalities which had long been customary in the ancient East in
commercial transactions, including land transfers. In Mesopotamia and Anatolia, as early as the beginning of the
second millennium B.C., contracts of sale were registered in cuneiform characters on a clay tablet in the presence
of witnesses, and the tablet was then sealed up in an earthenware container on the outside of which was written
an extract of the contents, also signed by the witnesses. One such contract, from the Assyrian colony of Kanish
(the modern Kültepe) in Anatolia and dating to the 19th-18th cent. B.C., is reproduced in the picture above.
In the Judah of Jeremiah's day, the agreement may have been recorded on parchment or papyrus, instead of clay,
as was the custom at Elephantine in Egypt in the 5th and 4th cent. B.C. There the contract of sale was written
twice over on a single piece of papyrus, the original document at the top and a copy at the bottom. The upper
half was then rolled up and sealed (Jeremiah's "sealed" deed?) (see the lower picture), while the lower part was
cut off, rolled up (but not sealed) and placed in a closed cylinder. In case of need, this copy, which was a kind
of "open deed", could be examined without any trouble. The double registration of a purchase, both in the case
of clay tablets and of papyrus, was therefore intended to make it possible for the terms of the agreement to be
studied without any risk of damage to the original document.

WHEN the army of the king of Babylon was fighting against Jerusalem and against all the cities of Judah that were left, Lachish and Azekah; for these were the only fortified cities of Judah that remained.

(Jeremiah 34 : 7)

The Babylonian army intensified its onslaught upon Judah until all the cities of the country, except Lachish (the modern Tell ed-Duweir) and Azekah (Tell Zakariyah), had fallen to it. Lachish, a fortress of note at the western approaches to the Judean hills (see Vol. II, p. 135), offered prolonged resistance to the Chaldean forces. Below is a view of the ancient city as reconstructed from the topographical data of the region, in accordance with the archaeological evidence found on the site and the pictorial details preserved in an Assyrian relief (see Vol. II, p. 286, top). The city was surrounded by a double wall, both sections of which were strengthened by towers and buttresses. Most strongly fortified of all was the entrance-keep with its two gateways — an outer and an inner one. These gateways were so placed as to force the troops assaulting them to expose their right flank to the wall, thus making themselves an easy target for the defenders, since the shield was carried on the left arm.

An echo of the increasingly critical military situation in Judah, as the Babylonians pressed home their attacks, can be heard in the letters excavated in the gateway of Lachish in a stratum from the time of the city's destruction (cf. p. 124). In one of them (No. 4, reverse side; see the reproduction above) the sender of the letter writes to Yaosh, who was apparently the military commander of Lachish, as follows: "Know that we are watching for the signals of Lachish according to all the indications that my lord has given, for we cannot see the signal of Azekah." In other words, the writer informs his superior that he and his men are faithfully carrying out the orders given by fire-signals (Heb. *massuoth*; cf. Jer. 6 : 1) from Lachish, but they have lost contact with Azekah. It is quite possible that, at the time of the writing of the letter, Azekah had already been cut off by the enemy's forces and may even have fallen, whereas Lachish itself continued to hold out for a little longer.

HE went down to the king's house, into the secretary's chamber; and all the princes were sitting there: Elishama the secretary . . .   (Jeremiah 36 : 12)

As the Babylonian army advanced upon Judah in the fifth year of Jehoiakim's reign, Baruch the son of Neriah read out to the people the words of rebuke which had been dictated to him by Jeremiah and written down in a scroll (Jer. 36 : 9-10). The prophet's indignant expostulations were brought to the notice of the princes of Judah who had just been called to the secretary's chamber, apparently for an emergency council of state. In Judah, as in all the other countries of the ancient East, this chamber was close to both the palace and the temple. The illustration below is a reproduction of a painting from the tomb of Tiy, the scribe and secretary of the Pharaoh Merneptah (end of the 13th cent. B.C.), in which the various departments of a royal secretariat can be clearly seen. Seated in the central room of the offices on the right is the god Thoth, the scribes' patron; ranged round both sides of the room are the shelves of the royal archives; and near the walls stand boxes for the filing of documents. In the central hall, the chief priest and his attendant are presenting an offering to the god Thoth. The three rooms on the left are the scribes' offices: the one in the centre is that of the head scribe who is giving out his instructions with a serving-boy, fan in hand, behind him. In the other two rooms, scribes are seen at work writing on papyrus scrolls which they hold on their knees.

The chief court scribes (see Vol. II, p. 207) had special seals of their own, marked with the name of their owner and his office. One of these seals, from approximately the time of Jeremiah, is reproduced at the top right. It is engraved with the following words in the ancient Hebrew script: "Amaz the scribe." Above this inscription there are two figures dressed in characteristically Babylonian fashion with, between them, a representation of what may be a sacred tree or perhaps the emblem of the moon-god, Sin, which was very common on Babylonian seals of that period. At the very top is the emblem of the god Ashur.

H<small>E</small> dictated all these words to me, while I wrote them with ink on the scroll.

(Jeremiah 36 : 18)

Jeremiah's confidant, Baruch the son of Neriah, who was also apparently the author of the biographical details included in the Book of Jeremiah, wrote down the prophet's words at the latter's dictation on a scroll (Jer. 36 : 4; 45 : 1), as described in this verse. The usual method of writing in the kingdom of Judah was with a reed-pen and in ink on potsherds or on papyrus scrolls called "books" (Heb. *sefer;* cf. p. 55). The ink consisted of a sticky lump of some carbonic substance which was wetted at the time of writing. It was of various colours: brown, black and red. The scroll was divided into columns or pages (called in Hebrew *delathoth* = "doors") as in the description of Jeremiah's scroll (Jer. 36 : 23; cf. the use of the same term in Lachish ostracon No. 4, line 3).

The scribe's craft is illustrated in detail in ancient Egyptian art. In the two pictures reproduced here — both of which are from Thebes and belong to the time of the New Kingdom — Egyptian scribes are seen at work with the instruments of their profession laid out before them. Above, a scribe is sitting at his desk on which there is a pot ("the scribe's ink-horn") containing ink and other writing materials. Below, a scribe is writing on a wooden board (apparently also known as a "door") with lines drawn on it. He is holding a reed-pen in his hand and has another stuck behind his ear. Lying on his desk there are various writing materials, including a palette (cf. p. 166).

F<small>OR</small> even if you should defeat the whole army of Chaldeans who are fighting against you, and there remained of them only wounded men, every man in his tent, they would rise up and burn this city with fire.

(Jeremiah 37 : 10)

Since Jeremiah regarded the destruction of Jerusalem as irrevocably decreed by God, he addressed Zedekiah's envoys in plain language, setting aside all prophetic symbolism. Neither temporary military successes, nor even the Egyptian army which was hastening to Judah's aid (Jer. 37 : 7; cf. p. 135), could save Jerusalem. Nothing could stop the Chaldeans from capturing the city and laying it waste.

It is implied in these verses that the Chaldean army used to encamp in rows of tents. A more detailed picture of the tents of the Assyrian (and Babylonian) armies and the lay-out of their camps is provided by the many reliefs excavated on ancient Assyrian sites. The one reproduced here was found at Nineveh and dates to the reign of Ashurbanipal (7th cent. B.C.) The tent — always shown in the reliefs in cross-section — was usually stretched over a central pole with, branching off it, two outriggers which supported the sides of the tent. The central pole and its outriggers were also used for hanging various vessels on, such as wine- and oil-skins, jars and the like. The diagonal lines at the bottom right of the tent are the guy-ropes for tautening the sides of the tent. The two soldiers in the tent are busy preparing food.

N ow when the Chaldean army had withdrawn from Jerusalem at the approach of Pharaoh's army.

(Jeremian 37 : 11)

It is reasonable to suppose that the Egyptians were privy to Zedekiah's plot against Babylon and therefore hastened to his aid when Jerusalem was besieged. To the ministers, and indeed to the whole people, the Pharaoh's hosts were an army of liberation and must obviously have aroused high hopes of speedy deliverance. Jeremiah, however, regarded the Egyptian intervention as a brief episode of no lasting military value. "Behold, Pharaoh's army which came to help you is about to return to Egypt, to its own land" (Jer. 37 : 7). Such joint political and military action on the part of Judah and Egypt, so far from being exceptional, was a constantly recurring feature of Judean foreign policy throughout the kingdom's history: every time Jerusalem was threatened from the north, its king looked to the Egyptian army to save the city (cf. 2 Kings 18 : 21; 19 : 9).

It was not only Judah that turned to Egypt for help. In an Aramaic papyrus found at Sakkarah (see the reproduction), one of the local Palestinian rulers makes an urgent appeal to the Pharaoh of the time for military aid against an invading Babylonian army which has already penetrated as far as Aphek (apparently the city of that name in the Sharon plain). The name of the ruler and the date of the letter are not given. However, in all likelihood the appeal was sent by one of the cities of Philistia, most probably Ashkelon, which, like Judah, had revolted against Babylonian overlordship; and its date may well have been 604 B.C. It was in the month of Kislev of this year that, as recorded in a Babylonian chronicle, Nebuchadnezzar sacked Ashkelon. In this case too, then, Egypt was "a broken reed of a staff."

BEHOLD, all the women left in the house of the king of Judah were being led out to the princes of the king of Babylon . . .   (Jeremiah 38 : 22)

At the height of Jerusalem's ordeal by siege, King Zedekiah sent secretly for Jeremiah to consult him about the course he should pursue. Jeremiah advised him to go out and surrender himself to the captains of the Babylonian king who were besieging the city. He further warned him that, if he did not give himself up to them, the Chaldeans would burn down the city, and the king and his family would be captured and carried off into exile (Jer. 38 : 23 ff.).

In ancient times it was customary for the conquered king to be brought captive, together with his courtiers, wives (cf. 2 Kings 24 : 12), sons and daughters, before his victorious rival. On a section of the bronze reliefs from the gates of Shalmaneser III's palace at Balawat (9th cent. B.C.), a Syrian prince and his daughter are shown being led into the Assyrian monarch's presence by one of his army officers (see the illustration above). The young princess is clothed in a dress girdled round the waist and is wearing shoes with pointed upturned toes — a Hittite fashion which had also become common in Syria. Her hands are raised in a gesture of greeting (for the whole relief see Vol. II, p. 174). The father, who holds a staff in his right hand, is presenting his daughter to the Assyrian captain.

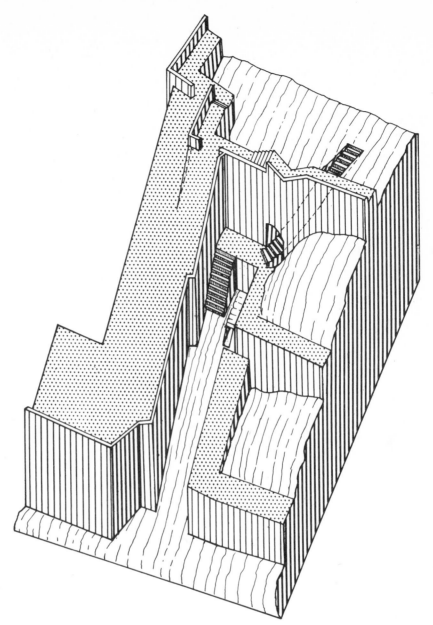

THEY fled, going out of the city at night by way
of the king's garden through the gate between the
two walls; and they went toward the Arabah.
(Jeremiah 39 : 4)

On the ninth day of the fourth month of the eleventh year of Zedekiah's reign (July 19th 586 B.C.) a breach
was made in the walls of Jerusalem through which the Babylonian army poured into the city, and the enemy's
commanders set up their headquarters in "the middle gate" (Jer. 39 : 2-3). This was apparently the central gate
in the wall running round the temple and the palace, between the Sheep Gate and the inner gateway of the temple
court. Zedekiah and his escort slipped out of the city by an escape route leading down to the Judean desert and
the Jordan valley, and got as far as the plains of Jericho before they were overtaken by the Chaldeans. This dash
for freedom was made at the dead of night through the gate between the two walls (cf. 2 Kings 25 : 4; Jer. 52 : 7).
In the opinion of some scholars, this gate stood between the ancient Jebusite wall, on the south-western slope
of the eastern hill of Jerusalem, and the new wall (the "other wall" of 2 Chron. 32 : 5) built by Hezekiah to
protect the pool of Siloam. According to our verse here, the gate was situated close to the royal garden (cf.
2 Kings 25 : 4; Neh. 3 : 9) which apparently occupied the junction of the Valley of Ben-Hinnom and the Brook
Kidron, and was watered from the pool of Siloam.
The picture above is a reconstruction of the gate "between the two walls" based on archaeological remains found
on the site. The low gate opened on to a flight of steps, from the bottom of which a path ran between the walls
alongside an ancient conduit. At the top right can be seen the Jebusite wall at the southern end of David's city,
and at the left the "other wall."

THEN Jeremiah went to Gedaliah the son of Ahikam, at Mizpah . . .
(Jeremiah 40 : 6)

After the sack of Jerusalem, the Babylonians appointed Gedaliah, the son of Ahikam, governor of the surviving remnants of the population left in Judah (2 Kings 25 : 22; Jer. 40 : 5). This Gedaliah was presumably chosen to be the representative of Babylonian authority in Palestine, because of his being the scion of an aristocratic Jerusalemite family which had held high offices in the royal court and was known for its pro-Babylonian leanings. Gedaliah himself had apparently occupied a very important administrative position in the kingdom of Judah before its downfall. It is probably the impression of his seal that was discovered at Lachish in an archaeological stratum from the time of the city's destruction (see the lower picture). Engraved on the seal there were two rows of letters separated by a double line: at the top was written "belonging to Gedaliahu", and at the bottom "who was over the house", i.e. the holder of the highest office in the royal court (cf. p. 48).

Gedaliah's residence was at Mizpah where the survivors from Jerusalem had gathered, amongst them the prophet Jeremiah and also the military commanders and the refugees who had fled during the war to Moab, Ammon and Edom (Jer. 40 : 6-13). Mizpah is generally identified with Tell en-Nasbeh, about 7 miles north of Jerusalem, on the main road to Shechem. Excavations of the tell have brought to light remains of settlements from the times of the Judges and the Monarchy and also from the Persian period. No signs of destruction dating to the beginning of the 6th cent. B.C. have been found on the site. Hence it has plausibly been conjectured that the city opened its gates to the Babylonians who made it one of their administrative centres, after the destruction of Jerusalem. The view of the city's fortifications in the upper picture is a reconstruction based on the archaeological remains from the latter days of the kingdom of Judah.

THEY went to Gedaliah at Mizpah — Ishmael the son of
Nethaniah, Johanan the son of Kareah, Seraiah the son of
Tanhumeth, the sons of Ephai the Netophathite, Jezaniah the
Maacathite, they and their men.

(Jeremiah 40 : 8)

Amongst the military commanders who joined Gedaliah at Mizpah, after the destruction of the Temple, there
was a certain Jezaniah, or Jaazaniah (2 Kings 25 : 23), who is sometimes identified with the Azaniah son of Hosha-
iah mentioned amongst the nobles that sought Jeremiah's advice after the assassination of Gedaliah (Jer. 42 : 1-2).
This particular officer may also have been the owner of the seal inscribed "Jaazaniahu, servant of the king" (see
the reproduction of the seal-impression above). This seal, which belongs roughly to the time of the conquest
of Judah, was found in a grave at Tell en-Nasbeh, Gedaliah's seat of government (see p. 138). If this identification
is correct, Jaazaniah was one of the chief ministers in the kingdom of Judah before the destruction of Jerusalem,
as is clearly implied by his title, "servant of the king." At the bottom of the seal there is a representation of a
fighting-cock tensed for combat, a fitting emblem for any warrior and one most appropriate to an officer of
Jaazaniah's high rank. This artistic portrayal of a cock from the beginning of the 6th cent. B.C. is the earliest
that has yet been found in Palestine, and proves that the bird was by that time known in the country, even though
it is not explicitly mentioned in the Old Testament. In Egyptian and Mycenean art the cock appears as early
as the middle of the second millennium B.C.

AND said to him, "Do you know that Baalis the king of the Ammonites has sent Ishmael the son of Nethaniah to take your life?"

(Jeremiah 40 : 14)

Ishmael, the son of Nethaniah, killed Gedaliah, the son of Ahikam, and fled to the country of the Ammonites (Jer. 41 : 15). Though we are explicitly told that Baalis, the king of Ammon, was the instigator of the assassination, the political motives for the crime must remain uncertain. The intention may have been simply to harm the surviving remnant of the Judean population, as the Edomites and Philistines had done at the time of the destruction; or, on the contrary, it may have been a genuine attempt to aid the forces of revolt against Babylon, as part of a joint anti-Babylonian policy. The second possibility receives some confirmation from Josephus' report of a campaign by Nebuchadnezzar against the Ammonites and Moabites in the year 582 B.C., i.e. five years after the destruction of the Temple.

Reproduced here is a statue of a local potentate, from the 8th or 7th cent. B.C., which was found at Rabbath-Ammon. It is only 19 in. high and is the earliest example of this type of plastic art so far discovered on either bank of the Jordan. The face is bearded and has side-curls hanging over the temples, but the upper-lip is clean shaven. There are indications that the figure was originally painted and the empty eye-sockets must once have contained a stone inlay. The lotus-flower in the left hand was a symbol of royal power and dignity. On the pedestal of the statue there is an only partly intelligible inscription engraved in the early Hebrew-Phoenician script.

HE shall kindle a fire in the temples of the gods of Egypt . . .
(Jeremiah 43 : 12)

Jeremiah prophesied that Nebuchadnezzar would overrun Egypt, dealing out slaughter and destruction and desecrating the temples of the Egyptian gods (Jer. 43 : 11-13). Ezekiel, too, similarly foretold the defeat of Egypt by the Babylonian monarch (see p. 188). Both these prophecies came true, at least in part, as is testified by a Babylonian inscription which describes an invasion of Egypt by Nebuchadnezzar in 568-567 B.C. and his war against the Pharaoh Amasis. Josephus also records a campaign of Nebuchadnezzar against Egypt (Antiquities x.9.7). But the actual conquest of Egypt was not accomplished till a later date, by the Persian king Cambyses.
A good idea of the appearance and size of the shrines whose destruction by fire was prophesied by Jeremiah may be obtained from the hall of pillars in the temple of Amon at Karnak, which was built during the reigns of Seti I and Ramses II (13th cent. B.C.). The centre of the hall is occupied by two parallel rows of pillars, six to a row, each pillar being sixty-nine feet high. On either side of this central nave there are another sixty-one columns, each about forty-two feet high, making one hundred and twenty two in all. All these pillars are ornamented and covered with hieroglyphic inscriptions (see the photograph). These gigantic monuments survived even the devastation of the cities of ancient Egypt.

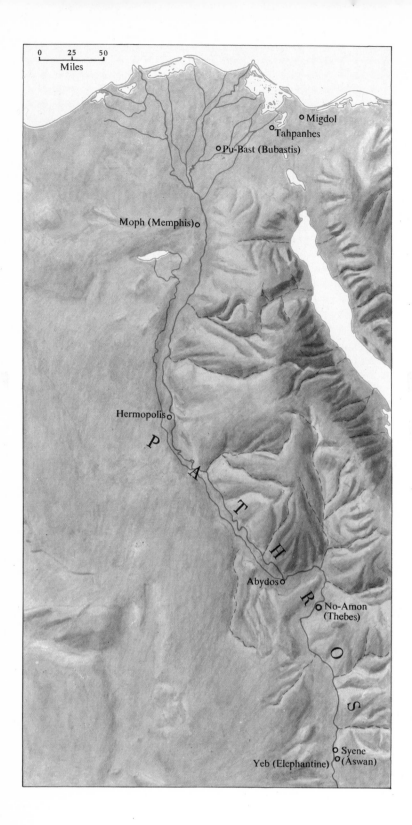

THE word that came to Jeremiah
concerning all the Jews that dwelt
in the land of Egypt, at Migdol, at
Tahpanhes, at Memphis, and in the
land of Pathros.

(Jeremiah 44 : 1)

Jeremiah's words to the Jews of Egypt (cf.
Jer. 24 : 8) imply that, at the time of the
destruction of the First Temple, Jews were
already settled in many parts of the country:
near Migdol (Tell el-Khair) and Tahpanhes
(Tell Dafna), in the north-eastern frontier
districts, at Memphis, and even in the region
of Pathros, i.e. in Upper Egypt (see the
map). This is confirmed by various pieces of
evidence from Egypt itself, some of them
from the 5th and perhaps even from the
6th cent. B.C., indicating the existence of
settlements of Jews in both Lower and
Upper Egypt at a slightly later period than
Jeremiah's lifetime.

The existence of a Jewish community at
Memphis (Heb. *Nof*) is testified by Aramaic
papyri found on the site containing such
patently Jewish names as Jonathan and Jehoram, and also by a letter written in Aramaic which was apparently sent from Memphis to Yeb (Elephantine). Papyri found at
Hermopolis in Middle Egypt also contain
Jewish names, such as Benaiah, Habib, Na-
than, Pedaiah and Raaiah, all of them
(except Habib) names known to us from
the period of the return from the Babylonian
exile. In addition, the Elephantine letters
(see p. 143) provide clear evidence of the
presence of a considerable Jewish community in this city in the 5th and 4th cent. B.C.
Amongst these letters there is one (see
photograph on p. 161) from Abydos in
Upper Egypt which was written by a Jew
named Maoziah and refers by name to his
assistants — Zaha, Hor and Anani. All these
various indications add up to a clear proof
that, in many Egyptian cities (including
some not mentioned by Jeremiah), there
were, at the beginning of the period of the
Second Temple, Jewish settlements (apparently founded in the first place as military
outposts) the origins of which went back to
the end of the First Temple and perhaps
even earlier. Additional evidence of a Jewish
settlement at Tahpanhes (one of the cities
mentioned by Jeremiah as having a Jewish
population) may be provided by the relics
of a Semitic cult excavated on the site (see
p. 143).

WHY do you provoke me to anger with the works of your hands, burning incense to other gods in the land of Egypt where you have come to live . . .　(Jeremiah 44 : 8)

The Judean refugees in Egypt continued, also in the land of their exile, to worship pagan gods, especially the "queen of heaven" (see p. 102), just as they had done in Judah and Jerusalem. Ever since the time of the New Kingdom, the cults of foreign, and particularly Semitic, deities had been widespread in Egypt. This religious syncretism took root above all in those parts of the country which had a population of mixed Assyrian, Phoenician, Aramaean and other stocks. It may have been this syncretistic atmosphere that encouraged the Judeans to continue their idolatry with still greater zeal in their new domicile (Jer. 44 : 15-20). The form taken by the cult of the Semitic gods worshipped in Egypt at the time of the destruction of the First Temple is illustrated on a stele from the 6th cent. B.C. which was found at Tell Dafna, i.e. Tahpanhes, one of the places where refugees from Judah settled (see picture on the right; and cf. p. 142). Depicted on the stele is a god, apparently the Babylonian deity Marduk, wearing Assyro-Babylonian dress. The staff he is holding in his left hand is Egyptian, but he is standing on the back of a lion after the manner of the Mesopotamian gods. In front of him there is an altar on which a priest is presenting an offering. At the top are the emblems characteristic of the gods of Mesopotamia. Further evidence that Semitic gods were worshipped at Tahpanhes is provided by a letter sent from there to Memphis in which the writer, a woman, swears a solemn oath by several gods, including the Semitic deity Baal Zaphon.

The Elephantine letters, which are written in Aramaic on papyrus, throw interesting light on the religious practices and forms of ritual observed in the shrine of the Jewish community in this city in the 5th cent. B.C. The papyrus reproduced at the left above contains a list of the contributors to the temple treasury and the sum total of their contributions. The money consisted of offerings made partly to "Yahu", and partly to "Ashambethel" and "Anathbethel" who were apparently pagan gods.

BEHOLD I will give Pharaoh Hophra king of Egypt into the hand of his enemies and into the hand of those who seek his life . . . (Jeremiah 44 : 30)

The Pharaoh Hophra ruled over Egypt in the years 588-568 B.C. It was in his reign that the First Temple was destroyed and the survivors from Judah took refuge in Egypt. He gave his support to the small nations of the Near East, like Judah and Ammon, that revolted against the king of Babylon, and apparently induced the Sidonians to join in this uprising. The Egyptian army marched out from Egypt to Zedekiah's aid, but was defeated and forced to withdraw to its land (see p. 135). Hophra's reign was, on the whole, a period of prosperity for Egypt. However, after the defeat of his armies in Cyrene, he was obliged to share the throne with his commander-in-Chief, Amasis. In the third year of their joint rule, their rivalry flared up into open war in which Hophra was killed. Thus Jeremiah's prophecy about Hophra's end proved to be true in every detail, a fact from which some scholars deduce that the prophet was still alive about 568 B.C. This particular prediction is inserted amongst Jeremiah's other prophecies about the refugees from Judah as a proof of their accuracy: "This shall be the sign to you, says the Lord, that I will punish you in this place, in order that you may know that my words will surely stand against you for evil" (Jer. 44 : 29).

A relief found at Abydos shows the Pharaoh Hophra presenting an offering to the gods of Egypt (see the reproduction above).

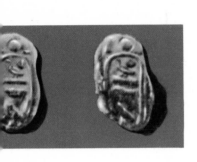

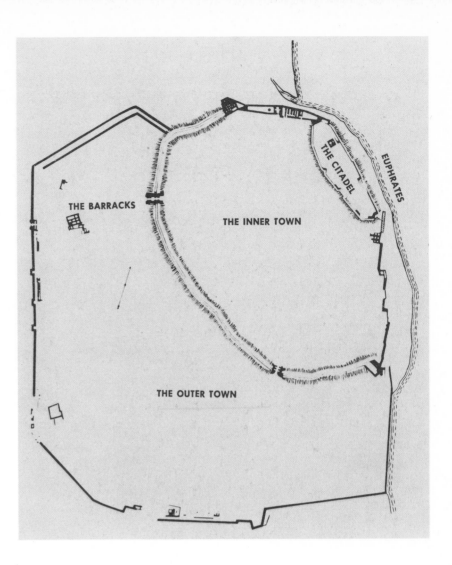

CONCERNING the army of Pharaoh Neco, king of Egypt, which
was by the river Euphrates at Carchemish and which Nebuchadrezzar
king of Babylon defeated in the fourth year of Jehoiakim the son of
Josiah, king of Judah.   (Jeremiah 46 : 2)

Jeremiah's collection of prophecies about the nations opens with an oracle concerning one of the major armed
conflicts of his time in which the armies of Egypt and Babylon contended for the mastery of the Near East.
The decisive battle was fought at Carchemish in the year 605 B.C., and ended in a brilliant victory for Nebuchadnezzar which opened the way for his conquest of Syria and Palestine. Jeremiah depicts the sudden downfall
of Egypt in poetic language: "Why have I seen it? They are dismayed and have turned backward. Their warriors
are beaten down, and have fled in haste; they look not back . . . in the north by the river Euphrates they have
stumbled and fallen" (Jer. 46 : 5-6). The battle of Carchemish and its consequences are also described in a Babylonian chronicle from the reign of Nebuchadnezzar and in the works of Josephus (Antiquities vi.1; Against Apion
i.19). These literary records are corroborated by the archaeological evidence found on the actual site of Carchemish.
Carchemish was situated on the right bank of the upper Euphrates, near the modern village of Jerablus. The
diagram above shows the lay-out of the city in the first half of the first millennium B.C. It will be seen that the
city had two sets of defence works. The outer, and later, wall was apparently built in the first millennium B.C.
at a time when the city's limits were extended, while the inner wall was already in existence in the second millennium. The citadel was protected by a third wall. There is clear proof that, shortly before the destruction of
Carchemish in 605 B.C., there were in the city Egyptian barracks which were subsequently burned to the ground.
Amongst the archaeological remains found in the main barrack-building were seal-impressions with the names
of the Egyptian monarchs Psamtik I and Necho. A set of Necho's seal-impressions, found in the stratum contemporary with the city's destruction, is reproduced above (pp. 144-145).

Baldness has come upon Gaza, Ashkelon has perished . . .   (Jeremiah 47 : 5)

In his wrathful prophetic arraignment of the country of the Philistines, Jeremiah singles out for special mention the coming doom of Ashkelon: "Ah, sword . . . How can it be quiet when the Lord has given it a charge? Against Ashkelon and against the seashore he has appointed it" (Jer. 47 : 6-7). The extant historical evidence confirms that Ashkelon was twice sacked in Jeremiah's lifetime. The first time, it was partly destroyed by the armed bands of Scythians which had stormed their way as far south as the Egyptian border and, as they withdrew northwards again, reduced to ruins the famous temple of "the heavenly Aphrodite" at Ashkelon (Herodotus 1 : 105). The second occasion was in 604 B.C., when it was sacked and this time completely destroyed by the Babylonians (see p. 135). Nebuchadnezzar, in the words of the contemporary Babylonian chronicle, "turned the city into a heap of ruins and a vineyard." There may be an echo of Ashkelon's double ordeal in Jeremiah's words.

Because of their geographical position astride the international highway connecting Egypt and Mesopotamia, the Philistine cities suffered, throughout their history, from the scourge of invasion, as is clearly shown by documents and plastic representations from the ancient East. For instance, a relief from the time of Ramses II (13th cent. B.C.), found at Karnak, gives a detailed picture of the capture of Ashkelon, which was built on a high mound, by the Egyptian army (see reproduction on p. 146). The fortifications of the city are represented schematically. Conspicuous amongst them is the entrance keep having, to the right and left of it, towers with galleries running round them from which anyone approaching the gate presented an easy target. The inside of the keep itself (with double gate) was divided into two horizontally by beams supporting a kind of upper chamber, the windows of which can be seen in a row on the relief. The roof of this chamber provided a vantage-point for soldiers who were stationed there to defend the gate. Clearly visible above the entrance keep is the citadel of the inner city, a kind of city within a city which was also heavily fortified. The Egyptians are shown trying to reduce Ashkelon by various methods: some of their troops are making a mass assault on the walls up long ladders, while other single soldiers, armed with axes and protected by long shields, endeavour to smash the bolts of the city's gates. The defenders of Ashkelon seem helpless in the face of the enemy's determined attacks. As a last desperate resort to save their city, they entreat the Pharaoh's mercy.

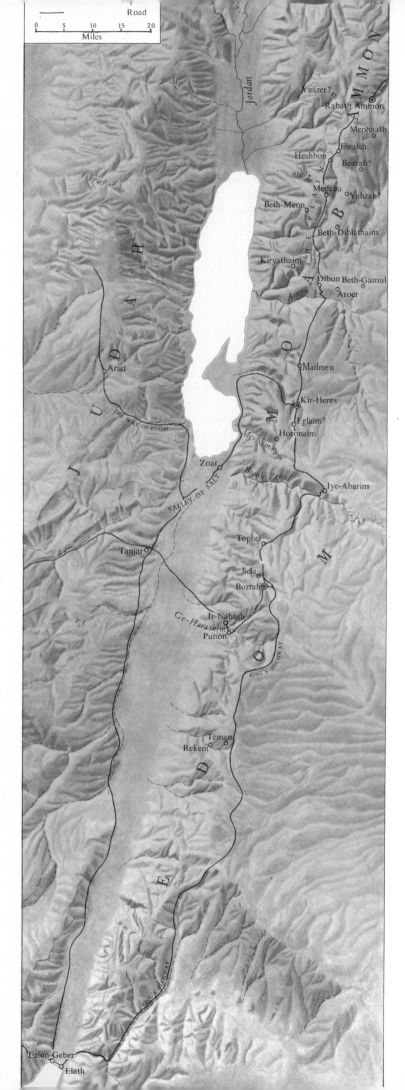

CONCERNING Moab. Thus says the LORD of hosts, the GOD of Israel: "Woe to Nebo, for it is laid waste! Kiriathaim is put to shame, it is taken; the fortress is put to shame and broken down."

(Jeremiah 48 : 1)

Embedded in the prophecies against the nations of Trans-Jordan — Edom, Moab and Ammon — contained in Jeremiah chaps. 48–49 (up to verse 23) there are ancient ballads about various disasters suffered by these kingdoms in the course of their long history. In addition, there are prophecies which are also included in the oracle concerning Moab in the Book of Isaiah (Jer. 48 : 1–8, 29–36 = Isa. 15 : 1–7; see pp. 40–41), and in Obadiah's vision about Edom (Jer. 49 : 7–11, 14–17 = Ob. 1; cf. p. 247). All these passages evidently go back to a common origin in the works of ancient bards (Nu. 21 : 27–31). The Old Testament characteristically explains the overthrow of these nations as a divine retribution for their arrogance (Jer. 48 : 7, 29, 30; 49 : 4, 7, 16). The note of savage delight which can be heard in the description of their downfall arises from the centuries' long enmity between the kingdoms of Trans-Jordan and the Israelites (cf. 2 Kings 24 : 2). The prophecies contain trustworthy information about the early settlements beyond the Jordan, with a specially full list of the cities of Moab. The places marked on the map here are those ancient inhabited sites in Ammon, Moab and Edom that can still be identified to-day.

MOAB is put to shame, for it is broken; wail and cry!
Tell it by the Arnon, that Moab is laid waste.

(Jeremiah 48 : 20)

In the oracle concerning Moab the devastation of the country and the headlong, panic-stricken flight of its inhabitants is depicted in vivid poetic images (Jer. 48 : 2-10, 15-25). No part of the land, neither valley nor plain, will be spared: "The destroyer shall come upon every city, and no city shall escape; the valley shall perish, and the plain shall be destroyed" (Jer. 48 : 8). Hordes of refugees will stream southwards towards the Arnon, fleeing from the ravages of the invader. But there will be no escape even for those who dwell in seeming security beside its banks.

The river Arnon, which, together with its tributary the Heidan, encircles the territory of Dibon, flows through a steep, twisting gorge in the mountains of Moab (see Vol. I, p. 253). As the natural defence of the heart of the country it was of great strategic importance. In times of political decline, the kingdom of Moab shrank to the area on the southern side of the river which thus became its natural border on the north. But, in its more vigorous and prosperous periods, the kingdom again expanded northwards beyond the river. The photograph shows the powerful grandeur imprinted upon the desert landscape of Trans-Jordan by the deep canyons of the Arnon.

BEHOLD, I will break the bow of Elam, the mainstay
of their might.   (Jeremiah 49 : 35)

The authenticity of Jeremiah's pronouncements about the downfall of distant Elam was regarded as dubious,
until it was recently confirmed by the discovery of a Babylonian chronicle which records a military campaign
undertaken by the Babylonian monarch Nebuchadnezzar against Elam, in the ninth year of his reign (596 B.C.).
Even such a detail as the date of the prophecy — "in the beginning of the reign of Zedekiah" (Jer. 49 : 34) — har-
monizes with the evidence of the non-biblical source. Elam was a mountainous country to the east of Babylonia.
Jeremiah's use here of the bow as the symbol of Elam's military strength shows that he was accurately informed
about the country: the bow was indeed the primary weapon of the Elamite army (cf. Isa. 22 : 6), as it was of
most of the mountain-dwelling nations of antiquity. In mountainous regions there was little possibility of hand-
to-hand combat and battles had sometimes to be fought out from the opposite sides of ravines or watercourses.
These were ideal conditions in which to exploit to the full the potentialities of the "composite" bow (see Vol. I,
p. 64) which had just been perfected technically. On the reliefs from the palace of Ashurbanipal at Nineveh (7th
cent. B.C.), portraying the conquest of Elam by the Assyrians, the Elamite army is shown as an army of bowmen,
some of whom are chariot-borne (see pp. 192-193).
In the section from these reliefs reproduced here, an Assyrian soldier is seen about to behead an Elamite officer
who his breaking his bow. This "composite" type, triangular shaped bow (see Vol. I, p. 75), is Assyrian in design,
having two duck's heads, one at either end, which serve as clasps to hold the bowstring taut.

H ER bulwarks have fallen, her walls are thrown down . . .
(Jeremiah 50 : 15)

Babylon will meet with the total defeat described in such detail in Jeremiah's prophecy (chaps. 50-51) on the city's appointed day of doom, as its just punishment by the God of Israel (Jer. 50 : 18-35). Babylon, the queen of cities, the impregnable fortress of the land of the Chaldeans, will in a moment be laid low while the nations look on in amazement. There is no evidence that Babylon was actually destroyed. On the contrary, according to one of Cyrus' inscriptions it fell to the Persians without resistance (see p. 75), as also seems to be implied by Jeremiah's words: "The warriors of Babylon have ceased fighting, they remain in their strongholds; their strength has failed, they have become women" (Jer. 51 : 30; cf. 50 : 37, 43).

Nebuchadnezzar made Babylon famous throughout the ancient world for the splendour of its buildings and the massiveness of its fortifications. Its walls were considered by classical authors to be one of the seven wonders of the world. Hence it is not surprising that the ruins of Babylon form one of the most extensive archaeological sites known in the East, covering an area of 320 square miles. Amongst the relics of the ancient city laid bare by the excavator's spade are remains of the outer and inner walls from the time of the Neo-Babylonian empire, and also remains of Nebuchadnezzar's palaces and temples. These ruins are seen in the photograph on the right. In the centre are the inner walls of the eastern portion of the Gate of Ishtar, with their facing of coloured, glazed bricks arranged to form representations of wild oxen and legendary serpents (see Vol. I, p. 21). The original appearance of the Gate of Ishtar, together with the "Street of the Processions" which led from it to the complex of Nebuchadnezzar's palaces, is shown in the reconstruction on the left. This ornamental gateway, standing amongst the splendid shrines of the city's sacred quarter, was one of the most magnificent achievements of Babylonian art.

PREPARE the nations for war against her, summon against her the kingdoms, Ararat, Minni, and Ashkenaz...

(Jeremiah 51 : 27)

Babylon s downfall will be a just retribution for her own misdeeds: even as in the past she herself had oppressed many peoples, so now many peoples and great kings will come to take their revenge on her (cf. Jer. 25 : 12-14). In particular, the prophet summons the nations of the north to batter Babylon with their blows. It is probable that the northern nations mentioned here — Ararat, Minni and Ashkenaz, all of which in the 8th and 7th cent. B.C. constituted a constant source of danger to the northern border of Assyria — were annexed to Media at the beginning of the 6th cent. B.C. and took part in the Medes' assaults on Mesopotamia. The domicile of the Minni *(Manaye* in Assyrian) was south of Lake Urmiah; the Ashkenaz *(Ashkuza* in Assyrian documents) were apparently the Scythians; and by the people of Ararat are meant the inhabitants of the kingdom of that name which is frequently mentioned in Assyrian inscriptions.

Ararat (Urartu in Assyrian) occupied a stretch of territory around Lake Van in Armenia (see map in Vol. I, p. 33) and reached the height of its power in the first half of the 8th cent. B.C. The kingdom was subsequently greatly reduced in extent by the expansive pressure of the Cymmerian and Scythian tribes, until finally, in the 6th cent., it became part of the Median, and later of the Persian, empire. Thus it will be seen that Jeremiah here appeals to nations that were no longer independent in his day. Ararat had a highly developed industry and was specially renowned for its fine metal-work. An example of the art of Ararat is provided by a bronze helmet, found in Armenia, with the name of the king Sarduri (who lived in the middle of the 8th cent. B.C.) engraved on its rim. Running round the helmet, in two broad ornamental bands, is an artistic representation of chariots and cavalry. Each chariot, in which there are two warriors, is followed by a horseman armed with shield and javelin (see the illustration).

THE fords have been
seized, the bulwarks are
burned with fire, and the
soldiers are in panic.
(Jeremiah 51 : 32)

The news of Babylon's fall (see pp. 151-152) will spread like wildfire throughout the country: "One runner
runs to meet another, and one messenger to meet another, to tell the king of Babylon that his city is taken on
every side" (Jer. 51 : 31). After the capture of the capital, the fighting will spread to the outlying parts of the
kingdom; the fords over the Euphrates will be seized and the "bulwarks" (RSV) or "reeds" (AV) set afire. The
reference here may be to the thick clumps of reeds that line the banks of the Euphrates; but it is also quite possible
that the "lakes" (Heb. *agammim)* in question were the reed-filled marshes which abounded particularly in the
region of the Persian Gulf in the south of the country. In either case, the biblical verse here describes the special
tactics employed in ancient warfare in marshy terrain overgrown with reeds: first, the closing of the fords — to
prevent the flight of the inhabitants; followed by setting fire to the reeds — in order to create confusion and panic.
This kind of warfare is illustrated on reliefs from the reign of Sennacherib (704-681 B.C.) which were excavated
at Nineveh. The section reproduced above shows the last stage of a battle against marsh-dwellers who are seen
in their boats made of reeds. Assyrian troops, armed with javelins and shields, are boarding the craft in the middle
to clear it of the enemy. The Assyrians had apparently made their assault on the boat from prepared positions
beside the fords. The occupants of the boat on the right are surrendering to the Assyrian soldiers. On the left
there is another craft hidden in the tangled undergrowth.

THIS is the number of the people whom Nebuchadrezzar carried away captive: in the seventh year, three thousand and twenty-three Jews.

(Jeremiah 52 : 28)

The description of the destruction of Jerusalem given in the Book of Jeremiah concludes with a precise statistical table — apparently based on official records (Jer. 52 : 28-30) — of the numbers deported from Judah after each of the various Babylonian campaigns against the country. There were three such deportations: the first, in the time of Jehoiachin, in 597 B.C.; the second, in the time of Zedekiah, in 586 B.C.; and the third and last, that ordered by Nebuzaradan in 581 B.C., of which nothing further is known from the Old Testament, but which was apparently connected with one of the anti-Babylonian revolts that broke out in Syria and Palestine. Josephus mentions a war fought by Nebuchadnezzar against the Ammonites and Moabites at this time and the deportation of the Jews of Palestine to Babylon (Antiquities x.6.7). It is noteworthy that, according to the numbers of exiles given in our verses, the main deportation was the one which took place in Jehoiachin's reign (cf. 2 Kings 24 : 14, 16).

The Babylonians, like the Assyrians before them, kept a tally of their captives, and some such numerical record probably underlies the figures given in these verses of the Old Testament. The method of counting captives is illustrated in a section from the reliefs of Sennacherib, which adorned the royal palace at Nineveh (see reproduction). Two Assyrian scribes standing in a palm-grove (at the right) are counting the captives who are fettered together in pairs and behind whom comes the animal booty. The captives are Chaldeans who were taken prisoner during Sennacherib's wars against Babylon, in c. 700 B.C. At the end of the period of the First Temple, the Chaldeans (i.e. Babylonians) rose to world power and the former captives now became the captors.

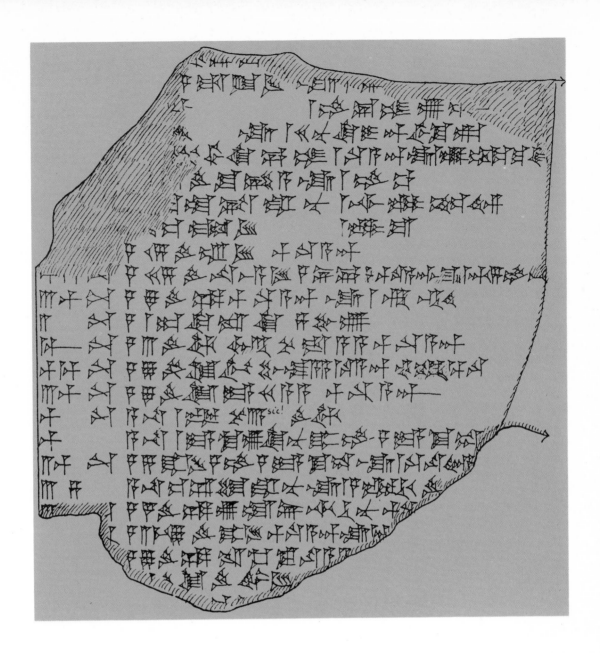

As for his allowance, a regular allowance was given him by the king according to his daily need, until the day of his death as long as he lived.　　　　　　(Jeremiah 52 : 34)

The Book of Jeremiah, like the Book of Kings, ends with an important event in the life of the exiled King Jehoiachin. Thirty seven years after Jehoiachin had been carried off captive, Evil-Merodach (561-560 B.C.), Nebuchadnezzar's successor on the throne of Babylon, released him from confinement "and gave him a seat above the seats of the kings that were with him in Babylon" (Jer. 52 : 32). The exiled monarch had evidently suffered various ups and downs of fortune during his captivity, depending upon the constantly shifting political aims of the Babylonian empire. In the reign of Nebuchadnezzar, some of the Jews still hoped that Jehoiachin would return to his throne in Jerusalem (Jer. 28 : 1-5; cf. Ezek. 17 : 22-24).

From contemporary economic documents, discovered in Nebuchadnezzar's palace, it is clear that Jehoiachin was treated with considerable respect at the court of the Babylonian king, in spite of his being reckoned one of the royal captives. Preserved in these documents (one of which is reproduced above) are lists of the daily rations of food given to royal prisoners and hostages from various lands, e.g. Ashkelon, Tyre, Gebal (Byblos), Egypt, Elam, Media and also Judah. The Judean exiles bear such names as Semachiah, Gadiel, Ormelech, and Shelemiah "the gardener." At the head of the list stand "Jehoiachin King of Judah" and his five sons, who were apparently born in Babylon. Jehoiachin's privileged status is evident from the quantity of rations that he received: for himself alone 10 measures of oil are provided, and another 2.5 for each of his sons; whereas eight prisoners from Gebal together get only 11.5 measures.

EZEKIEL

As for the likeness of their faces, each had the face of a man
in front; the four had the face of a lion on the right side, the
four had the face of an ox on the left side, and the four had
the face of an eagle at the back.   (Ezekiel 1 : 10)

The book of Ezekiel opens with a detailed description of the chariot of God seen by the prophet in his initiatory
vision. The central feature of the chariot is a flat surface supported by four living creatures each of which has at
its feet a wheel within·a wheel (Ezek. 1 : 16). Each creature has four countenances facing the four points of the
compass. They stand upright and have "the form of men" (ibid. 5). They have four wings on either side of their
body with "human hands" underneath them (ibid. 8), and the soles of their feet "were like the soles of a calf's
foot" (ibid. 7). Thus each creature is a combination of man, bird and beast.
Composite figures of this kind occur frequently in the mythology and plastic art of the ancient East. There we
find, for example, bulls and lions with human faces and wings, snakes with legs, and the like (see p. 165, and
Vol. I, pp. 21 and 22). One such mythological creature, called in Akkadian *lamassu*, is illustrated above. It has the
face of a man and wings of an eagle, with a bull's trunk and horns. This and similar figures were found in the
palace of the Assyrian monarch Sargon II (721-705 B.C.) at Dur-Sharruken (Khorsabad) flanking the entrance
to the throne-room. The statues of the *lamassu* stood facing each other, four on either side of the entrance. Their
function was apparently to protect the temple from evil spirits and to frighten away all the various demons
of destruction.

AND you, son of man, be not afraid of them . . . though briers and thorns are with you and you sit upon scorpions . . .

(Ezekiel 2 : 6)

At the time of his initiation as a prophet, Ezekiel is forewarned by God that he is being sent to a refractory and stubborn people. A similar warning is found in the passage describing the prophetic initiation of Isaiah and Jeremiah (Isa. 6 : 9-10; Jer. 1 : 19). Ezekiel, however, gives more forceful expression than either of these prophets to the heavy feeling with which he undertakes his thankless task by calling Israel "a rebellious house". The Israelites' active hostility to the prophet is compared to the stab of thorns and the sting of scorpions. Some scholars hold that the "scorpions" (Heb. *aqrabbim*) mentioned here are also a kind of thorn, but it seems more likely that the word has its natural meaning (cf. Vol. II, p. 228). The scorpion's sting is extremely painful and can be very dangerous.

Scorpions are found throughout Palestine, being particularly numerous in desert regions (see Deut. 8 : 15). The commonest of the ten indigenous varieties is *Buthus quinquestriatus,* which is yellow in colour and 3 to 4 in. long (see the picture above). By day the scorpion hides under stones, coming out at night to hunt its prey which consists of spiders and various other insects. It injects its poison through the thorn-like sting at the end of its tail.

AND when I looked, behold, a hand was stretched out to
me, and, lo, a written scroll was in it; and he spread it before
me; and it had writing on the front and on the back . . .

(Ezekiel 2 : 9-10)

Ezekiel's initiation into his prophetic task did not end with the verbal charge given him by God, after his vision
of the chariot (Ezek. 2 : 1-7). It is characteristic of this prophet that the true nature of his mission was brought
home to him by a symbolic act in which fantasy and reality are inextricably mingled. The hand that was stretched
out towards him from above the chariot unrolled before his eyes a scroll with "writing on the front and on the
back" and containing "words of lamentation and mourning and woe" (Ezek. 2 : 10). The prophet was commanded
to eat this scroll, as a symbolical demonstration that God's word had become part of his being.
Up to the first centuries of the Christian era, books were written in the form of scrolls (see Jer. 36 : 2-4; Ps. 40 : 7;
cf. p. 132), as the Jewish Scroll of the Law still is. The scroll was made of strips of hide, or papyrus (especially in
Egypt), and in the post-biblical period also of parchment (some of the Dead Sea scrolls). Usually only one side
of the strips was written on, and this was the inner side when the scroll was rolled up. Sometimes, however, on
account of the high cost of the material, both sides were written on, as illustrated in the photographs above of a
strip of papyrus from Elephantine in Egypt which has Aramaic writing "on the front and on the back" (5th
cent. B.C.).

ᴀɴᴅ you, O son of man, take a brick and lay it before
you, and portray upon it a city, even Jerusalem.

(Ezekiel 4 : 1)

Several of the deeds performed by Ezekiel at the beginning of his prophetic activity are meant to symbolize the
coming siege of Jerusalem and the punishment of its inhabitants. In one such case, the prophet is commanded to
draw Jerusalem — obviously meaning a plan of the city — on a brick and to lay symbolical siege to it (Ezek.
4 : 1-3). As bricks were the principal building material in Mesopotamia (see Vol. I, p. 44), this use of a brick
for the purpose of "drawing a city" clearly shows the influence of the material culture of Babylonia. Excavations
in Mesopotamia have brought to light "maps" of cities, buildings and plots of land incised on clay tablets or
statues, and dating from the third millennium B.C. onwards. Their purpose was mainly practical, occasionally
scientific and sometimes even ritualistic.
Reproduced above is such a map of the city of Nippur, one of the places in which the Judean exiles settled. It
was apparently drawn in the middle of the second millennium B.C. Marked on it with great accuracy are the
city's walls and gates, its main temple known as "the house of Enlil" (at the right), the water-channels by which
it was traversed, and the river Euphrates by which it was encircled (at the left). The remains of the city laid bare
by the excavations on the site accord, in general outline, with the details of the map which may have served as
a plan for the city's defence works.

AND you, O son of man, take a sharp sword; use it as a barber's razor and pass it over your head and your beard . . .

(Ezekiel 5 : 1)

The retribution in store for the people of Israel is demonstrated by another of the prophet's symbolical acts. At God's bidding, he shaves off his hair and his beard, as a sign that the enemy will pass over the land like a razor (cf. Isa. 7 : 20). He then divides his shorn locks into three parts: one he burns inside the city as a sign of its destruction together with the Temple; the second he strikes with his sword round about the city as a symbolical representation of those who are to fall outside its walls; and the third he scatters to the winds, to signify the dispersion of the exiles on foreign soil (Ezek. 5 : 2-4). It is also possible that this act of shaving harks back to the religious ceremonial so dear to the priest in Ezekiel. The purpose of the suffering that is to come upon the people of Israel is to remove their sin and purify them, just as the Levites and the Nazirites used to purify themselves by passing a razor over their hair and flesh (Num. 6 : 18-19; 8 : 7).

The razor (Heb. *taar*, or, as it is called in the Former Prophets, *morah*) was a finely sharpened knife used for shaving. The prophet is commanded to take a barber's razor, presumably because it was of superior quality to the ordinary razor. Ancient barbers are seen at work in the picture below, which is a reproduction of an Egyptian wall-painting found in a tomb at Beni Hasan (the Twelfth Dynasty, beginning of the second millennium B.C.). The barber on the right works sitting, while his colleague on the left stands. The two men being shaved are on their knees.

YOUR altars shall become desolate, and your incense altars shall be broken . . .

(Ezekiel 6 : 4)

Whenever the word here translated "incense-altars" *(hammanim)* occurs in the Old Testament, it is in connection with idolatry and usually together with high-places, altars and *asherim*. Hence it presumably denotes some ritual appurtenance. It was conjectured that the *hammanim* were pillars used in the worship of the sun *(hamah)* or in the cult of the Phoenician deity Haman. Their exact nature has now been made clearer through the discovery at Palmyra in the Syrian desert of an altar from the 1st cent. B.C. (see the reproduction). On one side of this altar (bottom left) two figures can be clearly seen with, between them, a kind of portable incense-altar. Engraved on the other side (bottom right) is a dedicatory inscription in Aramaic which runs as follows: "In the month Elul, the year 396 (according to the Seleucid era, i.e. 85 B.C.) this *hamman* and this altar have been made and offered by Lishamsh and Zebida the sons of Maliku the son of Yediabel the son of Nesa who was called Abd-bel, from the family of Migdat, to Shamash the god of their father's house for their life and the life of their brothers and children." This indicates that the *hamman* was a portable incense-altar which was placed on the main altar and which was not connected with the worship of any one particular deity. In that case, its name may be derived from the Hebrew root meaning "to heat" *(hmm)*, on account of the fire that was kindled on it.

So I went in and saw; and there, portrayed upon the wall round about, were all kinds of creeping things, and loathsome beasts, and all the idols of the house of Israel. (Ezekiel 8 : 10)

In a vision Ezekiel sees himself transported to Jerusalem, to the site of the Temple, that he may behold the abominations committed by the people of Israel. Through an opening in the Temple wall he sees seventy of the elders of Israel burning incense in front of various reliefs of insects and animals. These figures were undoubtedly of idolatrous, demonic significance, the reference apparently being to the rites of the Assyro-Babylonian cult which was widely practised in those days, as we know from archaeological finds.

Reproduced above are two stone panels from the temple of Kapara, king of Gozan (the modern Tell Halaf on the river Habur) from the end of the 10th or the beginning of the 9th cent. B.C. The demonic figures engraved on them are characteristic of the art of the region of northern Mesopotamia occupied in ancient times by the Hurrite-Mitanni peoples. On the left — a hybrid creature, part man part fish, holding a kind of snaky frame which is perhaps a primeval serpent. On the right — a winged creature with a man's head and a scorpion's tail.

AND with them was a man clothed in linen, with a writing case at his side . . .

(Ezekiel 9 : 2)

At the sight of the idolatrous abominations committed in Jerusalem (see p. 165) the prophet predicts the punishment in store for their doers. He has a vision of seven angels, in human form, descending from heaven to mete out retribution to the city's inhabitants. Six of them hold instruments of slaughter in their hands for the annihilation of the city. The task of the seventh, who was "clothed in linen, with a writing case at his side" (Ezek. 9 : 2), was to place a mark on the foreheads of those who had not participated in the acts of abomination, as a sign to the destroyers not to harm them.

The picture below is part of a wall-painting from the tomb of Khaemhet, the steward of the Pharaoh's estates, which was discovered at Sheikh Abd el-Gurnah (14th cent. B.C.). It portrays a scribe clothed in white linen, with a writing-case *(keset)* fastened to his waist. This case served as a container for the instruments required in writing. The two holes at the top of the case were used as palettes for mixing variously coloured ink-powders with water (cf. p. 133). The scribe's palette was called in Egyptian *gsti,* and this is apparently the source of the Hebrew word *keset* which is found only here in the Old Testament. The scribe in the picture is recording quantities of produce at the dictation of a messenger. At the same time, a second scribe, who holds a writing-case in his left hand, is turning round to pass on the information to his superior.

THEREFORE, son of man, prepare for yourself
an exile's baggage, and go into exile by day in
their sight . . .   (Ezekiel 12 : 3)

To bring home the stark reality of the exile in store for the people of Judah and their king, the prophet, complete
with exile's baggage, publicly enacts the fate of the deportees. The "exile's baggage", which is also mentioned in
Jer. 46 : 19, consisted of the bundles of personal possessions carried by exiles on their backs ("you shall lift the
baggage upon your shoulder", Ezek. 12 : 6). As might be expected, such bundles feature prominently in Assyrian
reliefs, since it was the Assyrians that first introduced systematic mass deportation as an instrument of policy
which was subsequently taken over by the neo-Babylonian empire.
The reproduction above is part of a relief from the palace of the Assyrian monarch Ashurbanipal (668–630 B.C.)
at Nineveh. It depicts three deportees, two men and a boy, being prodded along by an Assyrian soldier with a
staff in his hand. The pack-like objects on the backs of the two men and in the right hand of the one in front
are "exile's baggage."

Eᴠᴇɴ if these three men, Noah, Daniel, and Job, were in it, they would deliver but their own lives by their righteousness, says the ʟᴏʀᴅ ɢᴏᴅ.　　(Ezekiel 14 : 14)

In the course of the debate on the ways of God in His world, Ezekiel refers to the fate of Noah, Daniel and Job, those archetypes of righteousness in the traditional lore of the East who had also become part of the national literature of Israel. Noah, the just man who was saved from the Flood, is originally a Mesopotamian figure, the counterpart of Ziusudra in Sumerian tradition and Utnapishtim in Akkadian mythology. Job, the hero of the biblical Book of Job, apparently belongs to the very early days of Hebrew history close to the period of the Patriarchs. Unlike Noah and Job who are known to us from other passages in the Old Testament, Daniel is mentioned only in Ezekiel and is not to be identified with the Daniel of the biblical book of that name. However, he was a central figure in Canaanite lore, as is clear from the Ugaritic epics in which he appears as a righteous ruler whose custom it was to hold court on the threshing-floor in the city gateway and there "judge the case of the widow and see justice done to the orphan." It is related in the epic that he was childless, until his prayers moved God to grant him a son, named Aqhat, in his old age. Ezekiel mentions Daniel in another passage as the symbol of wisdom. Thus, he embodied in his person the two basic and complementary qualities of the true judge — wisdom and righteousness. Several tablets of "the epic of Daniel" (also called "the epic of Aqhat") have been discovered in the excavations at Ugarit.

The two sides of one of these tablets, each divided into two columns, are reproduced here. The writing is in the alphabetic cuneiform script peculiar to Ugarit.

Son of man, how does the wood of the vine surpass any wood, the vine branch which is among the trees of the forest? Is wood taken from it to make anything? . . .

(Ezekiel 15 : 2-3)

The vine was a popular prophetic symbol (cf. p. 217) and Ezekiel, too, frequently compares Israel and its rulers to a vine. When they are faithful to God they are compared to a well-set, fruitful and leafy vine (Ezek. 17 : 6-8; 19 : 10). But when they go astray, they are doomed to be torn up from their land and to wither away like a vine that has been uprooted (Ezek. 17 : 9; cf. Jer. 2 : 21). Unlike other trees and bushes whose wood, after they have been cut down, can be used for making various utensils, the vine is no good for any kind of woodwork: not even "a peg to hang a vessel on" can be made from its gnarled and brittle branches (Ezek. 15 : 3-4; cf. Isa. 22 : 23-25). The uprooted vine is good only for burning. Even so will be the fate of the inhabitants of Jerusalem; since they have exhausted God's forbearance by their sins, He will give them to the fire for fuel until they are utterly consumed (Ezek. 15 : 6-7).

In the photograph — a rough, twisted vine-stock, bare of leaves in the autumn.

A<small>ND</small> I put a ring on your nose, and
earrings in your ears, and a beautiful
crown upon your head.

(Ezekiel 16 : 12)

The covenant between God and the people of Israel is regularly likened by the prophets to a marriage contract.
Ezekiel too makes use of this simile, comparing the God of Israel to a traveller who found an abandoned infant
by the wayside, saved its life, cared for it and reared it and, when the now fully grown girl reached the age of
wedlock, clothed her in gorgeous raiment and decked her out with jewellery as befitted a bride (Ezek. 16 : 4–12).
Included here in the list of adornments is the crown which was placed upon the heads of the bride and groom on
their wedding-day, making them look like a king and queen (Song of Sol. 3 : 11).
The picture on the right is a painting of a crown worn by an Egyptian princess. The painting was discovered in
the tomb of Menna at Sheikh Abd el-Gurnah (15th cent. B.C.). The crown rests upon a diadem decorated with
lotus-leaves which fits over the princess's wig. The crown itself is composed of a series of frames, with leaf-
pendants. Above the lady's brow there is an ornamental gazelle's head and two gold feathers.
On the left — a fluted crown upon the ivory bust of a lady of rank which was discovered at Calah (Nimrud)
on the river Tigris (8th cent. B.C.).

A great vulture with great wings and long pinions, rich in plumage of many colours . . . (Ezekiel 17 : 3)

Ezekiel's fondness for parables and figurative expressions was so marked that, as he himself tells us, the people used to say of him: "Is he not a maker of allegories?" (Ezek. 20 : 49). It is indeed true that his book is full of picturesque similes and detailed allegories, one of the most striking of which is that quoted here from chapter 17. In his parable about Zedekiah's revolt against Nebuchadnezzar and his appeal to the Pharaoh Hophra for aid (cf. p. 144), Ezekiel compares the kings of Babylon and Egypt to mighty vultures, the symbols of pride and power.

From the dawn of Oriental history, the vulture has been considered the symbol of sovereignty and domination (see Vol. I, p. 292). In Egypt, it was the emblem of the goddess Mut, and its head and outspread wings formed one of the crowns worn by the queens of Egypt. In the picture above — which is reproduced from a wall-painting in the tomb of Queen Hatshepsut at Thebes (beginning of the 15th cent. B.C.) — a vulture is seen holding a ring which symbolizes the world's circuit.

THEN he took of the seed of the land and planted it in fertile soil; he placed it beside abundant waters. He set it like a willow twig.

(Ezekiel 17 : 5)

Ezekiel depicts the political events in Judah during the reigns of its last two kings in symbols taken from the animal and vegetable worlds (cf. Ezek. chap. 19, and p. 174). The Babylonian monarch, the great vulture (see p. 171), swooped upon the Lebanon — i.e. the land of Judah — and cut down "the top of the cedar", — i.e. Jehoiachin the exiled king of Judah (Ezek. 17 : 3). In place of this deported king, the Babylonian monarch set on the throne of Judah Zedekiah, a scion of David's line (see Vol. II, p. 297), who is symbolically described by the prophet as "the seed of the land." In one passage Zedekiah is likened to a willow that has grown from "the seed of the land" and is firmly planted by abundant waters; in another he is compared to a vine that has sprouted from the same seed in good, well-watered soil, but now bends its tendrils and shoots out its branches towards another vulture, who is the king of Egypt, thus betraying the first vulture, who is the king of Babylon. The purpose of this whole parable is to indicate that, by the fickleness and treachery of his revolt, Zedekiah had thrown away the fair chance offered him of living at peace under the protection of his treaty with the king of Babylon, and would be punished accordingly.

The willow *(zafzafah)* is mentioned only here in the Old Testament. Above is a photograph of the Euphrates willow *(Populus euphratica Oliv.)* which grows in large numbers on the banks of the Jordan, so close to the actual water-channel that its roots often draw their moisture straight from the river.

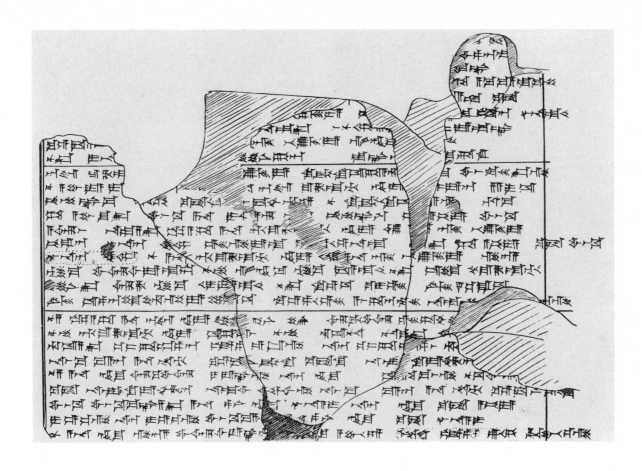

Bᴇʜᴏʟᴅ, all souls are mine; the soul of the father as well as the soul of the son is mine: the soul that sins shall die.

(Ezekiel 18 : 4)

The prophet disputes the doctrine of retribution held by his contemporaries, namely the deeply rooted belief that the fate of the children was decided by the deeds of their parents. This deterministic view found expression in a popular saying, the truth of which had already been contested by Jeremiah: "The fathers have eaten sour grapes, and the children's teeth are set on edge" (Ezek. 18 : 2; Jer. 31 : 29). Ezekiel too rejects this conception, which was still widely held by the Jewish exiles, replacing it by a doctrine of retribution based on personal responsibility: "The soul that sins shall die."

The problem of reward and punishment greatly exercised the minds of the sages of the ancient East, as can be seen from the numerous references to it in their writings. In the documents of the Hittite king, Mursilis, for example (second half of the 14th cent. B.C.), there is a forceful statement of the doctrine of collective responsibility, according to which the deeds of the sinner bring retribution not only upon himself, but upon his whole family as well. Thus, Mursilis regards the plague afflicting his land as the consequence of his father's sins and he therefore says in his prayer to the Hittite storm-god: "My father sinned and transgressed the word of the Hattian storm-god, my lord. But I have not sinned in any respect. It is only too true, however, that the father's sin falls upon the son. So my father's sin has fallen upon me" (this section of the prayer is reproduced above). Ezekiel takes issue with those who hold such a belief, which was still common in his time, and categorically denies its validity.

WITH hooks they put him in a cage, and brought him to the king
of Babylon . . .   (Ezekiel 19 : 9)

In Ezekiel's lament over the princes of Israel, the two kings of Judah, Jehoahaz and
Zedekiah, are compared to two lion-cubs reared by the lioness, their mother. The lioness
in this simile apparently stands for the kingdom of Judah, or perhaps for the mother of
the two kings, the princess Hamutal the daughter of Jeremiah from Libnah. One of the
cubs grew into a young lion which learnt to rend its prey and became a man-eater, until
it was caught in a trap and dragged by hooks to the land of Egypt. This is an allegorical
reference to King Jehoahaz who was captured by the Pharaoh Necho and carried off to
Egypt (see 2 Kings 23 : 34). Now the lioness devoted all her care to the second cub
(Zedekiah). He too grew into a young lion and met the same fate as his brother: he was
caught in a net laid to ensnare him and brought in a cage to the king of Babylon.
The reality which underlies this figure of a caged lion being brought before a king is
vividly illustrated in Assyrian reliefs, where the king is sometimes shown enjoying the
sport of hunting in a game-reserve. Reproduced above is one such relief from Nineveh
in which the Assyrian monarch Ashurbanipal (668-630 B.C.) is seen engaged in a lion-
hunt. As is usual in Assyrian reliefs, the various stages of the event are portrayed in
sequence. A lion, which has just been released from its cage, hurls itself at the king who
draws his bow and shoots an arrow into the beast. Beside the king stands his shield-
bearer who is protecting his royal master.

Aɴᴅ I said to them, Cast away the detestable things your
eyes feast on, every one of you, and do not defile yourselves
with the idols of Egypt . . .   (Ezekiel 20 : 7)

The prophet regards the past history of the Israelites as one long series of acts of apostasy which have inevitably
brought down the wrath of God upon their heads. Even before the exodus from Egypt the children of Israel had
already defiled themselves with idols and other abominations. The Israelites' sin of idolatry while in Egypt is not
usually so explicitly described in the Bible, but only hinted at (e.g. Deut. 29 : 16-17; Josh. 24 : 14).
The gods of ancient Egypt were often represented in the forms of various animals (cf. pp. 64 and 171; Vol. I,
pp. 137, 171; Vol. II, p. 274). The two Egyptian idols reproduced here clearly illustrate the absurdity of these
representations. The picture on the left is a statue of the goddess Taweret, found at Karnak, from the time
of the Twenty-Sixth Dynasty (7th-6th cent. B.C., not long before the time of Ezekiel). The goddess is represented
as a woman with a heavy, sagging body and the head of a hippopotamus, on which there is a wig and a cylindrical
headdress like those worn by Egyptian ladies of rank. Her hands and feet have lion's claws. On the right is a statue
of a dwarf-like demon known to the Egyptians as Bes. His broad, bearded face is contorted into a hideous grimace,
with his tongue stuck out. On his head there is a crown of feathers, in his arms a child-dwarf like himself, and
all around him the figures of twelve monkeys and two geese.

FOR the king of Babylon stands at the parting of
the way, at the head of the two ways, to use
divination; he shakes the arrows, he consults the
teraphim, he looks at the liver.   (Ezekiel 21 : 21)

Wheu Nebuchadnezzar stood at the junction of the roads to Rabbath-Ammon and Jerusalem, he had recourse, according to Ezekiel, to various methods of divination in order to decide which of the two cities he should march on and besiege (Ezek. 21 : 18-22). The "oracle of the liver" mentioned here by the prophet was one of the commonest forms of divination in Mesopotamia. When the ancients wished to divine the future, they slaughtered an animal (usually a sheep) and carefully examined its colour and its special anatomical features. In this "looking at the liver" the augurs were assisted by clay models of the organ on which the various "omens" were marked. Models of this kind, dating from the beginning of the second millennium B.C. onwards, have been excavated at Babylon and are also known from other parts of the ancient world, such as the Hittite empire, Etruria and even Canaan.

The picture at the top of p. 177 shows such a model of a liver from Babylon, belonging to the time of the First Dynasty (first half of the second millennium B.C.). In each one of the squares engraved on it (about fifty in all) the "omen" is marked in two sections: first, the anatomical signs by which it may be recognized; and secondly, its significance — whether favourable (a blessing and the victory of the king and his land), or unfavourable (misfortune, plague, military defeat). In the picture at the top of p. 176 there are two fragments of a liver-model which were found in a Canaanite temple at Hazor (apparently from the 15th or 14th cent. B.C.). On this liver from Hazor only the meaning of the "omen", which foretells coming disasters and the city's deliverance from them, is given.

To set battering rams against the gates, to cast up mounds, to build siege towers.
(Ezekiel 21 : 22)

In his vision of the capture of Jerusalem, the prophet gives a detailed picture of the way in which the city was besieged and of the highly efficient methods employed by the Assyro-Babylonian army to breach its walls. Siege operations of this kind against a fortified city are illustrated in great detail on Assyrian reliefs, one of which, from the palace of Tiglath-Pileser III (744-727 B.C.) at Nineveh, is reproduced below. In the centre of the picture an Assyrian battering-ram is seen in action. In appearance this siege-engine, with its two protruding "horns" for breaking down the wall (a common feature at this period) and its protective covering of pieces of leather and metal plates, was very similar to a ram, hence its name *(kar* or *ayil)*. It was rolled up to the tower of the defensive wall on an embankment of earth. The construction of this embankment was a complicated piece of engineering, since the earth had to be piled up on a ramp of wooden beams, the function of which was to bind together the earth of the inclined surface and thus prevent the whole from disintegrating when the rams were rolled over it. To ensure that the wheels of the engine did not sink into the earth, the ramp was covered with wooden planking and other materials. The ram-team sat inside its protective casing, working the two "horns" forwards and backwards by means of ropes attached to the inner side of the roof above their heads. At the right Assyrian bowmen, protected by large shields, are providing covering fire for both the ram and the attacking infantry. The latter are assaulting the walls up long ladders placed in the moat surrounding the city (For other types of battering-ram see p. 52, and Vol. II, p. 192 and the top of p. 287). In the centre and at the right of the picture are representations of the brutal acts committed by the Assyrians after the capture of the city.

As men gather silver and bronze and iron and lead and tin into a furnace, to blow the fire upon it in order to melt it . . .   (Ezekiel 22 : 20)

Other prophets (Isa. 1 : 25; Zech. 13 : 9; Mal. 3 : 3), had used metal-smelting as a metaphor to describe the purification of the house of Israel from its moral dross. In Ezekiel, on the contrary, it is a symbol of the complete destruction of the wicked who are beyond redemption and must be melted away in the fire: "I will gather you and blow upon you with the fire of my wrath, and you shall be melted in the midst of it" (Ezek. 22 : 21). The process described in our verse above is not the smelting or refining of the ore of a certain metal, but the fusing of many metals into a single alloy. The assorted metals were to be fused together "as silver is melted in a furnace". The "furnace" *(kur)* in question was a special large kiln for the smelting of metal in which a hotter flame than in the ordinary kiln was obtained by a forced draught from bellows (cf. p. 101).

An example of such a smelting-furnace is provided by the kiln from the Philistine period (11th cent. B.C.) found at Tell Qasileh on the banks of the Yarkon river. This particular specimen was used for the smelting and processing of copper. The picture is a reconstruction of the kiln, based on the archaeological finds. At the bottom can be seen the air-channel which supplied the draught for the fire. Standing on the charcoal are two clay containers ("crucibles" in modern terminology) in which the copper was smelted, and which were still found to contain traces of the processed metal.

SHE saw men portrayed upon the wall, the images of the Chaldeans portrayed in vermilion.

(Ezekiel 23 : 14)

Samaria and Jerusalem, which have sinned by entering into alliances with the idolatrous empires after soliciting their favours so ardently, are compared here to two lewd sisters — Oholah and Oholibah — who lust for foreign paramours from Egypt and Assyria (cf. Ezek. chap. 16). When Oholibah, who represents Jerusalem, sees portraits of Chaldeans engraved on the wall, she becomes so inflamed with passion for them that she finally sends messengers to Babylon to entice them to come and share her bed. The prophet's allegory here is based on the widespread custom in ancient Mesopotamia of decorating the walls of large chambers with reliefs, on stone slabs, of all kinds of figures (cf. p. 165), amongst them human forms which were sometimes executed in more than life-size. It was also customary to paint these reliefs in various colours such as the vermilion mentioned by Ezekiel here.

The picture above is a reconstruction of a wall-painting found in the house of a senior Assyrian official at Dur-Sharruken (Khorsabad), the capital of the Assyrian monarch Sargon II (721-705 B.C.). On it the king is seen standing before the statue of the god Ashur who is holding in his hand the symbols of sovereignty — a staff and a circle with his own likeness inside it. Sargon's right hand is raised towards the god in a gesture of adoration while in his left he holds a mace. Behind the king stands one of his ministers, perhaps the official in whose house the painting was found. In the arched border surrounding the picture, and on the frieze below it, there are winged figures separated by stylized rosettes.

YOU bathed yourself, painted your eyes, and decked yourself with ornaments.   (Ezekiel 23 : 40)

The faithless city of Jerusalem is depicted by the prophet as a wanton woman who deploys all her charms to seduce men of other nations (see p. 179, and cf. pp. 22-23). Here Ezekiel describes her as putting on all her finery to inflame the passions of "the men who come from far" (cf. Jer. 4 : 30). Many pictures from the ancient East, together with archaeological finds, provide us with detailed knowledge of the forms taken by feminine adornment in antiquity and of the methods employed by the women of those days to heighten their natural charms (cf. Vol. II, p. 267).

The picture above is a section of a wall-painting from the tomb of an Egyptian notable of the time of Thutmose IV (end of the 15th cent. B.C.). In it two waiting-women are seen grooming a lady of rank who is seated on a low chair. One of them is arranging her mistress' hair, while the other is holding out a necklet of flowers and lotus-leaves to her. All three women have a ribbon and a lump of ointment on their heads. The plate at the right on p. 181 is a photograph of the toilet-box of Tutu, the wife of the scribe Ani, which was found at Thebes (14th cent. B.C.). In the upper compartments there are jars which contained unguents for anointing the body, a tube of kohl with wooden and ivory sticks for painting the eyes, and an ivory comb. On the bottom shelf there is a bronze spoon for stirring the unguents, a pair of sandals and three little elbow-cushions,

SET on the pot, set it
on, pour in water also.
(Ezekiel 24 : 3)

On the day when Nebuchadnezzar commenced the siege of Jerusalem the prophet was commanded to perform the symbolical act of putting a pot on the fire and filling it with pieces of meat and bones (cf. Ezek. 11 : 7-13). The flesh and bones stand for the inhabitants of Jerusalem (Ezek. 11 : 7,11), while the pot is the city itself. The flesh and bones will be burnt to cinders; and the pot, too, together with the dirt and rust inside it, will be scorched and melted in the fire kindled by God's wrath (Ezek. 24 : 9-11), since it is too encrusted with filth to be cleaned any more and must be left on the fire until the incrustations have been burnt away. In the same way, Jerusalem, "the city of blood", is so foul that it can only be cleansed of its impurity by being utterly destroyed.

The picture above is taken from a relief in the palace of Sennacherib (704-681 B.C.) at Nineveh portraying a large, two-handled copper cauldron in an Assyrian army camp. The cauldron is held in place over the fire by two stones, one on either side. Below is a photograph of a clay hearth with fragments of cooking-pots on it. This hearth was found at Hazor in an Israelite house from the 8th cent. B.C., roughly one or two generations before the destruction of the city by the Assyrians.

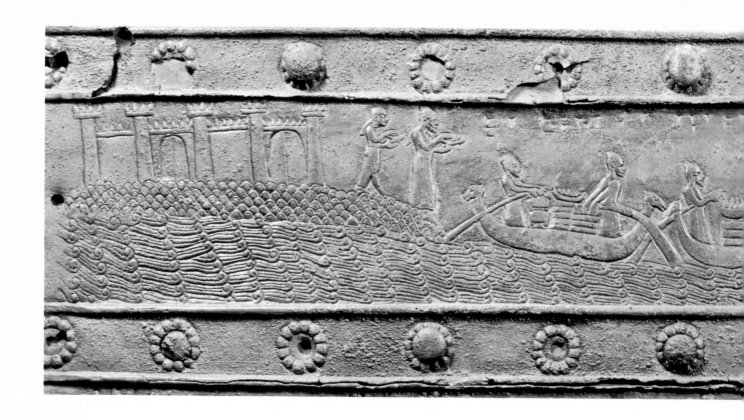

THEY shall destroy the walls of Tyre, and break down her towers; and I will scrape her soil from her, and make her a bare rock.

(Ezekiel 26 : 4)

In his prophecies concerning the nations, Ezekiel devotes the largest space to Tyre (Ezek. chaps. 26-28). He may have obtained his information about this kingdom from the groups of Tyrian deportees in Babylonia who were apparently settled in special enclaves near to the Judean exiles. Because of its unique strategic position on a rocky island just off the Phoenician coast (see p. 49) and the strength of its powerful fortifications, the city was able to withstand the various attacks made upon it in the course of its long history. In Ezekiel's day, it even resisted the armies of Nebuchadnezzar for thirteen years (cf. p. 123). It was Tyre's overweening confidence in its impregnability that provoked the prophet into pronouncing its coming doom.

Reproduced above is a section of the bronze gates discovered at Balawat, showing the surrender of Tyre to the Assyrian monarch Shalmaneser III (858-824 B.C.). At the left the city's fortifications are seen towering above the rocky island. Two boats (of which the one on the right is being hauled to the shore) are bringing the tribute of the citizens of Tyre: a large pot and trays full, apparently, of ivory. At the right are other tribute-bearers carrying heavy loads on their backs.

AND say to Tyre, who dwells at the entrance to the sea, merchant of the peoples on many coastlands . . .   (Ezekiel 27 : 3)

Tyre's unique geographical situation enabled it to become the centre of a far-flung commercial empire. The trade and wealth of Tyre are frequently referred to in the Bible (cf. pp. 49-50), above all in the lament over the city which is contained in the twenty-seventh chapter of Ezekiel. In this chapter there is a list of the many nations, cities and lands with which Tyre entered into commercial relations, together with the goods that she imported from them. It thus constitutes an important source of information about the economic geography of the ancient East.

Tyre's trade extended over a vast area stretching from the Persian Gulf to beyond the Straits of Gibraltar, and from southern Arabia to the shores of the Black Sea (see the map; and for the identification of the various sites cf. "The Table of the Nations", Vol. I, pp. 36 ff.). At its western end stood the biblical Tarshish (Ezek. 27 : 12), which was a Phoenician colony either in the Iberian peninsula (in the region of Gadara, the modern Cadiz), or on one of the large islands in the western basin of the Mediterranean (perhaps Sardinia). Other places mentioned are, in the eastern basin of the Mediterranean, the isles of Cyprus (Elishah) and Javan (Ezek. 27 : 6-7, 13); and in Asia Minor, Tubal, Meshech and Beth-Togarmah (ibid. 13-14). Further on in the same chapter comes a list of peoples and places lying along the borderland of the Arabian desert from north to south: Aram, Damascus, Dedan, Arabia, Kedar, Sheba and Raamah (ibid. 16-22). Then there is a reference to cities and districts of northern Mesopotamia: Haran, Canneh, Ashur (the city of that name) and Eden (ibid. 23). Judah and the land of Israel also appear amongst the lands with which Tyre traded: "they exchanged for your merchandise wheat, olives and early figs, honey, oil and balm" (ibid. 17).

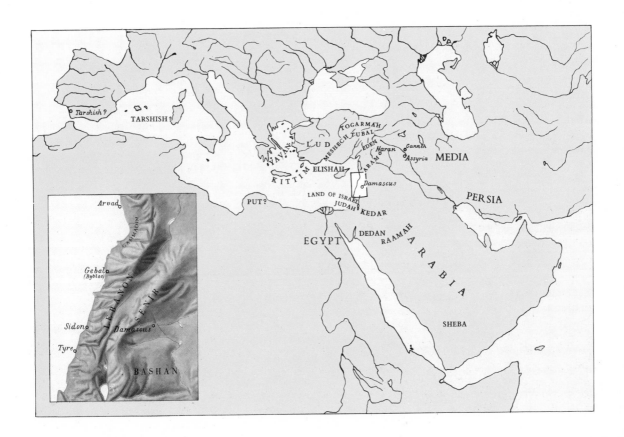

THE inhabitants
Sidon and Arvad we
your rowers; skille
men of Zemer were
you, they were yo
pilots, the elders
Gebal and her skille
men were in yo
caulking your seams.
(Ezekiel 27 : 8-

Tyre's strength and security lay in its far-ranging fleet of merchant vessels (see p. 183). Hence the prophet, in his lament, likens the city's downfall to the shipwreck of a surpassingly beautiful vessel on the high seas. In so doing he describes in detail the various fittings of the ship, the choice materials that were imported for its construction, and the allocation of nautical tasks amongst the sailors who were pressed into service from the neighbouring countries of the Phoenician seaboard — Sidon, Arvad and Gebal (Ezek. 27 : 5-9; see map on p. 183). The inhabitants of the Phoenician cities were renowned far and wide as shipbuilders and seafarers. Solomon made use of their skill in the building and sailing of the Israelite merchant fleet (see Vol. II, pp. 222-223). Even the great Assyrian kings had recourse to Phoenician experts for the construction of river-craft to ply up and down the Euphrates and the Tigris.

In the centre of the illustration above is a sketch of a Tyrian man-of-war, prepared from a relief in the palace of Sennacherib (704-681 B.C.) at Nineveh (see the designs in the background of the picture). The oarsmen sat in two rows along the hull of the vessel, which was steered by two long oars protruding from its stern. In case of need, a sail could be hoisted on this type of ship (cf. p. 60). For ramming in battle a metal spike was fitted to the prow below the water-line. The soldiers sat on the upper deck and their shields were hung along both sides of the ship.

BECAUSE your heart is proud, and you have said, "I am a god, I sit in the seat of the gods, in the heart of the seas," yet you are but a man, and no god, though you consider yourself as wise as a god ... (Ezekiel 28 : 2)

The sin which, according to the prophets' conception, characterized the kings of idolatrous nations was their arrogant boasting of their own divinity (Isa. 10 : 12-15; 13 : 11; 31 : 3 and elsewhere). Ezekiel too rebukes the king of Tyre for this same sin, after first portraying him in all his wealth and wisdom. Since his sea-girt city was impregnable to foreign assault (see p. 182), he had become so puffed up with pride that he regarded himself as a god *(el)* dwelling in the heart of the seas. The reference here seems to be the actual god El, the chief divinity of the Canaanite pantheon (see Vol. I, p. 269) who is described in the Ugaritic epic as having his abode "at the source of the rivers, in the channels of the two deeps."

Photographed above is a silver shekel from Tyre minted at the end of the Persian period (4th cent. B.C.). On it can be seen the chief deity of the city (Melkarth) in the form of a bearded man with a royal crown on his head. In his left hand he holds a bow and in his right the reins of a mythical beast which he is riding. The beast has a horse's head and forefeet, a fish's tail, and wings with upturned ends. It is galloping over the sea waves which are represented by two undulating lines with a dolphin under them.

Y OU were in Eden, the garden of GOD; every precious
stone was your covering... (Ezekiel 28 : 13)

In his highly-coloured description of the king of Tyre's pride and
splendour, Ezekiel compares him — in a prophetic figure of speech —
to a more than mortal creature dwelling in the garden of God. This
poetic allegory is embellished with themes and word-pictures taken
from various traditions about paradise which were part of the folklore
of Israel and other nations (Ezek. 28 : 12-19; cf. the story about the
Garden of Eden in Gen. 2-3; Vol. I, pp. 20-22).
Mesopotamian traditions about the garden of God similar to those
found in the Bible may have been incorporated into a wall-painting,
reproduced here, from the royal palace at Mari (18th cent. B.C.).
This painting depicts the coronation of the king of Mari who is seen
standing before the goddess Ishtar and receiving the emblems of
sovereignty from her (see the upper panel in the centre of the picture).
The ceremony is performed in a garden where there are various trees,
all of them remarkably beautiful (Ezek. 31 : 8-9; cf. Gen. 2 : 9).
Next to the two central trees there are mythical creatures, amongst
them cherubs (see Vol. I, p. 162, right-hand plate). In the lower panel
in the centre of the picture two figures can be seen holding jars with
a column of water rising from each, and splitting to form "four
rivers" (Gen. 2 : 10; cf. Ezek. 31 : 4, 15-16).

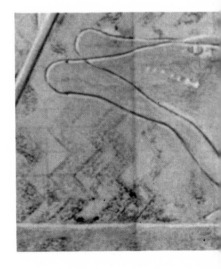

S PEAK, and say, Thus says the LORD GOD: "Behold, I am against you, Pharaoh king of Egypt, the great dragon that lies in the midst of his streams . . ." (Ezekiel 29 : 3)

The Hebrew word here translated "dragon" *(tannin)* was first used to designate a mythological beast which is mentioned in the Old Testament, together with the Leviathan and Rahab, as one of the primeval monsters defeated and crushed by God (Isa. 27 : 1; 51 : 9; Ps. 74 : 13; Job 7 : 12). Only later did it come to signify the crocodile — *Crocodilus niloticus* — which was especially common in the Nile and therefore appears in the Old Testament as a characteristic feature of the Egyptian landscape. Thus, when Ezekiel likens the king of Egypt to the great *tannin,* the simile, though mainly derived from the natural features of the land of the Nile, also contains overtones from the ancient myth. It is, furthermore, a symbol of the idolatrous arrogance of the Pharaoh in arrogating God's powers to himself and claiming to have created the Nile: "that says, 'My Nile is my own; I made it'" (Ezek. 29 : 3; and for the symbolical use of Rahab cf. Isa. 30 : 7; Ps. 87 : 4).

The picture below is a reproduction of one section of a relief discovered at Sakkarah in the tomb of Mereruka, an Egyptian minister of the time of the Sixth Dynasty (second half of the third millennium B.C.), showing a crocodile in one of the marshes of the Nile. In the other parts of the relief (which are not seen here) fish are being caught and a hippopotamus hunted, but the crocodile squats on the marshy ground unmolested.

The crocodile was also known on the shores of Palestine. Strabo and Pliny mention a place called "Crocodilon-polis" (the city of crocodiles), not far from Caesarea, which is to be identified with Tell el-Malat. The creature was hunted there up to the beginning of the present century.

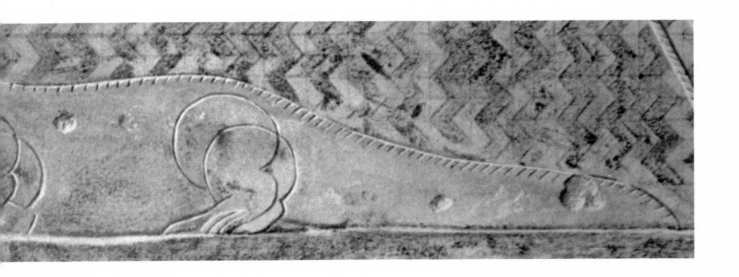

Thus says the LORD: Those who support Egypt shall fall, and her proud might shall come down; from Migdol to Syene they shall fall within her by the sword, says the LORD GOD.   (Ezekiel 30 : 6)

Like Jeremiah (see p. 141), Ezekiel too prophesied the defeat of Egypt by the king of Babylon (Ezek. 29 : 17-21; 30 : 10-26). To make it clear that Egypt's destruction would be complete, the prophet defined the extent of the country by the expression "from Migdol to Syene" (cf. ibid. 29 : 10), its two northernmost and southernmost points. This recalls the similar expression "from Dan to Beersheba" which is used in the Old Testament to describe the limits of Israelite settlement in Palestine. Migdol, the modern Tell el-Kheir at the north-western end of the Sinai peninsula, lay on the line of fortified posts built from Pelusium to Sileh for the defence of the Egyptian border with Palestine (see Vol. I, p. 141). Syene, which marks the southernmost limit of Egypt, stood on the site of the modern city of Aswan, on the eastern bank of the Nile just below its northern cataracts (see map on p. 142). On account of its special strategic position as a natural fortress on the river bank, Syene had been settled as early as the middle of the second millennium B.C., and from then onwards played an important part in Egyptian history. Close by the city was the island of Yeb (Elephantine) where, in the 6th and 5th cents. B.C. a garrison force of Jewish soldiers was stationed in the service of the Persian kings (see p. 142).

The photograph shows the Nile near Aswan. The barrenness of the slopes in the background is due to their distance from the Nile's waters.

BEHOLD, I will liken you to a cedar in Lebanon, with fair branches and forest shade, and of great height, its top among the clouds.   (Ezekiel 31 : 3)

In the course of his message to Pharaoh, Ezekiel utters an allegorical dirge over the king of Assyria whom he compares to a cedar of Lebanon, one of his favourite similes (see Ezek. 17 : 3-4). The prophet gives a glowing description of a magnificent tree of this kind which was so renowned throughout the ancient East that "no tree in the garden of God was like it in beauty" (Ezek. 31 : 8). But when the tree grew too proud, the woodcutter came and laid its branches low on the ground (ibid. 10-12). The fate of the Assyrian monarch was like that of the tree, and his end is held up as a warning to the king of Egypt.

The cedar of Lebanon *(Cedrus libani Loud),* which is seen in the photograph above, is one of the tallest species of tree. It may grow to a height of 120-150 ft.; and the trunk of a very old cedar may measure as much as 40-45 ft. in diameter. A particularly striking feature of the cedar is the arrangement of its branches. At a certain point in its growth its top seems, as it were, to flatten out, so that its branches no longer thrust upwards but grow out from the trunk horizontally, tier above tier. The cedar never grew in Israel, but only in the mountains of Lebanon; indeed, it is always referred to in the Bible as the "cedar of Lebanon". If the sparse remnants of the cedar forests in Lebanon can still charm us with their beauty to-day, it is not surprising that this tree filled the ancients with awe-struck wonder and was regarded by them as a symbol of royalty and nobility. Solomon, like the kings of Mesopotamia and Egypt, used the durable and fragrant wood of the cedar in the construction of his Temple (cf. Vol. II, p. 212). So did Zerubbabel, when he built the Second Temple (Ezra 3 : 7).

THIS is a lamentation which shall be chanted; the daughters
of the nations shall chant it; over Egypt, and over all her
multitude, shall they chant it . . .   (Ezekiel 32 : 16)

The mourning-rites customary in Israel can be reconstructed from various passages in the Old Testament (e.g.
Jer. 16 : 5-8). These passages also provide detailed information about the public dirge, in the performance of
which professional wailing-women were employed (see p. 104). It is this latter rite, which was also practised by
the other peoples of the ancient East, that is referred to by Ezekiel when he calls on "the daughters of the nations"
to bewail the destruction of Egypt and its multitude.

The group of wailing-women illustrated above is taken from a wall-painting in the tomb of a high Egyptian
official at Thebes, from the reign of Amenhotep IV (14th cent. B.C.). The women are making gestures of grief
with their arms and tear-stains can be seen on their cheeks. Standing amongst them is a naked young girl, whose
nakedness may also be a sign of mourning (cf. Mic. 1 : 8, "I will lament and wail; I will go stripped and naked").
Some of the wailing-women are fully clothed, while others are bare-breasted with their dresses fastened round
their waists so as to cover only the lower part of their bodies (cf. Isa. 32 : 11).

E<small>LAM</small> is there, and all her multitude about her grave; all of them slain, fallen by the sword . . .   (Ezekiel 32 : 24)

In his dirge over the downfall of Egypt the prophet gives a list of various nations which the doomed "multitude of Egypt" is to meet in "the nether world". Prominent amongst them is Elam, the mountain kingdom bordering on Babylonia, whose people "spread terror in the land of the living", but in the end, after their downfall, bore their shame "with those who go down to the Pit" (Ezek. 32 : 24). The defeat of the Elamites is vividly recorded in the magnificent series of reliefs excavated in the palace of the Assyrian monarch Ashurbanipal at Nineveh (middle of the 7th cent. B.C.; see p. 150), in which the turmoil of the battle between Assyria and Elam and the rout of the Elamite army have been realistically portrayed by the artist.

On one of these reliefs (see the reproduction), the progress of the battle is shown from left to right in three registers which are allowed to run into each other so as to represent the tumult and confusion more forcefully. The Assyrian army is composed of a cavalry force, armed with javelins and bows, and heavy infantry whose equipment consists of long spears, bows, clubs, breastplates and large shields. The Assyrian troops are everywhere slaughtering the routed Elamite forces. Teumman, the king of Elam, is shown still drawing his bow, and again being slain by an Assyrian soldier (middle of the second row). The Elamite soldiers are trying to escape by every means at their disposal — principally on horses and in large horse-drawn waggons. These heavy vehicles have two wheels with numerous spokes (see top left). The Assyrian army is driving the enemy towards the river at the right of the relief in which the Elamite hosts and their steeds are seen drowning.

I will feed them with good pasture, and upon the mountain heights of Israel shall be their pasture; there they shall lie down in good grazing land, and on fat pasture they shall feed on the mountains of Israel.

(Ezekiel 34 : 14)

The comparison of the nation to a flock of sheep and its God, or king, to the shepherd is common in biblical literature, being particularly popular with the prophets (see p. 68). A similar figure of speech is found in the literature of the ancient East, as also in that of the western world (for example, in the Homeric epic). The prophecy in chap. 34 of Ezekiel is an allegorical development of this simile (cf. Ezek. 37 : 24). In the economy of Israel, which is an agricultural country in all those of its regions that have an adequate rainfall, an important part has, from the earliest times, been played by sheep- and cattle-rearing. This branch of husbandry was eminently well suited to the natural conditions of the country, since it could make use of the areas of scrub and woodland in the hills, and it was therefore always taken as a symbol of prosperous farming. The sheep and goats provided milk, both for drinking and for making butter and cheese; wool for clothing; and sacrifices and food on religious festivals.

Photographed above is a flock of sheep in the Galilean hills in springtime. To-day, as of old, the shepherds still seek out rich pasturing-grounds on the lower hill-slopes that are unsuitable for cultivation.

Aɴᴅ the land that was desolate shall be tilled, instead of being the desolation that it was in the sight of all who passed by.   (Ezekiel 36 : 34)

Ezekiel's consolatory promises differ, to a certain extent, from those of other prophets in being exclusively concerned, in their essentials, with the life of Israel. In his prophecy, Ezekiel does not mention the conversion of the nations to the belief in the Lord at the coming of the millennium, or the dominion of the king of Israel over the whole world. His vision of redemption is distinguished by the unpretentiousness of its main features: the ingathering of exiles, a life of undisturbed peace in the holy land, material plenty, the renewal of the Davidic monarchy, and the worship of the Lord in the Temple. The main points of this prophecy are based on the blessings of the Mosaic Law and the promises contained there (Lev. 26 : 3-13; cf. Ezek. 36 : 27-31, and elsewhere). A constant refrain in Ezekiel's consolatory prophecies is the future great fertility and fruitfulness of the land. Thus, in other passages he says: "I will make the fruit of the tree and the increase of the field abundant" (Ezek. 36 : 30); "and the trees of the field shall yield their fruit and the earth shall yield its increase" (34 : 27); "but you, O mountains of Israel, shall shoot forth your branches, and yield your fruit to my people Israel" (36 : 8). The photograph above is a view of rocky terrain in Judah which has been reclaimed for agriculture and is now yielding fruit, much as in the prophet's vision.

THE hand of the LORD was upon me, and he brought me out by the Spirit of the LORD, and set me down in the midst of the valley; it was full of bones..........(Ezekiel 37 : 1)

In his vision of the dry bones, Ezekiel gave powerful expression to the hope for the eventual restoration of Israel and Judah. In his inspired imagination the prophet sees himself borne by the spirit of the Lord to a valley full of dry bones and ordered to prophesy to them that they will be restored to life. The bones symbolize the scattered exiles of Israel whose redemption is assured and who will return to their land where the nation will, by God's grace, be revived (cf. Isa. 26 : 19). At the same time, it may be possible to find in this vision the germ of a belief in the resurrection of the dead.

The profound influence exercised by the vision of the dry bones on later generations of Jews is illustrated by a fresco on the wall of a synagogue from the 3rd cent. A.D., which was excavated at Dura-Europus on the Euphrates. The fresco occupies the whole lower part of the northern wall and is thus the largest and most detailed of all the paintings in the ancient synagogue. It depicts the vision of the bones in a consecutive series of episodes (see the reproduction, from left to right): first the prophet is lifted up by the hair by the hand of the Lord and set down in the valley of the dry bones; then comes the valley, drawn as a dark cleft between mountains, full of severed human heads and limbs; next, at the prophet's command these severed portions unite to form whole bodies; and finally, the souls of the dead, which are represented in accordance with Hellenistic tradition as women with butterfly wings, return to their former abode of flesh and blood. The last picture on the right shows the prophet — dressed now in a long Greek cloak in contrast to the short Parthian garment that he had worn previously — and the company of the resurrected (dressed like him) together singing the praises of the Lord who restores the dead to life.

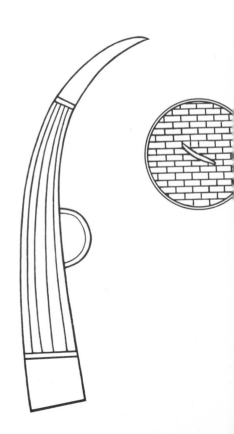

AND come from your place out of the uttermost
parts of the north, you and many peoples with you,
all of them riding on horses, a great host, a mighty
army.   (Ezekiel 38 : 15)

The nation that is to come from the north is a well known
theme of Old Testament prophecy (see p. 99, and also Joel
2 : 20). Ezekiel works this motif into his vision of the millennium and invests it with an apocalyptic colouring. Gog
descends suddenly from the far corners of the north, "like a
storm . . . like a cloud covering the land" (Ezek. 38 : 9),
leading a horde of nations who fall upon a land of unfortified
villages, plundering and ravaging as they go. Angered by this
wanton assault, the Lord will utterly overthrow Gog and his
hosts on the mountains of Israel (see p. 199), thereby sanctifying
His name in the sight of all the nations. Amongst the barbarian
northern tribes described as accompanying Gog on his march
are the peoples of Gomer (Ezek. 38 : 6), the Gimirai of the
Assyrian documents and the Cymmerians of the Greek sources.
These tribes, who came from the Caucasus mountains, were
the terror of Armenia and Asia Minor from the 8th to the 6th
cent. B.C., and even fought pitched battles with the Assyrian
army.
The reproduction above is of a painting on a sarcophagus from
Clazomenae, a Greek town in western Asia Minor, dating to
the 6th cent. B.C. (contemporary with Ezekiel). Amongst the
figures portrayed on it, the Cymmerians can be seen (bottom
row) on horseback, with dogs beside them, fighting against
their Greek foes.

THEN those who dwell in the cities of Israel will go forth and make fires of the weapons and burn them, shields and bucklers, bows and arrows, handpikes and spears, and they will make fires of them for seven years.

(Ezekiel 39 : 9)

The magnitude of the defeat of Gog and all his horde upon the mountains of Israel (see p. 198) is depicted by the prophet in terms that would have been readily understood by the inhabitants of those hilly regions who, in the winter months, needed firewood to warm their hearths. The wooden weapons of the armies of Gog will fall to the Israelites in such great quantities as to provide them with fuel for seven years. Of all the weapons listed in this passage the only one to require elucidation is the "hand-stick" *(makkel yad)*. Perhaps this expression is used here to designate the "throw-stick" *(makkel yediyyah)* (cf. "a weapon of wood in the hand" — Nu. 35 : 18), or boomerang, which was widely used by the peoples of the ancient East, especially in hunting. Photographed at the bottom right is a collection of such throw-sticks which was found in the tomb of Tutankhamon in Egypt (middle of the 14th cent. B.C.). To their left are drawings of a bow, a javelin and a quiver of arrows, in that order. On p. 198 there is an elongated shield (left) and a round shield (right), both of them plaited from rushes and therefore most suitable for burning. The drawings were made from Assyrian reliefs from the 9th and 8th cents. B.C. excavated at Calah and Nineveh.

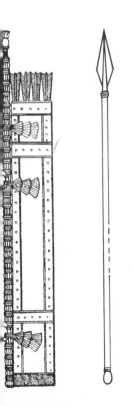

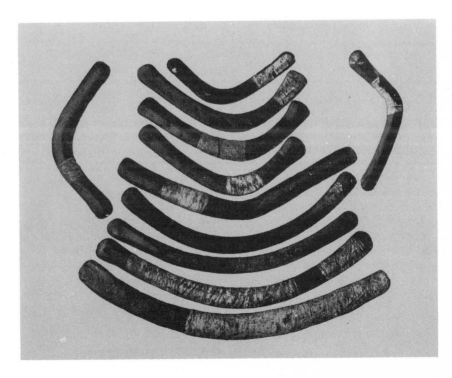

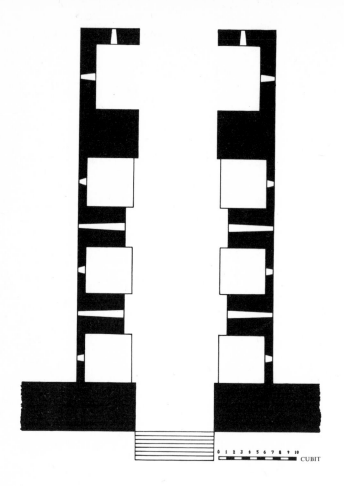

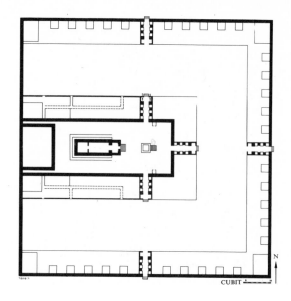

THEN he went into the gateway facing east, going up its steps, and measured . . .   (Ezekiel 40 : 6)

The description of the Temple as seen by Ezekiel in his vision opens with the plan of the gateways. It was usual, in the architecture of the ancient East, for the gateway to be flanked by towers which were designed to protect the approaches to the city. In Ezekiel's description every gateway has an entrance porch ("the vestibule of the gate"), leading to a passage with side-chambers running off it ("the side-rooms of the gate"), the latter being arranged in two parallel rows, three to a row (Ezek. 40 : 6-13; see the plan on the left). There were six such gateways in the courts of Ezekiel's Temple (see the plan on the right); three in the wall of the outer court and three in the wall of the inner court. In every one of the outer gates the porch was on the side of the court, away from the wall and the entrance; in the inner gates, on the contrary, the porch was close to the entrance. Seven steps led up to the outer gates (Ezek. 40 : 22, 26), and eight to the inner gates (ibid. 31, 34, 37). Although, taken as a whole, Ezekiel's architectural designs are visionary, they nevertheless have a realistic basis. This is particularly true of the plans of the gateways which are apparently modelled on those of the gates in the courts of Solomon's Temple, and also accord with the details of the actual gate-structures excavated at Hazor, Megiddo and Gezer, which were also built by Solomon (see Vol. II, p. 221).

AND he measured the court, a hundred cubits long, and a hundred cubits broad, four-square; and the altar was in front of the temple. Then he brought me to the vestibule of the temple and measured . . .   (Ezekiel 40 : 47-48)

As Ezekiel proceeds from place to place in "the visions of God" a clear picture emerges of the lay-out of his visionary Temple. The description follows the direction of the prophet's own progress — from the outside to the centre, and from east to west. First, he describes the outer gates and the outer court, with its rooms and and paving (Ezek. 40 : 6-27); after that, the inner gates and the inner court, with its rooms (ibid. 25-47); next, the Temple with its chambers and appurtenances (Ezek. 40 : 48 — 41 : 26); and finally, the holy offices which were separated from the outer court, at the western end of the compound, (Ezek. 42 : 1-14). The whole description ends with a summary of the total dimensions of the Temple area (ibid. 15-20; see plan on the right). This lay-out appears to be based, in its essentials, on the plan of the Temple built by Solomon in Jerusalem (see Vol. II, p. 213). Solomon's Temple also had two courts, one inside the other; and Ezekiel's temple resembles it in other technical and architectural details too. At the same time however, Ezekiel's visionary structure differs from the plan of the First Temple in various particulars, there being two reasons for these modifications: a) the prophet's desire to give both the courts and the chambers a completely symmetrical form; b) his desire to bring the lay-out of the temple and its courts into accord with the special priestly laws and prohibitions which he himself enumerates in the following chapters of his book.

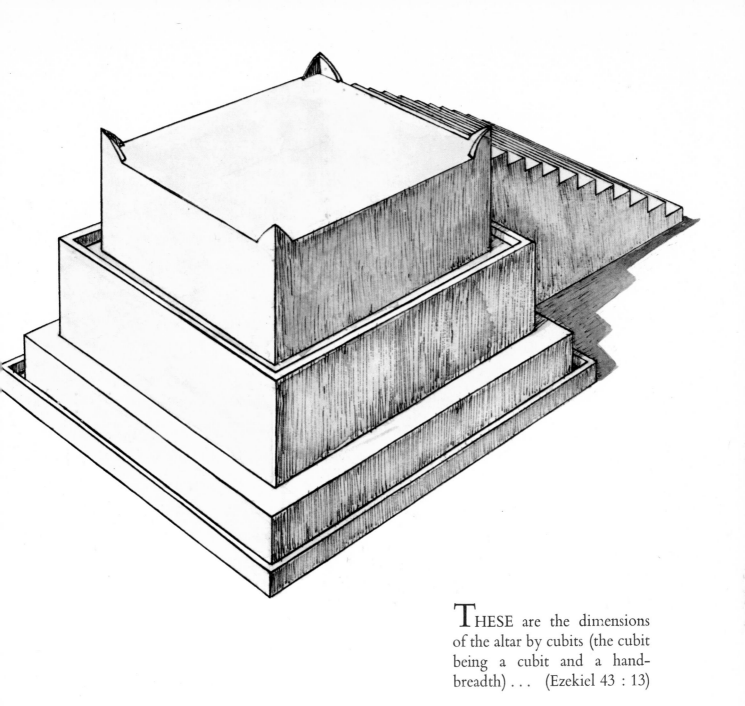

THESE are the dimensions of the altar by cubits (the cubit being a cubit and a handbreadth) ... (Ezekiel 43 : 13)

Ezekiel's visionary altar (Ezek. 43 : 13-17), a reconstruction of which is shown above, consisted of four square courses of masonry, one on top of the other. The lowest of these four courses, called by Ezekiel "the base of the altar," was one cubit high. The next, "the smaller ledge" or "lower ledge", was two cubits high. The course above that, "the larger ledge" or simply "the ledge," was four cubits high, as was the uppermost course which which was called "the altar hearth." On this altar hearth there were four horns each of which, according to the Septuagint translation (to Ezek. 43 : 15), was one cubit high. Thus the total height of the whole altar, including the horns on the altar hearth, was twelve cubits. In area the altar hearth was "a square, twelve cubits long by twelve broad." Along the lower edge of the base ran a raised rim one span high, called "the border," which formed a runnel all round it. This latter is what is referred to by Ezekiel as "the recess on the ground." There was another recess of this kind running round the edges of the larger ledge, and this apparently formed the base of the altar (Lev. 4 : 7) onto which the blood of the victims was poured (Ezek. 43 : 20; 45 : 19). Steps led up to the altar on its eastern side. The altar described here differs in shape from that which stood in the court of the Tabernacle (Ex. 27 : 1-8), and also from those built on the Temple Mount by Solomon, the returning Babylonian exiles, and Herod respectively. Some scholars find Babylonian affinities in the design of Ezekiel's altar and the names given to its parts, and it is possible that Mesopotamian traditions have been incorporated in his description.

Y OU shall have just balances, a just ephah, and a just bath ... The shekel shall be twenty gerahs ... (Ezekiel 45 : 10, 12)

In the restored Jewish kingdom of the future, which is seen by Ezekiel in his vision, justice and morality will reign supreme. One of the foundations of this new society will be strict honesty in all commercial transactions, as manifested in the punctilious use of exact weights and measures. The falsification of weights and measures was a constant fear with the peoples of the ancient East and is denounced as a crime in numerous documents. The Mosaic law also warns against acts of this kind (cf. Vol. I, pp. 194, 285), a warning which is repeated in the prophets and wisdom writers.

The reproduction on the left is a relief from northern Mesopotamia (8th cent. B.C.) on which a man is shown holding two sets of small hand-scales. Those in his right hand are opened out ready for use, while those in his left are folded up. The lower plate on the right is a fragment of a jar from Lachish (8th cent. B.C.) inscribed with the words "the king's *bath*", i.e., a *bath* that has been certified as accurate by royal authority. The *bath*, a wet measure, was equivalent to six *hin* (see Vol. I, p. 194) and of roughly the same volume as an *ephah*, the dry measure. Above this plate there is a spherical stone weight, so shaped to make falsification difficult. Incised on it there is a sign which, in the opinion of some scholars, denotes the *shekel,* the unit of weight that was in common daily use (= approx. 1/3 oz.).

THUS says the LORD GOD: "These are the boundaries by which you shall divide the land for inheritance among the twelve tribes of Israel . . ."

(Ezekiel 47 : 13)

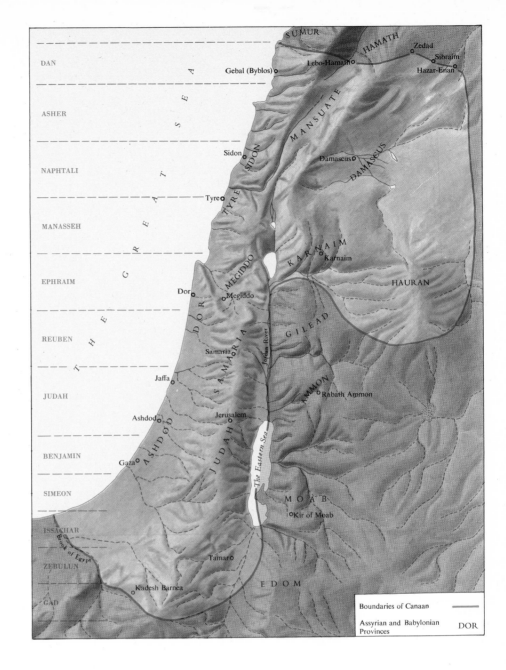

The Promised Land, as seen by Ezekiel in his divinely inspired vision, covers a larger area than the territory actually occupied by the Israelite tribes, its borders being identical with those of the land of Canaan as described in the thirty-fourth chapter of the Book of Numbers (see Vol. I, p. 239). However, the prophet does not merely repeat the more ancient source word for word but has superimposed upon it geographical terms of his own time, most noticeably in his use of the names of the Assyro-Babylonian administrative districts in the north of the country. His northern border passes between the districts of Hamath and Damascus (Ezek. 47 : 16), while on the east the boundary line embraces the districts of Damascus and Hauran and borders the district of Gilead (ibid. 18; see map, and cf. p. 32). The Land of Israel of Ezekiel's vision is divided up amongst the twelve tribes of Israel in a purely imaginary way which takes no account of the natural geographical conditions of the country. The tribal territories are marked off from north to south by parallel lines arbitrarily drawn "from the east side to the west." In the centre of the country there are special enclaves, called "portions" (terumah), including one for the priests in which stands the Temple ("the holy portion"), and another for the Levites, the City (Jerusalem) and "the Prince," as the future king is to be called. Seven of the tribal territories are to the north of "the holy portion" and five to the south of it.

MINOR PROPHETS

HOSEA

THE LORD said to Hosea, "Go, take to yourself a wife of harlotry and have children of harlotry, for the land commits great harlotry by forsaking the LORD."　　(Hosea 1 : 2)

Hosea the son of Beeri prophesied in the dark days that came upon the kingdom of Ephraim after the glorious reign of Jeroboam the son of Joash (784-748 B.C.; see p. 230). He thus saw Israel in its moral decline, its eager adoption of pagan creeds, and its social and political demoralization. The nation's betrayal of its true God was, for the prophet, like a woman's faithlessness to the husband of her youth, and was symbolically reflected in the conduct of his dissolute wife, Gomer the daughter of Diblaim. Gomer is called "a wife of harlotry" even before her marriage to the prophet, just as the children she is still to bear are already referred to as "children of harlotry." These terms may be used in anticipation of what she eventually became, or may indicate that her behaviour was similar to that of the woman of easy virtue described by Ezekiel: "you bathed yourself, painted your eyes, and decked yourself with ornaments; you sat upon a stately couch with a table spread before it" (Ezek. 23 : 40-41; cf. p. 180). The prostitutes of the time had a passion for ostentatious self-adornment and their heavy use of eye-paint and rouge became proverbial. Cosmetic preparations of this kind are depicted on an Egyptian papyrus, reproduced here, from the time of the New Kingdom (second half of the second millennium B.C.). It shows an Egyptian woman painting her lips with a brush held in her right hand. In her left hand she is holding a mirror, and what may be a tube of kohl for painting her eyes. Her hair is elaborately groomed and her eyes appear enlarged, evidently through the use of kohl (cf. Vol. II, p. 267). Around her neck she is wearing a double necklace.

SHE is not my wife, and I am not
her husband . . .　　　(Hosea 2 : 2)

Hosea's private life, even more than the private lives of other prophets, served him as an allegory of the relations between God and His people (Hos. 1 : 2, 6, 9) and a symbol for contemporary political and military events (ibid. 4, 5). The "wife of harlotry" whom he married represents Israel, which had been betrothed to the Lord (Hos. 2 : 19-20; cf. p. 207) but now "has played the harlot . . . for she said, 'I will go after my lovers' " (ibid. 5), and will therefore be banished from His sight. No details of divorce proceedings are given in the Old Testament. The Mosaic Law merely mentions a "bill of divorce" which was presented by the husband to the wife when he put her out of his house, "if she finds no favour in his eyes" (Deut. 24 : 1-4). This bill of divorce is also referred to in other passages of the Old Testament, but again without any explanatory details (Isa. 50 : 1; Jer. 3 : 8). The prophet's words in our verse here may help to fill this gap in our knowledge, since they apparently contain an ancient form of the declaration made by the husband in divorcing his wife. Similar divorce formulae have been found in documents from the ancient East from the second half of the third millennium B.C. onwards. Reproduced here, for example, is a document from Nuzu dating to the 15th cent. B.C. in which it is explicitly stated that when the husband (Kikkinu) says to his wife (Bitti-Dagan), "Thou art not my spouse", or the wife says to her husband, "Thou art not my husband", the marriage is thereby dissolved. This formula corresponds to that used in the marriage ceremony, as we find it in the Elephantine letters: "She is my spouse and I am her lord."

THEY sacrifice on the tops of the mountains, and make offerings
upon the hills, under oak, poplar, and terebinth, because their shade
is good. Therefore your daughters play the harlot, and your brides
commit adultery.

(Hosea 4 : 13)

Hosea sternly condemns the Israelites for their sins of moral corruption and religious backsliding: "For there is
no faithfulness or kindness, and no knowledge of God in the land" (Hos. 4 : 1). The pagan rites performed on
the high places are, for the prophet, the result of the failure of the people's spiritual guides — the prophets and
priests — who have allowed God's Law to be forgotten (ibid. 5-6). The orgiastic and licentious nature of these
rites, in which sacred prostitutes played a prominent part, made them similar to those Canaanite practices which
had been forbidden the Israelites (Deut. 23 : 18): "harlotry, wine and new wine take away the understanding"
(Hos. 4 : 10-11). The altars of pagan cults, in Israel as amongst the Canaanites, stood "on the tops of the mountains" and, in most cases, under a spreading, shady tree. Sometimes an *asherah* (sacred tree) was set up beside
them (Deut. 16 : 21; cf. Vol. I, p. 270). Hence the oft-repeated combination in the prophetic books of the Old
Testament: "on every high hill and under every spreading tree." Sacred trees were a regular feature of many
ancient religions. In Palestine it was principally the common oak (Heb. *allon*, see Vol. I, p. 92) that was invested
with sanctity, though other trees too, such as the poplar and the terebinth, played a part in various cults.
The storax tree *(Styrax officinalis L.;* cf. Vol. I, p. 82) is a bush or small tree that grows in the woodlands of
Palestine. Its Hebrew name *(libneh)* contains a reference to two of its distinctive features: the under side of its
leaves is white *(laban),* as are its fragrant flowers (see the photograph above on the right). The resinous gum of its
trunk and bark may have provided the stacte (Heb. *nataf; styrax)* used as incense in the Tent of Meeting (Ex.
30 : 34). The terebinth *(Pistacia palaestina Boiss.)* is also very common in the woodlands of Palestine. It is usually
no more than a bush (see top left), but occasionally develops into a tall, handsome tree.

THE princes of Judah have become like those who remove the landmark; upon them I will pour out my wrath like water.

(Hosea 5 : 10)

In Hosea's words here there is an allusion to the wars fought at various times between Judah and Israel over frontier disputes (see e.g., 2 Chron. 13 : 19; 16 : 6), in the course of which both kingdoms sometimes appealed for military aid to Aram, Assyria and Egypt, as happened for instance in the reigns of Ahaz and Pekah the son of Remaliah (see Vol. II, p. 282; Vol. III, p. 30). Possibly Hosea is referring to the events that followed the death of Jeroboam the son of Joash, when the rulers of Judah thought to take advantage of the weakened condition of the Northern Kingdom resulting from the rapid succession of usurpers on its throne, and tried to extend their territory northwards by force.

By comparing the rulers of Judah to "those who remove the landmark", Hosea is expressing his opposition to their political acts in the language of civil law. In the lands of the ancient East it had been customary, from the earliest times, to mark the boundaries of a field by the erection of single stones or cairns at each of its corners (see Vol. I, p. 274). Since these boundary-stones served as evidence of ownership, their removal was naturally forbidden (Deut. 19 : 14; 27 : 17). In countries subject to frequent flooding, where the stones were often washed away by water, as in Egypt, the plots of land were remeasured at regular intervals and the boundary-marks replaced in their proper position so as to obviate disputes. In any such litigation, the owner of the land in question would swear that he had not removed his neighbour's landmark. In the painting reproduced here, from the tomb of Nebamon at Thebes (time of the Eighteenth Dynasty, 14th cent. B.C.) a farmer is seen, at the left, swearing by the great god in the heavens that the boundary-stone which he is touching has not moved from its place.

THEN Ephraim went to Assyria, and sent to the great king . . .   (Hosea 5 : 13)

Hosea opposed the attempts made by the kings of Israel in his time to base their foreign policy on Assyrian protection. The prophet considered that such a policy was neither sound nor practical, and could only end in complete disaster for the whole nation. No good could come of trying to curry favour with "the great king", since the gifts lavished upon him would only impoverish the country, without bringing it any corresponding assurance of military aid in time of need. It was in these days that the then king of Israel, Menahem the son of Gedi, sent to Pul (i.e. Tiglath Pileser III) the Assyrian monarch "a thousand talents of silver, that he might help him to confirm his hold of the royal power" (2 Kings 15 : 19). Hosea the son of Elah, the last ruler of the Northern Kingdom, also sent presents to the king of Assyria (ibid. 17 : 3). The same policy was pursued by the kings of Judah, Ahaz and Hezekiah (ibid. 18 : 13-15), who tried to gain the support of the Assyrian monarchs by "gifts" and protestations of loyalty: "I am your servant and your son" (ibid. 16 : 7-8; cf. Vol. II, p. 282).

Scenes of tribute being brought to an Assyrian king by the emissaries of subject peoples are portrayed on the four sides of the black obelisk of Shalmaneser III (857-824 B.C.). Shown in the second row, reproduced above, is the deputation from Jehu the "son of Omri", king of Israel (cf. Vol. II, p. 269). At the left two Assyrians are seen leading forward three tribute-bearers from the land of Israel, followed, at the right, by five more tribute-bearers. The bearded Israelites are clothed in long tunics covered by a kind of fringed cloak. They are wearing characteristically Syrian headdress and shoes with upturned, pointed toes. The inscription on the obelisk gives a list of the various articles of tribute sent by Jehu, which can also be clearly seen in the picture: "Silver, gold, a gold cup, gold vessels with a pointed base, goblets of gold, buckets of gold, a staff for the king and a wooden *puruhtu* (an unknown object)".

THEY are all adulterers; they are like a heated oven, whose baker ceases to stir the fire, from the kneading of the dough until it is leavened.

(Hosea 7 : 4)

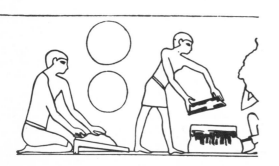

Hosea does not spare his criticism of the internal condition of the kingdom either. After the overthrow of Jehu's dynasty, the stability of the Samaria throne was severely shaken by a rapid succession of usurpers' plots and palace revolutions. The plotting courtiers are described by the prophet as treacherous men who deceive the king by their lies, "by their wickedness they make the king glad" (Hos. 7 : 3), and execute their evil designs with carefully thought-out cunning. The conspiratorial nature of their deeds is described by a simile taken from baking. Just as the baker first kneads the dough, then sits and waits for it to rise, and finally, at the right moment, completes his work by placing the risen dough in the oven, so the plotters first draw up their plan of action with great care down to the last detail, and then wait patiently for the time pre-arranged for its execution.

Detailed information about the bakers' craft as practised in antiquity can be obtained from Egyptian art. The upper plate is a scene from the tomb of Antefoker at Thebes (beginning of the second millennium B.C.) in which two bakers are shown at work. The one on the left is on his knees kneading the dough; while his companion is holding what looks like a lid, apparently to cover the round, flat loaf which is being baked on the oven. Two such loaves, already baked, can be seen on the wall. In the lower picture, which is from the tomb of Kenamon, also at Thebes (15th cent. B.C.), the process of baking is illustrated in great detail. At the right of the lower register two men are kneading dough on a kind of baking-board. Next to them (centre of the row) a third man is fashioning the dough into round shapes, while below him a colleague is arranging these rounds in piles, before carrying them in a basket to the oven (top left). The bread is then baked in an open oven, as can be seen in the middle of the upper register. From there the finished loaves are handed to the man at the right who puts them into the large bin standing beside him.

THE calf of Samaria
shall be broken to pieces.
(Hosea 8 : 6)

Hosea is here protesting against the bull-cult which had been practised in the Northern Kingdom at Bethel and Dan ever since the reign of Jeroboam the son of Nebat (1 Kings 12 : 28-29; cf. Vol. II, p. 230), and which the people had come to regard as a legitimate form of the worship of Jahweh. Not so the prophet, who pours scorn upon what is for him a thoroughly idolatrous ritual. The "calf" is the work of human hands, "a workman made it" (Hos. 8 : 6), and its cult contains acts of adoration such as were performed in the actual worship of idols (ibid. 13 : 1-3). In the day of trial, the calves will be of no avail to Israel. They will be captured by the enemy and carried off into captivity, "yea the thing itself shall be carried to Assyria, as tribute to the great king" (ibid. 10 : 6). There they will finally be broken into pieces, since the Assyrians were in the habit of destroying the temples of the nations conquered by them and smashing their idols (see p. 34).

The illustration is a section of a relief portraying the campaigns of Sargon II against the land of Ararat (714 B.C.). The Assyrian forces have conquered the city of Muzazir and its temple (see p. 66). At the top Assyrian troops are seen looting the temple vessels and royal servants are weighing the booty. Below, other soldiers are using long-handled axes to hack a statue in pieces.

N ETTLES shall possess their precious things of silver; thorns shall be in their tents.

(Hosea 9 : 6)

The wanton sinfulness of the Northern Kingdom is to be punished by a two-fold exile. Since Ephraim has, like a silly dove, wooed both Egypt and Assyria (Hos. 7 : 11; 12 : 1; cf. pp. 212-213; 218), its people will be deported to both these lands: "Ephraim shall return to Egypt, and they shall eat unclean food in Assyria" (ibid. 9 : 3). The property of the exiled Israelites will be taken from them, and their abandoned lands and fields will become a wilderness. Thorns will spring up from the soil where formerly crops grew; while the luxurious dwellings of the deported inhabitants will be overgrown with nettles and thistles (cf. p. 31). The thorn and nettle are commonly used in the Old Testament as symbols for field and vineyard left to run wild, as also to indicate ruin and neglect in general: "Thorns shall grow over its strongholds, nettles and thistles in its fortresses" (Isa. 34 : 13). Sometimes the thistle is placed in opposition to the cultivated produce of the soil: "let thorns grow instead of wheat" (Job 31 : 40).

The thistle *(hoah)* is a plant of the *Compositae* species which multiplies very rapidly in ground that is not cultivated. Two types are found in Palestine: the *Scolymus hispanicus,* and the *Scolymus maculatus* which appears in the photograph above. The thistle-plants may grow as high as one metre, or even more.

The exact identity of the second plant mentioned (Heb. *qimosh,* here translated as "nettle") is uncertain.

ISRAEL is a luxuriant vine that yields its fruit. The more his fruit increased the more altars he built . . .   (Hosea 10 : 1)

Like other prophets, Hosea too compares Israel to a choice vine. But whereas Isaiah, Jeremiah and Ezekiel in their similes speak of a vine that dashed its owner's hopes by producing only sour wild grapes (Isa. 5 : 1-7, and see pp. 24-26; Jer. 2 : 21, cf. p. 169), Hosea compares the people to a "luxuriant vine" *(gefen boqeq)* with abundant grapes — "that yields its fruit" (cf. Ezek. 17 : 6). At first the people of Israel were like that favoured vine whose fruits are a delight to behold — "like grapes in the wilderness I found Israel" (Hos. 9 : 10; cf. Ps. 80 : 8-13). However, in Hosea's simile too Israel is doomed to be destroyed, since the enjoyment of God's great bounty has made "their heart false; now they must bear their guilt" (Hos. 10 : 2).

Known in Palestine from the time of the Early Bronze Age (the third millennium B.C.), the vine became in the Old Testament a symbol of plenty and prosperity (see Gen. 49 : 11). Its remarkable luxuriance and the profusion of its grape-clusters are well illustrated in a painting from the ceiling of the tomb of Senufer, the governor of Thebes in the reign of Amenophis II (second half of the 15th cent. B.C.). With firm, sure strokes, the artist has drawn the vine with its intertwining leaves and tendrils and the bunches of grapes that grow on it (cf. Vol. I, p. 102).

THEY make a bargain with Assyria, and oil is carried to Egypt.   (Hosea 12 : 1)

Hosea reiterates his warning to the people of Ephraim against their attempts to obtain political support from both Assyria and Egypt. While the Israelites form an alliance with Assyria, they seek to placate Egypt with gifts of oil. This commodity was chosen because, from the earliest times, it was always in great demand in the land of the Nile where there were no olive-trees. Hence olive-oil was one of the principal Palestinian exports in the time of the Old Testament (see 1 Kings 5 : 11; Ezek. 27 : 17).

The export of oil from Palestine to Egypt can be traced back to the third millennium B.C. On Egyptian wall-paintings there are representations of men from Syria and Canaan bringing oil to Egypt. In a section of one such painting from a tomb at Thebes (see the illustration below), apparently belonging to the reign of Amenophis III (first half of the 14th cent. B.C.), two Syrian trading ships are seen anchored in an Egyptian port, one of them laden with large jars. The traders are carrying their produce down ladders from the ship to the booth of an Egyptian merchant. A Canaanite is offering the merchant a large jar which probably contains oil. Above is a photograph of an ostracon found at Tell Qasileh bearing an inscription in the cursive Hebrew script of the 8th cent. B.C., as follows:

> For the king, one thousand ...
> and one hundred [log of] oil ...
> A]hijahu.

This may be an account of a quantity of oil sent, in the charge of an official (Ahijah), from the royal stores to Phoenicia or Egypt (cf. 1 Chron. 27 : 28; 2 Chron. 2 : 10,15).

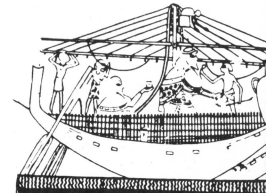

THEREFORE they shall be like the morning
mist or like the dew that goes early away . . .
(Hosea 13 : 3)

The spread of bull-worship amongst all sections of the
people of Ephraim (see p. 215) will bring about the
kingdom's destruction. All its former greatness and
power will vanish as if it had never been. The political
downfall of the Northern Kingdom is depicted by the
prophet in similes drawn from his hearers' own experience, which thus lend vividness and force to his teaching
(cf. p. 220). Ephraim's glory and splendour, the proud
boast of its kings and people (cf. Amos 6 : 13), will all
fade away like the thin wisps of dew-cloud which sometimes appear at dawn in the skies of Palestine, only to
disperse rapidly as the sun rises, leaving no trace behind
(cf. Hos. 6 : 4). Early morning clouds of this kind over
the Dead Sea are seen in the photograph above, which
was taken at the foot of the rock of Masada.

LIKE the chaff that swirls from the threshing floor or like smoke from a window.
(Hosea 13 : 3)

The punishment of the Israelites will be swift and merciless. They will vanish like smoke rising up from a chimney and be swept away like chaff winnowed in the wind on a threshing-floor. The comparison of the wicked to chaff is a common simile in the poetical language of the Old Testament (Isa. 29 : 5; Zeph. 2 : 2; Ps. 35 : 5). It was particularly apt to bring home to the people of Ephraim the severity of the retribution in store for them, since it is drawn from a feature of the daily life of the Palestinian farmer which has remained unchanged throughout the ages. At the end of the harvest the corn is brought to the threshing-floor to be threshed and winnowed. The winnowing is usually done when a wind is blowing. Sheaves of threshed corn are lifted on winnowing-shovels and pitchforks (see Isa. 30 : 24) and flung into the air. The lighter chaff is carried some distance away by the wind, while the heavier grains of corn fall back into a constantly growing heap on the threshing-floor (see the picture).

I WILL be as the dew to Israel; he shall blossom as the lily ...   (Hosea 14 : 5)

The destruction of Israel has been described by Hosea in a word-picture taken from the plant world: the de-populated land was to be overgrown with nettles and thistles (see p. 216). So now the Lord's redemption of Israel and its future greatness are also depicted in similes from nature. After Israel has returned to its true God and renounced its pagan creeds, it will be like the cedar of Lebanon with its deep-set roots, spreading branches and refreshing shade (Hos. 14 : 5-7). Or again, the nation will once more flourish like the lily which excels all the other flowers in beauty and is the absolute antithesis of the thistle, that symbol of neglect and desolation (Song of Sol. 2 : 1-2).

The lily (Heb. *shoshannah*; *Lilium candidum L.*), which is perhaps the loveliest, though to-day also one of the rarest, of Palestinian flowers, grows in Upper Galilee and on the Carmel. At the beginning of autumn, the lami-nated bulb sends out a rosette of leaves. With the coming of the rains, this rosette opens out into a fringe of smaller leaves from the midst of which the stem thrusts itself upwards, topped by large, but at the same time strikingly graceful, snow-white flowers that catch the eye with their stately stance amongst the woodland trees. In its full glory, there is no finer symbol of renewed splendour than this flower.

IT is I who answer and look after you. I am like an ever-green cypress, from me comes your fruit. (Hosea 14 : 8)

When Ephraim returns to its God, the Lord will also renew His lovingkindness to His people. Israel will then be like the cypress, the evergreen tree which, with its slender majesty, was a biblical symbol of strength and grandeur (Isa. 37 : 24; Ezek. 31 : 8). The cypress (called in Hebrew, as in Akkadian and Aramaic, *brosh — Cupressus sempervirens L.*) is a handsome, tall conifer. Two types grow in Palestine: the pyramidical *(var. pyramidalis)* and the horizontal *(var. horizontalis)*. The branches of the former all grow straight upwards, thus giving the tree the appearance of a narrow, high pyramid (see the photograph); whereas in the latter the branches grow outwards, so that the tree has a squatter outline. The cypress is a native of the eastern Mediterranean. The ancients knew it as both a wild and a cultivated tree, but it is doubtful if any wild specimens are still to be found in Palestine to-day. In Old Testament times, the wood of a species of cypress common in the Lebanon was used in the construction of splendid buildings, in much the same way as cedar-wood (1 Kings 6 : 15). At the top right is a photograph of the small, cone-like fruit of the cypress.

JOEL

WHAT the cutting locust left, the swarming locust has eaten. What the swarming locust left, the hopping locust has eaten, and what the hopping locust left, the destroying locust has eaten.

(Joel 1 : 4)

The whole prophecy of Joel is dominated by the indelible impression made on the prophet by a particularly disastrous locust-invasion of the country in his own lifetime, "the like of which has never been from of old, nor will be again after them through the years of all generations" (Joel 2 : 2). In the twinkling of an eye and with a mighty beating of wings, swarm upon swarm of the insects spread over the land, moving in orderly array like a hostile army marshalled for battle (ibid. 4-9). They darkened the sky in their millions and stripped the trees bare of their foliage (see the middle photograph), till it seemed "that the day of the Lord is near, and as destruction from the Almighty it comes" (ibid. 1 : 15; cf. 2 : 2). The inhabitants of the country looked on helplessly at one of the most terrible of all natural scourges, against which only divine intervention could avail. Hence the prophet calls on them to fast and pray, blowing on the ram's horn and rending their garments, till their imploring cries rise to the intensity of a wailing over the dead (ibid. 1 : 13-14; 2 : 12-17). Similar special prayers for deliverance from a plague of locusts are found in Assyrian documents.

Of the many kinds of locust known in biblical lands, only three multiply enormously and periodically invade distant regions. Foremost among these, in its visitations of Palestine and Egypt, is the desert locust *(Schistocerca gregaria Forsk)* which breeds in the wastes of Arabia and the Sahara (see Vol. I, p. 137), and, when climatic conditions are favourable, multiplies a myriad-fold (cf. Judg. 6 : 5). In such years huge swarms unite to spread their ravages over vast areas, from the Atlantic Ocean to India and including the countries of the Mediterranean, winging their destructive way sometimes more than a thousand miles from their breeding-ground. The locust moves mainly by day, resting at night on plants and hedges (Nahum 3 : 17). This winged insect has several names in the Old Testament. In its fully grown form, (see the illustration at the left of p. 224: No. 9 — female, No. 10 — male) it is referred to both by the collective term *arbeh* and also by the more specific names, *gobay* (Amos 7 : 1; Nahum 3 : 17) or *gebim* (Isa. 33 : 4) and *hagab* (Lev. 11 : 22). Joel also picturesquely calls it "the northerner" *(zephoni)* (Joel 2 : 20), apparently because of its resemblance to a conquering army sweeping down from the north. In addition, the following names are found to denote the various stages in the insect's development: *yeleq* (see No. 4) which is sometimes also used as a synonym for the collective term *arbeh* (Nahum 3 : 16); *hasil* (Isa. 33 : 4; see Nos. 5-6); and *gazam* (Amos 4 : 9; see Nos. 7-8). No. 3 is a newly born insect, No. 2 a single egg, and No. 1 a cluster of eggs.

At the right of p. 225 there is a photograph of a locust-horde such as has frequently invaded Israel in recent years.

FIRE devours before them, and behind them a flame burns . . .   (Joel 2 : 3)

Covering the hill tops in a dark cloud (Joel 2 : 2) the locust consumes every speck of greenery and vegetation, like a devouring flame. Fire is no less dreaded by the farmer in every place and in every age than the locust, and it is a specially grave menace in a country like Palestine where water is scarce. The danger is greatest in the blazing summer days when the farmer is bringing in the harvest and fire can suddenly sweep through his corn-fields and orchards, destroying all the fruits of his labours. Like the locust, fire is too powerful for man to control and its ravages change the countryside out of all recognition: "the land is like the garden of Eden before them, but after them a desolate wilderness, and nothing escapes them" (Joel 2 : 3). Hence the scourge of fire and the plague of locusts are found combined together in other prophets too (see Amos 7 : 1-6).
Seen in the foreground of the photograph are black, fire-scorched fields in the Jezreel Valley, with Mount Gilboa at the back left.

YOU have sold the people of Judah
and Jerusalem to the Greeks, removing
them far from their own border.

(Joel 3 : 6)

Joel here denounces the Tyrians and Sidonians and the people of Philistia for despoiling the war-ravaged land
of Judah and carrying off many of its inhabitants to sell them as slaves to the Ionians (Greeks) (cf. Amos 1 : 6, 9).
In the 7th cent. B.C., the Greeks pressed outwards from the countries and islands of the Aegean Sea and reached
the eastern coasts of the Mediterranean. At the end of this century they founded the colony of Naukratis in the
Nile delta, and not long afterwards Cyrene in Libya. In the 6th cent. B.C., they entered into close commercial
relations with Tyre and Sidon. Though the Greeks traded in a wide variety of commodities, they are referred
to by the prophets principally as slave-dealers, traders in human souls (Ezek. 27 : 13).
A scene of commercial activity — to which great importance was attached by the authorities of the Greek cities —
is artistically portrayed on the base of a Laconian kylix, dating to the first half of the 6th cent. B.C. (see the reproduction above). It shows merchants loading their vessel with sacks full of silphion, a vegetable for which there
was a great demand in antiquity and one of the main sources of the wealth of the Greek colony at Cyrene. On the
ship's deck, the sacks are being counted in the presence of a clerk who is calling out the weight of each sack.
A second clerk is repeating the weights to Arkesilas, the king of Cyrene (at the left), who is supervising his
country's export trade in person. In the ship's hold porters are piling up the sacks on top of each other. The
monkey and birds on the yardarm indicate that the scene represented is set in Africa.

PUT in the sickle, for
the harvest is ripe . . .
(Joel 3 : 13)

Joel gives a vivid description of the great and terrible Day of the Lord, when God will avenge the wrongs done to His people. Then He will gather together all its enemies among the nations in the valley of Jehoshaphat, the steep ravine close to Jerusalem (Joel 3 : 2, 14) where He will judge them for their crimes against Israel, their plundering of its treasured possessions and their selling of its sons into slavery in distant lands (see p. 227). The day of reckoning has come, the time when ploughshares will be beaten into swords and pruning-hooks into spears (ibid. 10), for the measure of the nations' sinfulness is full to overflowing. Now the avenging sword will cut them down in multitudes as the reaper at harvest-time cuts down the grain-laden ears with his sickle.

This simile of Joel's is taken from one of the most important of all agricultural implements, the use of which by man goes back to prehistoric times. The blade of the earliest sickle was made of stone. It was first crudely attached to the jaw-bone of an animal and was given a wooden handle only at a later stage of its development. This is the type of sickle used by the reaper in a relief from the tomb of Werarna at Sheikh Said in Egypt, dating to the time of the Fifth Dynasty (middle of the third millennium B.C.; see the illustration above). The man is seen holding the ears in his left hand while he cuts the stalks at about their middle. thus leaving quite a high stubble behind him. When, from the middle of the second millennium B.C., metal scythes began to come into use (see Vol. II, p. 130 at the left), the reaper could cut the stalks of corn with a free swinging stroke, without having to take hold of the ears.

AMOS

THE words of Amos, who was among the shepherds of Tekoa . . .   (Amos 1 : 1)

The prophet Amos was one of the sheep-rearers of Tekoa in Judah. Unable to resist God's summons, he was forced to give up "following the flock" and was sent from his native land to prophesy against the kingdom of Israel (Amos 7 : 15), which was then — in the reign of Jeroboam the son of Joash — at the height of its power and prosperity (cf. 2 Kings 14 : 25; and see Vol. II, p. 277). However, all this wealth and material splendour were being rotted away from within by social injustice and moral corruption, and behind the glittering facade signs of decline and decay were already visible. Amos, the prophet from the sister kingdom of Judah, denounced the king of Israel, his ministers and the whole people for the oppression rampant in their land, and sought to warn them, while there was yet time, of the destruction that it was soon to bring upon them.
Tekoa (to-day Khirbet Taqua), Amos' native city, stood about 5 miles south of Bethlehem and about 10 miles south of Jerusalem, on the dividing-line between the desert and the sown. To the east of it lay the Judean wilderness and to the west the fertile agricultural region of the Hebron hills. The city was also on the caravan-route from Bethlehem to En-Gedi and the shore of the Dead Sea (2 Chron. 20 : 20).
The ruins of Tekoa are seen in the foreground of the photograph above. Away to the right of them, in the background, rise the bare slopes of the Judean wilderness with, in the distant centre, Herodion, the fortress and tomb of King Herod.

TWO years before the earthquake. (Amos 1 : 1)

The earthquake that occurred in the reigns of Jeroboam the son of Joash in Israel and Uzziah in Judah was apparently one of the most severe and destructive of the tremors to which Palestine has been periodically liable throughout its history. Hence the period of Amos' prophetic activity was dated by it (cf. p. 51). So great and lasting was the impression made on men's minds by this earthquake that, hundreds of years later, it served the prophet Zechariah as an outstanding example of the terror and panic inspired by the catastrophic convulsions of nature: "And you shall flee as you fled from the earthquake in the days of Uzziah king of Judah" (Zech. 14 : 5). In the prophecies of Amos himself this impression is only dimly felt in various poetical similes: "The Lord, God of Hosts, He who touches the earth and it melts, and all who dwell in it mourn, and all of it rises like the Nile, and sinks again, like the Nile of Egypt" (Amos 9 : 5; cf. ibid. 8 : 8; 9 : 1).

Visible evidence of this devastating upheaval has been found in the excavations at Hazor, where the houses in the stratum corresponding in date to the time of Amos appear to have been destroyed by a violent earthquake. Photographed below is a large dwelling-house which caved in as a result of the seismic shocks. The ceilings of the rooms collapsed, covering the floors with a shower of plaster. The pillars supporting the roofed-in section of the courtyard were found flat on their sides. The walls were all cracked and some of them had been forced out of alignment.

"I WILL break the bar of Damascus... and the people of Syria shall go into exile to Kir," says the LORD.

(Amos 1 : 5)

Amos' prophecy against Aram, like all his other prophecies against the nations, is concerned with the just retribution to be meted out to its people by God for the wrong they have done to Israel. The Arameans caused frequent trouble to Israel in the reigns of Jehu and his son Jehoahaz, which was the time when Aram was ruled by Hazael and his son Ben-Hadad (2 Kings 10 : 32; 13 : 4; cf. Vol II, p. 273). For this their country is doomed to destruction and its people to deportation: "So I will send a fire upon the house of Hazael, and it shall devour the strongholds of Ben-Hadad" (Amos 1 : 4). This prophecy came true when Aram Damascus was laid waste by the Assyrian king, Tiglath-Pileser III, in his campaigns against Syria in the years 733-732 B.C. The population were carried off into captivity and the country itself was split up into Assyrian provinces, one of them the province of Damascus (see Vol. II, pp. 280-281). Amos depicts the fall of Damascus in a series of poetic images. Once the bar of the gate, which was the weakest point of a besieged city, has been broken, the capital of Aram will fall to its foes. This bar, or bolt, might be broken off in various ways; for example by soldiers armed with axes (see pp. 146-147), or by technically the most developed of ancient siege-engines, the battering-ram (see pp. 52, 177).

In the relief reproduced above — which is from the palace of Sargon II (721-705 B.C.; for the second half see p. 52) at Dur Sharruken (Khorsabad) — a battering-ram can be seen, at the right, advancing up the embankment of the gateway to assault its towers, doors and bars. The defenders on the walls are hurling blazing torches down at the ram in an attempt to set its bodywork on fire (cf. Vol. II, p. 286, top). Below is a section of the Bronze Gates of Shalmaneser III, which were found at Balawat, showing Arameans from the city of Karkar in Syria who were taken captive in Shalmaneser's campaign in the year 853 B.C.

BEHOLD, I will press you down in your place, as a cart full of sheaves presses down.

(Amos 2 : 13)

The severity of the divine punishment that the people of Israel is bringing upon itself by its crimes is vividly depicted by the prophet in images taken from daily life and its tasks. Himself born and bred in a community of farmers and shepherds, Amos makes frequent use of such word-pictures. In this there is more than mere conformity to the traditional style of prophetic utterance: it is the prophet's way of reaching the hearts of his hearers whose lives were devoted to the working of the land. Here, for example, the invading enemy, from whose relentless oppressive advance there will be no escape for anyone, is likened by the prophet to a farm-cart weighed down with a full load of corn (cf. Amos 6 : 14).

The prophet's simile is illustrated by the picture above. In the farming districts of Anatolia, where the photograph was taken, use is still made to this day of the most primitive of all forms of wheel, the solid wooden disc, which was found unsuitable for light war-chariots as early as biblical times (see Vol. II, pp. 41, 80) but continued to be fitted to the slower, more ponderous farm-waggons. The cart in the photograph is piled high with the produce of the fields and is drawn by a pair of oxen.

233

DOES a bird fall in a snare on the earth, when there is no trap for it? Does a snare spring up from the ground when it has taken nothing?

(Amos 3 : 5)

Amos employs seven short parables — each worded as a rhetorical question — to prove to his audience that everything has a cause (Amos 3 : 2-6), and that the ultimate cause is God the Creator. This conception of causality is clearly expressed in the double parable from fowling. If a bird falls to the ground, there must be a trap there; conversely, if a snare springs up from the ground, a bird must have been caught in it.

Bird-traps in the ancient East were of two main types: a snare hidden on the ground in which the bird was caught when it unsuspectingly alighted on it; or an unconcealed trap into which the bird was tempted by seeds placed inside it as a bait (cf. Prov. 7 : 23). The latter kind is illustrated in a painting from the Middle Kingdom in Egypt (19th cent. B.C.) found at Beni Hasan (see the reproduction below). The trap consists of a net stretched taut over a metal ring that folds into two on a transverse hinge on which the bait is placed. When the bird, in swooping down on the seeds, touches the hinge, the upper half of the net closes on the lower and the bird's head is caught between the two halves of the ring. The fowler is lying in wait at the left. His hands are stretched out to collect the birds as they are caught, and to re-set the trap.

T HE lion has roared; who will not fear?... (Amos 3 : 8)

Among the parables employed by Amos to demonstrate the working of cause and effect in God's world is one about the lion. Just as the lion's triumphant roar, when it has caught its prey (Amos 3 : 4), strikes terror into the hearts of all who hear it, so does the word of the Lord fill all its hearers with awe and compel the prophet to perform his prophetic mission. These similes were no doubt based on Amos' own personal experiences in the days when he was a shepherd (ibid. 12; 5 : 19; cf. p. 238). The shepherd's constant struggle with the wild beasts that attack his flock is described by other prophets (Isa. 31 : 4; Jer. 49 : 19) and is used elsewhere in the Old Testament as a symbol of human strength and courage (1 Sam. 17 : 34-36; 2 Sam. 23 : 20; cf. Vol. II, p. 101), as is the lion itself which has many Hebrew names *(laish, kefir, shahal, shahaz, lavi, gur-aryeh ;* see Vol. I, p. 229). In Old Testament times there were lions in the Jordan valley and also in the hilly regions of Israel and Judah (see Jer. 50 : 44). From the contemporary biblical stories it is clear that, in those days, the inhabitants of the country still went in fear of the beasts' ravages (1 Kings 13 : 24-28; 2 Kings 17 : 25-26).
The statue of a roaring lion reproduced in the photograph above is from the time of the Assyrian monarch Ashurnasirpal (883-859 B.C.). It stood at the entrance to the palace of the goddess Belit-Mati at Calah (Nimrud).

WHO say to their husbands,
"Bring, that we may drink!"
(Amos 4 : 1)

The prophet Amos repeatedly castigates the population of the Northern Kingdom for the habits of pampered and luxurious living which became widespread in Samaria in the reign of Jeroboam the son of Joash. Enjoying the fruits of a wealth gained largely by oppression and extortion, the pleasure-loving citizens of the capital let themselves be lulled by their material comfort into a false sense of security (Amos 3 : 10; 6 : 1-7). The social injustice and lax morality prevailing in Samaria were regarded by the prophet as largely due to the women of the city with their habits of sensual indulgence, gluttony and intemperance. Hence his abusive reference to them as "cows of Bashan" — a specially fattened breed of animal renowned for the succulence of its meat (cf. Deut. 32 : 14; Ps. 22 : 13). In the true prophetic manner, Amos roundly condemns the indolent lives lived by the idle rich and pours scorn upon the appurtenances of luxury which fill their possessors with such overweening pride (cf. Isa. 3 : 16-24; and see pp. 22-23).

The art of the ancient East has preserved for us records of the splendour in which the aristocracy of those far-off days lived. For example, on the Hittite stele from Marash (8th cent. B.C.) which is reproduced above, two women are seen clothed in gorgeous, long fringed garments, and wearing tall, cylindrical headdresses. They are seated on chairs at a small table on which there are a cup and three cakes, with their feet resting on footstools. The woman on the left is holding a pomegranate in her right hand and a cup in her left; her companion is holding a pomegranate and a mirror. Their dress and manners clearly show them to be ladies of high rank.

"I SMOTE you with blight and mildew . . ."   (Amos 4 : 9)

The plant-diseases of blight *(shiddafon)* and mildew *(yerakon)* are regularly mentioned together in the Old Testament in maledictory formulae (see Deut. 28 : 22; 1 Kings 8 : 37; Hag. 2 : 17). Often they are coupled with other scourges which plagued the farmers of Israel in biblical times: famine, drought, locust, plague, war and earthquake (Amos 4 : 6-11; cf. 2 Chron. 6 : 24, 26, 28). The prophets regarded these disasters as God's retribution for the sins and crimes of the Israelites.
Though primarily diseases of the various grain-crops, blight and mildew may also attack other kinds of vegetation. The kernels of an affected ear of corn do not grow to their normal size, but gradually lose their green colour and finally shrivel up completely (see the pictures).

As if a man fled from a lion, and a bear met him;
or went into the house and leaned with his hand
against the wall, and a serpent bit him.

(Amos 5 : 19)

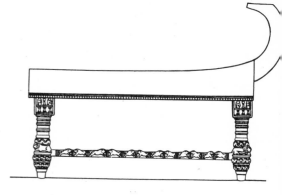

Israel's doom on the Day of Judgment, when the Lord will overwhelm the nation with natural calamities and human foes from all sides, is likened to the fate of a man who flees from one danger only to fall victim to another scourge and meets his doom where he least expects it, just when he thinks that he has escaped and is safe. A similar figure of speech is also found in Isaiah: "He who flees at the sound of the terror shall fall into the pit; and he who climbs out of the pit shall be caught in the snare" (Isa. 24 : 18; cf. Jer. 48 : 44). Amos makes frequent use of similes taken from the experiences of wayfarers, especially from that of the shepherd in his wanderings in waste places. Hence he compares Israel to a man who, fleeing from one wild beast — the lion, suddenly finds himself face to face with another — the bear. And when, by a desperate effort, he has managed to escape to his house and is leaning on the wall to recover from his exhausting flight, a snake glides out from the cracks in the masonry and bites him.

An attempt to give plastic form to an idea of this kind was made by an ancient artist in Mesopotamia. A decoration in relief on a vessel found in the temple at Eshnunna (Tell Asmar) in Babylonia, from the third millennium B.C., shows two men who have suddenly been attacked by snakes, while at the same time a lioness is bearing down on them. A third man (at the left) has his hands raised in a helpless gesture of entreaty. It may perhaps be deduced from this that the combination of the lion (and bear) with the snake in Amos' parable was a standard feature, in the ancient East, of any description of the dangers lurking for the shepherd.

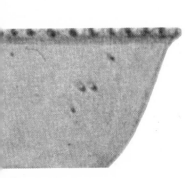

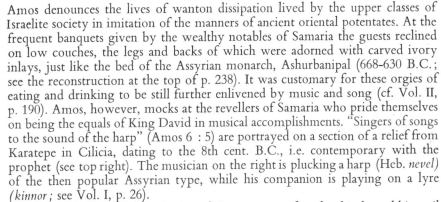

THOSE who lie upon beds of ivory, and stretch themselves upon
their couches . . .   (Amos 6 : 4)

Amos denounces the lives of wanton dissipation lived by the upper classes of
Israelite society in imitation of the manners of ancient oriental potentates. At the
frequent banquets given by the wealthy notables of Samaria the guests reclined
on low couches, the legs and backs of which were adorned with carved ivory
inlays, just like the bed of the Assyrian monarch, Ashurbanipal (668-630 B.C.;
see the reconstruction at the top of p. 238). It was customary for these orgies of
eating and drinking to be still further enlivened by music and song (cf. Vol. II,
p. 190). Amos, however, mocks at the revellers of Samaria who pride themselves
on being the equals of King David in musical accomplishments. "Singers of songs
to the sound of the harp" (Amos 6 : 5) are portrayed on a section of a relief from
Karatepe in Cilicia, dating to the 8th cent. B.C., i.e. contemporary with the
prophet (see top right). The musician on the right is plucking a harp (Heb. nevel)
of the then popular Assyrian type, while his companion is playing on a lyre
(kinnor; see Vol. I, p. 26).
Another widespread fashion in Amos' time was to soften the skin by rubbing oil
of high quality into it — "they anoint themselves with the finest oils" (Amos
6 : 6; cf. Mic. 6 : 15; Ps. 23 : 5). This may be what is meant by the term "fine oil"
(shemen rahas) which occurs in the ostraka found at Samaria, apparently from the
time of Jehoahaz the son of Jehu (815-801 B.C.). The inscription on the sherd
reproduced above places it in the tenth year of the reign of the king of Israel: "In
the tenth year. Belonging to Shamaryau from ha-Tel, a jar of fine oil".

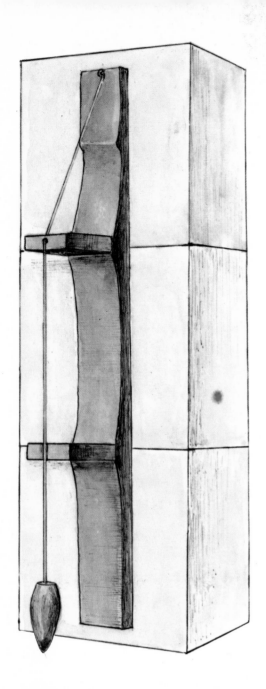

He showed me: behold, the LORD was standing beside a wall built with a plumb line, with a plumb line in His hand.

(Amos 7 : 7)

In five visions Amos is shown the various forms that God's chastisement of Israel will take: natural calamities, such as locust and fire, and disasters due to human agency, such as war and destruction (Amos 7 : 1-9; 8 : 1-3; 9 : 1-4). God has borne with Israel's sins and forgiven His people for a long time. But, now that the hour of retribution has come, they will be judged without compassion. Just as a builder tests a wall to see whether it is straight and, if it is not, knocks it down, so God will pass a measuring-line of justice over His people and, finding that they have gone astray from the straight path, will condemn their land to ruin (cf. Isa. 28 : 17; 34 : 11).

The primary meaning of the Hebrew word *anakh* (Assyrian, *anakku),* here translated "plumb-line", is "tin" or "lead". In our verse it denotes a weighted line used by a builder to test the alignment of a wall. Hence "a wall built with a plumb-line" was evidently a high wall such as had to be tested with a plumb-line. The use of this line is illustrated in the reconstruction on the left, which is based on an Egyptian original. Two ledges of wood were joined, one above the other, at right angles to a plank. The line was attached to the end of the plank and passed through a hole in the upper ledge. If the line touched the edge of the lower ledge when stretched taut by the weight of the plumb, the wall was properly built. The plumb-line was in use in Egypt as a builder's tool as early as the first half of the third millennium B.C.

Reproduced below are stone plumb-weights from the time of the Twelfth Dynasty in Egypt (20th-18th cent. B.C.).

THEN Amos answered Amaziah, "I am no prophet, nor a prophet's son; but I am a herdsman, and a dresser of sycamore trees." (Amos 7 : 14)

Amos roundly rejects the insinuation made by Amaziah, the priest of Bethel, that he was one of the popular oracle-mongers and soothsayers who made a living from their prophecies (Amos 7 : 12). A true prophet like Amos treats payment with contempt (cf. Mic. 3 : 5). Amos has nothing at all in common with the bands of ecstatic visionaries, nor was his prophecy a craft that he inherited or learnt from his ancestors. God's word was suddenly revealed to him; and it was at God's personal command that he gave up shepherding his flocks to prophesy to the people of Israel (Amos 7 : 15). Till that moment, Amos had lived by breeding sheep and tending sycamores, the fruits of which presumably provided animal-fodder. The sycamore (Ficus sycomorus L.), a large, handsome tree with a thick trunk, is common in the Shephelah (1 Kings 10 : 27) and is also found in the plains of the Negev (see the picture). Its fruit is something like a fig, only smaller and not particularly tasty. Clusters of this fruit grow in large numbers on all the branches of the tree and even on its trunk. To improve their taste and to make them ripen more quickly, it is usual to-day, just as it was no doubt in ancient times, to prick them with a sharp instrument. Hence the meaning of the Hebrew word boles (translated "dresser" above) would appear to be "one who pricks and makes holes", as rendered by the Septuagint.

"AND on that day," says the LORD GOD, "I will make the sun go down at noon, and darken the earth in broad daylight." (Amos 8 : 9)

At the beginning of Amos' prophetic mission there was a total eclipse of the sun in the skies of Palestine. This striking natural phenomenon, which occurred on June 15th 763 B.C., has left its mark on the language of Amos' prophecy, as has the earthquake which also took place in his lifetime and may even be directly referred to in the verse before us. The same eclipse was also seen in Assyria, where it was interpreted as a sign of the gods' wrath and regarded as the source of the epidemics and internecine warfare that subsequently broke out in the country.

The eclipse of the year 763 B.C. is mentioned in the Assyrian list of eponyms which is a year by year record of the history of the kingdom, each year being named after one of the royal officials (see the reproduction below). The list is inscribed on clay tablets that were found at Nineveh. Each tablet is divided into four columns in which are recorded the name of the eponym, his title, and the main event of the particular year, in that order. In the seventh row from the top of the tablet reproduced here, we find the following words: "In the year of the eponym Buru-Sagale, the governor of Gozan: an uprising in the city of Ashur. In the month of Sivan there was an eclipse of the sun". It is worthy of note that this eclipse, which has been exactly dated by astronomical calculations, provides a fixed point of reference for Assyrian chronology in the first half of the first millennium B.C., and indirectly also for the chronology of the Old Testament.

"ARE you not like the Ethiopians to me, O people of Israel?" says the LORD. "Did I not bring up Israel from the land of Egypt, and the Philistines from Caphtor and the Syrians from Kir?"

(Amos 9 : 7)

For Amos, God's choice of Israel has meaning only in terms of the nation's moral mission (Amos 3 : 2). He is therefore opposed to the belief, widespread among his contemporaries, that Israel is the chosen race by virtue of certain inborn natural qualities. On the contrary, all the nations are intrinsically equal in God's eyes, so that if the Israelites violate the covenant made with them by God, there is no longer any difference between them and a far-off, strange people like the Nubians. These black natives of Africa (Heb. *kushim*) are frequently represented in the art of ancient Egypt. At the top right, for example, there is a section of a wall-painting found at Thebes in the tomb of the prince Huy, who was Tutankhamon's viceroy in Nubia (14th cent. B.C.). The dark-skinned men shown in it are the escort of a Nubian princess who is presenting a gift to the Pharaoh (cf. Vol. I, p. 114).

Even the exodus from Egypt was not, for Amos, a sign that the Israelites were under God's special protection. Other nations too, such as the Philistines, had been divinely assisted in their migrations from one land to another. According to the Old Testament the Philistines came from Caphtor (Jer. 47 : 4), which is apparently the island of Crete (Ezek. 25 : 16; cf. p. 278, and Vol. I, p. 252). This identification is thought by some scholars to be supported by a pottery disk found at Phaistos in Crete, and which dates, at the earliest, to the 15th cent. B.C. Amongst the as yet imperfectly understood pictograms inscribed on both sides of this disk (see top left), there are drawings of a male head wearing a feathered crown characteristic of the "Sea Peoples", including the Philistines (see Vol. II, p. 118). These Sea Peoples were carried along to the shores of Asia, as were the Philistines to Egypt and Canaan, by the great wave of migrations that swept across the ancient world in the 13th cent. B.C. (cf. Vol. II, p. 98).

FOR lo, I will command, and shake the house of Israel among all the nations as one shakes with a sieve, but no pebble shall fall upon the earth.

(Amos 9 : 9)

The sieve is still used by the peasants of Palestine, as it was in ancient times, to separate out the grains of corn from the accumulations of earth and refuse with which they are mixed after threshing. It consists of a network of holes stretched across a frame in which the corn is placed and then shaken to and fro, so that the finer grains fall through the perforations while the coarser impurities remain inside the sieve (see the illustration). This simile, with which Amos closes his prophecy of retribution, has a double significance. It is both a threat of punishment for the wicked and a promise of consolation to the righteous. When God shakes out the house of Israel amongst all the nations, as corn is shaken out in a sieve, the sinners, who are the refuse, will remain in the sieve, while the righteous will pass through all the dire calamities and fall safely to the ground like the good grains. God will sift His people so thoroughly that the wicked will have no chance of escaping their doom: "All the sinners of my people shall die by the sword" (Amos 9 : 10). The righteous, however, will be saved and will behold the restoration of "the booth of David that is fallen" (ibid. 11).

OBADIAH

YOU who live in the
clefts of the rock, whose
dwelling is high . . .
(Obadiah 1 : 3)

In the sixth, and still more so in the fifth, cent. B.C., the tribes of the Arabian desert poured into the territory of Edom and forced its inhabitants to flee northwards to the borders of Judah. The overthrow of Edom is described by the prophet Obadiah, in his vision, with such mocking contempt, because he regards it as a divine retribution for the Edomites' unrelenting hostility to Judah and their savage delight at the downfall of the Judeans "in the day of their ruin," when Jerusalem was laid waste and its population carried off into captivity (Obad. 1 : 10-14). In the spirit of the other prophecies of Edom's destruction (Amos 1 : 11-12; Jer. 49 : 7-22; cf. pp. 148, 296) and in the language of the Psalms and Lamentations (Ps. 137 : 7; Lam. 4 : 21), Obadiah's vision gives expression to the age-long hatred of the Judeans for Edom, a hatred that grew all the stronger the more the Edomites pressed northwards and encroached on the territory of Judah (cf. Ezek. 35 : 1-11; 36 : 5). Even the rock-built citadels perched on the mountain-tops of Edom (amongst the highest in Palestine), those fortresses which had been the country's proud boast and sure defence from of old, will no longer avail to deliver it from its foes.

Since the brittle Nubian sandstone of Edom is easily worked and shaped, the Edomites were able to build their houses and fortifications in "the clefts of the rock", that is to say in rock-fissures high up the mountains. But the greatest achievements in this art were those of their successors, the Nabateans, who built the rock-city of Petra (the Rekem of the Old Testament), which, with what remains of its dwellings, temples and tombs, all cut with great skill out of the many-coloured sandstone, stands as a silent witness to the lives of those ancient communities. The centre of Petra is dominated by a great rock (Umm el-Biyarah) on the top of which were found potsherds and the remains of a settlement from the time of the Edomite kingdom. Photographed above is the tomb of a Nabatean king of the Hellenistic period which is called by the Arabs el-Khazneh, i.e. "the Treasury." On the left is another Nabatean tomb at the approaches to Petra, with four obelisks towering high above its entrance.

AND the exiles of Jerusalem who are in Sepharad . . .   (Obadiah 1 : 20)

The retributory oracles uttered by the later prophets against the nations are characterized by their expectation of the apocalyptic war between Gog and Magog and the subsequent restoration of Israel to its former glory (cf. pp. 198-199). Obadiah too eagerly awaits the coming of the Day of the Lord, when judgment will be passed on the nations and Israel will be redeemed (Obad. 1 : 15-17). He proclaims the glad tidings that the reunited people of Israel, Judah and Ephraim together, will rise victoriously against their wicked neighbours, who had tormented them in time of misfortune, and wreak vengeance upon them. The kingdom of David and Solomon will be restored as of old, and on the judgment day in the mountains of Jerusalem "saviours shall go up to Mount Zion to rule Mount Esau; and the kingdom shall be the Lord's" (ibid. 21). Then too will come the ingathering of the exiles of Judah dispersed in the distant regions of the north. From Obadiah's words we learn that, in his time, there were Judean exiles as far away as Sepharad. In rabbinical literature this place name was translated as Aspamia (i.e. the Iberian peninsula), an identification which passed into medieval Hebrew and thence into the modern language. Probably, however, the Sepharad of the Old Testament is the less remote city and district of Sardis (Sapparda in Persian) in Asia Minor.

Sardis, the capital of Lydia, was famous for its great wealth. In the Persian period — the time of Obadiah — it was the principal city of the second Persian satrapy and the seat of the Persian governor of Lydia. The ruins of the city, seen in the foreground of the photograph above, lie in the Hermos valley in western Anatolia, at the foot of Mount Tmolus which rises steeply in the background, its summit crowned by a citadel.

JONAH

BUT Jonah rose to flee to Tarshish from the presence of the LORD. He went down to Joppa . . .

(Jonah 1 : 3)

When the prophet Jonah was sent to make the dire proclamation of the coming destruction of Nineveh (see p. 253), he sought to escape from his distasteful task. Other prophets before him had at first shrunk back from the mission imposed on them (Ex. 3 : 11; Isa. 6 : 5; Jer. 1 : 6), but in the end they had all submitted to God's command; whereas Jonah persisted in his rejection of the divine summons and tried to flee far away from God's presence. He therefore went down to Joppa, with the intention of sailing across the sea. Joppa was one of the principal ports of Palestine in biblical times. In Egyptian documents from the second half of the second millennium B.C. and in the Amarna letters, it is referred to as one of the most important of the Pharaoh's dependencies in Canaan. In another Egyptian source, which is generally known as the Papyrus Anastasi I and which dates to the 13th cent. B.C. (see Vol. II, p. 55), Joppa is described as a bustling centre of merchants and craftsmen. At the end of the second millennium B.C., it came under Philistine control and remained a foreign city throughout the period of the Israelite monarchy. In Solomon's reign, the cedars of Lebanon used in the construction of the Temple at Jerusalem were sent "to the sea of Joppa" (2 Chron. 2 : 16), where perhaps the reference is to the mouth of the Yarkon which marked the boundary between the united kingdom of Israel and Philistia. In the time of Sennacherib, the Assyrian ruler (704-681 B.C.) Joppa was apparently within the confines of the kingdom of Ashkelon. After Sennacherib's campaign against Judah, it passed under Assyrian control (cf. p. 35). The Phoenician elements in the population now became so numerous that, in the Persian period, Joppa was considered a Tyrian city. When Zerubbabel set about rebuilding the Temple, cedar-wood was once more brought from Lebanon to the sea of Joppa (Ezra 3 : 7). Under the Hasmoneans, Joppa became a Jewish city and the port of Jerusalem.

The photograph shows the tell of Joppa, enclosed on the land side by the buildings of the modern city which lies on the only natural bay in the southern part of the Palestinian coastline. The remains of a settlement from the Late Canaanite period have been excavated on the site. The archaeological finds include the walls and gates of the Canaanite city, and an inscription of the Pharaoh Ramses II.

THE men rowed hard to bring the ship back to land ...

(Jonah 1 : 13)

The vessel on which Jonah embarked was no doubt one of the large ships which, in biblical times, sailed across the open sea. The Hebrew word used to describe it *(sephinah;* Jon. 1 : 5) shows that it had a deck *(sippun).* Ships of this kind, which were usually manned by Phoenician sailors, were propelled by both oars and sails (see p. 184; and cf. Vol. II, pp. 222-223). A single vessel might have as many as fifty to sixty rowers. The use of oars was known to the inhabitants of Crete in the Mycenean period (14th-12th cent. B.C.) and was taken over from them and perfected by the Phoenicians, who sailed the length and breadth of the Mediterranean in their ships, hugging the coast as they went. In a sudden storm, the crew would hurriedly furl their sails and row with all their might for the nearest point of land (Jon. 1 : 13).

The illustration is a relief of a ship on a panel discovered in the citadel of the king of the Dadanu at Karatepe, in Cilicia (second half of the 8th cent. B.C.). The ship has a rounded hull, like the Phoenician merchantmen (and in contrast to the long-hulled vessels intended primarily for warfare). The rowers, symbolically represented by two men, are sitting facing the stern which is portrayed as an inward turned horse's head. This, the customary figurehead of the oared vessels of Greece from the Minoan period onwards, was apparently preserved by the Dadanu, the latter-day descendants of Dedan, one of the "Sea Nations" (see p. 278). The prow of the vessel is in the form of a butting ram (cf. the ships on p. 182), which was also a common feature of the ships of the Aegean islands in the Mycenean period. The steersman is sitting in the stern, holding a goblet in his hand, while the captain is standing on the prow and scanning the surface of the sea. The figures of men and fish that can be seen underneath the ship call to mind the story of the prophet Jonah.

N_{OW} Nineveh was an exceedingly great city, three days' journey in breadth. (Jonah 3 : 3)

Jonah's attempt to evade God's command by flight (see p. 251) ended in his being brought back and in his after all proclaiming to Nineveh its imminent destruction: "Yet forty days, and Nineveh shall be overthrown!" (Jon. 3 : 4). From the prophet's words it appears that, in his day, Nineveh was at the height of its power and prosperity (ibid. 1-8; 4 : 11). This was the case in the period between the end of the 8th cent., and the end of the 7th cent. B.C.; that is to say, from the time the city became the capital of Assyria in the reign of Sennacherib, till its destruction by the Babylonian and Median armies (see p. 264). Nineveh stood on the eastern bank of the upper Tigris close to the river's ancient channel (the remains of the city are some distance from the river's present course), opposite the modern town of Mosul. The site of the ancient city is marked by two high tells: Kuyunjik, which is close to one of the tributaries of the Tigris; and Nebi Yunis (so named after the prophet Jonah), further to the south (see the picture below). The city itself was traversed by the tributaries of the Tigris (cf. the words of the prophet Nahum, 2 : 8: "Nineveh is like a pool of waters"). The remains of the wall, which are still visible above the surface of the ground, enclose an area of roughly oblong shape, about 3 miles in length and varying in width from $1\frac{1}{2}$ miles at its northern end to 1100 yards at its southern end (see the plan of the city at the top right). This means that the city had a walled-in area of no less than 2000 acres, which makes it very large by ancient standards.

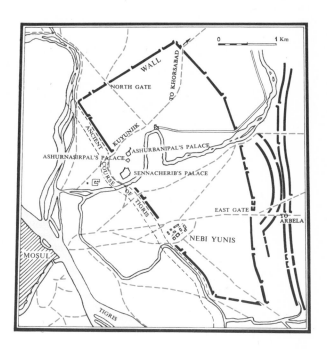

AND the LORD GOD appointed a castor plant, and made it come up over Jonah, that it might be a shade over his head . . .   (Jonah 4 : 6)

The castor-plant (Heb. *qiqayon; Ricinus communis L.*) is normally a bush, but sometimes attains the height of a tree. As it is extremely fast-growing and has leaves large enough to provide shelter from the burning rays of the sun, it was chosen to spring up overnight and give shade to the embittered prophet. Hence we are told: "So Jonah was exceeding glad because of the plant" (Jon. 4 : 6). The parable of the castor-plant is forcible and incisive. If the withering of this bush, which shot up quickly and effortlessly, upsets the prophet so much, how much the more will the Creator be distressed by the destruction of so great a city as Nineveh, "in which there are more than a hundred and twenty thousand persons who do not know their right hand from their left, and also much cattle" (ibid. 11). This parable gives expression to one of the central themes in the Book of Jonah: God's compassion for His creatures. Nineveh was not overthrown, because its inhabitants repented of their evil deeds (ibid. 3 : 5-8). The lesson of this is that it is never too late to repent, and that whole-hearted contrition may make atonement even for the sins of a city like Nineveh which, in the vision of another prophet, is ill-famed as "the bloody city, all full of lies and booty — no end to the plunder!" (Nah. 3 : 1).

MICAH

THE word of the LORD that came to Micah of Moresheth . . .   (Micah 1 : 1)

Micah's prophetic activity covered the reigns of Jotham, Ahaz and Hezekiah in Judah; that is to say, the first half of the 8th cent. B.C. Like his contemporary, Isaiah, Micah too sternly censures the perversion of justice and social oppression which were rampant in the kingdom. He denounces the nobles and judges who batten upon the simple folk (Mic. 3 : 2-3), blandly confident that the mere existence of the Temple in Jerusalem will absolve them from sin: "Is not the Lord in the midst of us? No evil shall come upon us" (ibid. 11). Hence the violence of the doom pronounced by the prophet: "Zion shall be ploughed as a field; Jerusalem shall become a heap of ruins, and the Temple Mount a wooded height" (ibid. 12; cf. Jer. 26 : 18).

Micah's birthplace, Moresheth Gath, was one of the cities of the Shephelah, in the region of Lachish and Mareshah, though its exact site has not been identified with certainty. On the basis of a statement in Byzantine sources, that a church to the east of Beth-Guvrin was called after Micah, it has been proposed to locate Moresheth Gath at the nearby Tell el-Jedeideh, one of the most important tells in the whole district, which dominates the road running from Lachish up into the Judean hills (see p. 256). Reproduced at the bottom of p. 257 is part of a mosaic map of the Holy Land, showing a section of the Judean hills between Beth-Zur and Beth-Guvrin. This map, which was found at Medeba in Trans-Jordan, is the earliest known example of Palestinian cartography (from the 6th cent. A.D.). Seen at the bottom right-hand corner of the reproduction is a picture of the city of Beth-Guvrin (Eleutheropolis), represented as a stronghold containing numerous churches. To the north of the city (on the left) a village is depicted with, beside it, the following inscription: "Moresheth, from which came Micah the prophet." Above the village there is a church, next to which are the first letters of another inscription: "Of (Saint Micah)."

I WILL make lamentation like the jackals, and mourning like the ostriches. (Micah 1 : 8)

One of Micah's first utterances was a prophecy against Samaria. The prophet denounces the northern capital for its sins — the impurity and sexual promiscuity of its idolatrous worship. The penalty to be paid by the kingdom of Ephraim for its crimes is its total destruction by Assyria which, under the rule of Tiglath-Pileser III (745-727 B.C.). was at time already casting the dreaded shadow of its power over southern Syria and Palestine (see pp. 212-213). Samaria, the pride and glory of the kings of Israel, will be razed to the ground: "I will make Samaria a heap in the open country, a place for planting vineyards; and I will pour down her stones into the valley and uncover her foundations" (Mic. 1 : 6). So vivid is this vision of utter devastation that the wrathful prophet from Judah is himself moved to compassion. In his grief, he mourns for Samaria like the ostriches, he laments and wails like the jackals whose far-echoing howls in the night make both man and beast shudder. The mournful, sobbing cry of the jackal is used symbolically in the Old Testament of a man lamenting his bitter fate (Job 30 : 29).

The jackal (Heb. *tan*; *Vulpes vulpes*; see the picture) is a carnivorous animal found in most parts of Palestine and in Egypt. It usually prowls by night, uttering its characteristic howls, in the vicinity of human habitation, where it finds the carrion and garbage which form its staple diet.

BUT they do not know the thoughts of the LORD, they do not understand His plan, that He has gathered them as sheaves to the threshing floor.

(Micah 4 : 12)

To his apocalyptic vision of the day of judgment, Micah appends a prophecy of consolation to Zion. On that day the Lord will gather the surviving remnant of Israel to Jerusalem, as a shepherd brings home his flock, and there He will rule over them for evermore (Mic. 4 : 6-8). But God's kingdom on earth will be ushered in by siege and war, with the armies of many nations converging upon Jerusalem to lay it waste (ibid. 11). The prophet evidently envisaged these nations in the form of the hosts of Sennacherib, the Assyrian monarch, which were advancing upon Jerusalem under the deluded belief that it was the Lord's will that they should destroy Judah (cf. Isa. 36 : 10). In fact, the Lord was bringing them there only to pass judgment upon them.
Micah describes the fate of these nations in a simile taken from harvesting. As the swaths (Heb. *amir* = the number of ears reaped at a single stroke, Jer. 9 : 22) are cut, the ears are bound into sheaves which are laid out all over the field. At the end of the reaping, the sheaves are loaded on to camels (see the photograph) or on to a cart (see p. 233), and brought to the threshing-floor to be threshed. Even such will be the fate of the nations who have been gathered in their multitudes around Jerusalem, only for the inhabitants of Zion to thresh them (Mic. 4 : 13).

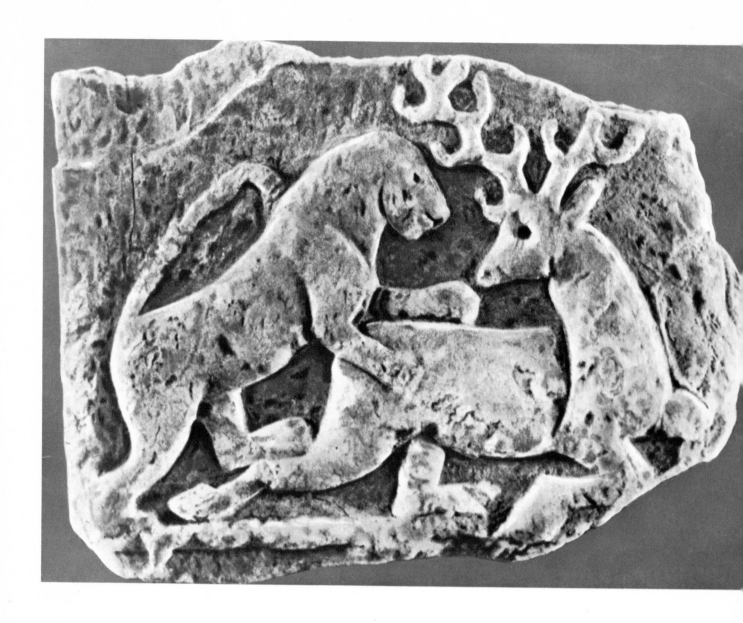

AND the remnant of Jacob shall be among the nations, in the midst of many peoples, like a lion among the beasts of the forest, like a young lion among the flocks of sheep, which, when it goes through, treads down and tears in pieces, and there is none to deliver.

(Micah 5 : 8)

Israel's future deliverance from the might of Sennacherib and his armies (cf. p. 259) is also depicted by Micah in another simile, this time from animal life. Not only will Judah be saved from its foes, but the remnant of Jacob will actually go over to the attack against Assyria: "They shall rule the land of Assyria with the sword" (Mic. 5 : 6). The prophet likens Zion to a lion and its cub that prey upon both the wild life of the forest and upon domestic animals (cf. Gen. 49 : 9; Deut. 33 : 22).

The art of the ancient East, and particularly that of Mesopotamia, is rich in representations of lions hunting their prey (see Vol. I, p. 120). Reproduced here is a fragment of a relief from the third millennium B.C. found at Kish, on which a lion is seen pouncing upon a stag. The victim is sinking to the ground under the weight of its attacker whose claws are already firmly fixed in its flesh, much as described by Micah: "it tears in pieces, and there is none to deliver."

ＡND I will cut off your
images and your pillars from
among you, and you shall bow
down no more to the work of
your hands.   (Micah 5 : 13)

Micah foresees the renewal of Israel's
belief in the one God, when the
surviving remnant of Jacob will trust
no longer in its old apparent sources
of strength, neither in man and the
works of man (Mic. 5 : 7), nor in
horses, chariots and fortifications, the
symbols of military might (ibid.
10-11), and when its idol-worship,
with all its sorceries, images and
pillars, will be no more. The prophet
is here referring to the popular religion that required no priests or
idolatrous pomp, but was essentially a
domestic cult performed within the
family circle. Most of the household
idols that the Israelites are to destroy
were apparently dedicated to the
goddess of fertility and were regarded,
especially by the women, as talismans
against barrenness. Such a cult was
widespread amongst the Canaanites
and subsequently took root in Israel
too, as indicated by the numerous
idols from the end of the second
millennium B.C. that have been excavated in Palestine, mostly in the
form of a nude goddess with prominent breasts (see p. 34).

The illustration is of one such clay
household image of the goddess of
fertility, from the period of the Judean
monarchy. The hands are supporting
the large breasts which emphasize the
idol's function. The goddess' hair has
apparently been carefully dressed (cf.
p. 23).

SHALL I come before Him with burnt offerings, with calves a year old? Will the LORD be pleased with thousands of rams, with ten thousands of rivers of oil? . . .   (Micah 6 : 6-7)

Micah, like other prophets, sets justice and humanity above formal worship and sacrifice: "What does the Lord require of you, but to do justice and to love kindness, and to walk humbly with your God?" (Mic. 6 : 8; cf. Hos. 6 : 6; Amos 5 : 24). He therefore pours scorn on those of his people who are mainly concerned about the performance of all the various kinds of sacrifice. The Israelite who in all sincerity wishes to perform God's will, but is too ignorant to understand how best to please his Maker, mistakenly thinks that God requires numerous and lavish sacrifices: burnt-offerings of calves, thousands of rams, libations of oil, and even human sacrifice (Mic. 6 : 7; cf. Jer. 7 : 31).
Scenes of sacrifice feature prominently in ancient Egyptian art (cf. Vol. I, p. 185; Vol. II, p. 115). The relief reproduced here is from the temple of Queen Hatshepsut at Deir el-Bahri, from the time of the Eighteenth Dynasty (beginning of the 15th cent. B.C.). On it row upon row of servants are seen bringing to the temple a rich assortment of offerings — produce, animals and birds.

NAHUM

AN oracle concerning Nineveh. The book of the vision of Nahum of Elkosh. (Nahum 1 : 1)

Nahum of Elkosh prophesied in Judah at the end of the 7th cent. B.C. He thus lived through one of the most critical periods in the history of the ancient East, when the Assyrian empire, which had been founded in the 9th cent. B.C., on the spoliation and oppression of conquered countries, was tottering to its fall. Its magnificent capital, Nineveh (see p. 253), was sacked in the year 612 B.C. by nations that only a few years previously had been its vassals. In Nahum's "oracle concerning Nineveh" the overthrow of the Assyrian capital is represented as an act of vengeance by the Lord, who appears on the day of judgment "in whirlwind and storm" (Nah. 1 : 2-6) to punish "the bloody city" (ibid. 3 : 1). The tidings of its destruction bring comfort to Judah and gladden the nations with the hope that it will never again reduce kingdoms to slavery (ibid. 2 : 13).

Fresh light has been thrown on "the oracle concerning Nineveh" by a Babylonian record, known as the Gadd Chronicle (after the English scholar who published it in the year 1923; see the reproduction), which recounts the wars of the Chaldean ruler Nabopolassar (625-605 B.C.), the founder of the Neo-Babylonian empire, and his victories over Assyria. From this document we learn that a decisive part in the overthrow of Nineveh was played by Nabopolassar's Median allies, led by their king Umakishtar (the Cyaxares of Herodotus' history). The chronicle describes the capture of Nineveh as follows: "They advanced up the bank of the Tigris ... (encamped) against Nineveh ... launched a powerful attack on the city, and in the month Abu the city was taken. They made great (slaughter) of the princes... They took a heavy weight of booty from the city and the temple, (and turned) the city into a mound and a ruin ..."

THE crack of whip, and rumble
of wheel, galloping horse and boun-
ding chariot! Horsemen charging,
flashing sword and glittering spear...
(Nahum 3 : 2-3)

With a few powerful strokes, the prophet paints a vivid picture of the destruction of Nineveh and of the great
slaughter in the Assyrian camp: "Hosts of slain, heaps of corpses, dead bodies without end" (Nah. 3 : 3). The
city was stormed by the enemy's chariots and horsemen (see p. 264). The power of this combined assault by
chariot and cavalry units (which formed part of all the armies of the Near East at that time) was such as to sweep
away any attempt at resistance by the foot-soldiers. Few of the opposing army survived such a devastating
charge, and even they, cowering in woods and ravines, were usually cut down by the hotly pursuing horsemen.
The illustration above is a section of the Bronze Gates from Balawat (9th cent. B.C.), showing the Assyrian
chariot-force in action. The chariots depicted here, with their six-spoked wheels, are still light vehicles. By
Nahum's day (end of the 7th cent. B.C.) they had become considerably heavier (with eight spokes to a wheel)
and "the rumble of wheel" made by them in full career must have been very loud. In the lower picture horsemen
are seen at full gallop, thrusting their spears and javelins into their desperately fleeing foes.

Nahum compares the downfall of Nineveh to the fate of Thebes, the capital of Egypt and one of the greatest and most famed cities of the ancient East. The kings of Assyria, in the course of their conquests, had reached the northern frontier of Egypt as early as the 8th cent. B.C., but were for a long time unable to penetrate into the interior of the country. After two attempts at invasion, the Assyrian monarch Esarhaddon (680–669 B.C.) finally succeeded in conquering Lower Egypt in the year 671 B.C., and divided it up into subject princedoms. However, the Egyptian kings of the Twenty Fifth Dynasty still continued to rule over Upper Egypt from their capital at Thebes, until Esarhaddon's son, Ashurbanipal, eventually advanced upon the city and took it by assault in 663 B.C. It is this famous conquest that is referred to here by Nahum. Ashurbanipal's own record of the victory runs as follows: "From Thebes I carried away booty heavy and beyond counting ... I pulled two high obelisks, cast of shining bronze, the weight of which was 2,500 talents, standing at the door of the temple, out of their bases and took (them) to Assyria." The reference here is to the metal obelisks that were placed at the entrance to Egyptian temples. Amongst the surviving examples, though in this case made of stone, are the monoliths which rose to the skies in the temple of the god Amon at Karnak (the temple quarter of Thebes), the ruins of which are seen in the picture on p. 267. This temple was built in the time of the Eighteenth Dynasty (second half of the second millennium B.C.) and, after various improvements and structural enlargements, served as the centre of the Amon-cult right down to Nahum's lifetime and the days of the Ptolemies.

Reproduced above is a relief from the palace of Ashurbanipal at Nineveh portraying the capture of an Egyptian city by the Assyrian army. The gate-fortress, with its upward tapering towers, can be seen in the centre. Instead of using heavy and unwieldy siege-engines, the Assyrian troops are breaking down the walls with picks and other breaching-tools. Screened by long (top left) or round shields (top centre), they are making their way up on to the walls by ladders, under covering fire provided by the bowmen. One soldier is setting fire to the gate with a lighted brand, protecting his back with his round, convex-shaped shield as he does so. In the procession of captives (bottom) Egyptians are seen with their wives and children; those with their hands and legs fettered are "their great men."

ARE you better than Thebes that sat by the Nile, with water around her . . . Yet she was carried away, she went into captivity . . . and all her great men were bound in chains.

(Nahum 3 : 8, 10)

DRAW water for the siege . . .
(Nahum 3 : 14)

The prophet's description of Nineveh's ordeal by siege is full of savage irony (Nah. 3 : 13-15). It is now the tyrant's turn to suffer the agony of thirst which formerly it had inflicted on the cities beleaguered by its hosts (cf. the words of the Rabshakeh, 2 Kings 18 : 27; Isa. 36 : 12). The provision of an adequate supply of water in time of siege was one of the most difficult problems confronting the cities of the ancient East. Since most of these cities were built on artificial mounds or on hills, the natural sources of water, whether springs or rivers, were outside their walls. The ancients were thus compelled to display considerable ingenuity in bringing the water from its source into the city by means of conduits cut through the rock, a feat calling for great engineering ability. Access to the conduit was provided by vertical shafts. Installations of this kind have been excavated at Jerusalem (see Vol. II, p. 169), Gezer, Gibeon, Ibleam and Megiddo. The conduit at Megiddo (see the upper picture), which is from the end of the Canaanite period, is approximately 230 ft. long and the shaft as much as 82 feet deep.

Another method of obtaining "water for the siege" is illustrated on a relief from the palace of the Assyrian monarch, Ashurnasirpal II (883-859 B.C.) at Calah (see the picture below). Here the inhabitants of the besieged city can be clearly seen drawing up their water in a bucket by means of a rope and drum set up on one of the towers. The besieging Assyrian soldiers are trying to cut the rope to which the bucket is attached.

HABAKKUK

FOR lo, I am rousing the Chaldeans, that bitter and hasty nation, who march through the breadth of the earth, to seize habitations not their own.   (Habakkuk 1 : 6)

Habakkuk prophesied in the days when the Chaldean empire was at the height of its power. The hopes raised throughout the Near East by the fall of Nineveh were quickly dashed when the conquering Chaldeans adopted the Assyrian methods of power politics and established a great empire of their own, also based on the oppression of subject peoples (see p. 122). In his oracle concerning the Chaldeans, Habakkuk is amazed by the doom in store for these peoples and their states with the rise of "the bitter and hasty" nation. Just as Isaiah and Jeremiah had proclaimed that the mighty idolatrous empires were merely the rod of God's wrath and that, therefore, their task completed, they would vanish from the world, so Habakkuk regards the Chaldeans as a nation sent by the Lord to deal out divine retribution to sinful peoples. Unlike Isaiah and Jeremiah, however, Habakkuk cannot resign himself to the dominion of Babylon (Jer. 27 : 6-7), and bitterly complains to God: "Why dost Thou make me see wrongs and look upon trouble? Destruction and violence are before me" (Hab. 1 : 3).

The Chaldeans of Habakkuk's description came to be used symbolically, by later generations of Jews, of any merciless enemy. Amongst the writings of the Sect of the Judean Desert, found at Qumran close to the western shore of the Dead Sea (from the end of the period of the Second Temple), there is a commentary on the Book of Habakkuk in which the prophet's words are applied to the sectarians' own history and the events of their own period. In this scroll the "Chaldeans" are interpreted as being "Kittim" — apparently meaning the Romans (cf. Dan. 11 : 30) — who come from afar, "from the isles of the sea to devour all the nations like a vulture that is never sated . . ."

The picture is a reproduction of the third and fourth columns of the Commentary of Habakkuk.

Is he then to keep on emptying his net, and mercilessly slaying nations for ever?

(Habakkuk 1 : 17)

The neo-Babylonian empire, which was founded in 626 B.C., quickly overthrew Assyria and thereby became mistress of all its subject lands (see p. 271). After their decisive victory over Egypt at the battle of Carchemish, the Chaldeans swept through the regions to the west of the Euphrates (Syria and Palestine) to make themselves the undisputed rulers of all the countries of the Fertile Crescent, from the Persian Gulf to the shores of the Mediterranean (cf. pp. 122, 145). In Habakkuk's prophecy, Babylon is compared to a fisherman who hauls up catch after catch in his net: "He brings all of them up with a hook, he drags them out with his net, he gathers them in his seine" (Hab. 1 : 15). Intoxicated by the dizzy speed of its victories and conquests, Babylon places its trust in its armies and bows down in worship to its own military power: "Therefore he sacrifices to his net and burns incense to his seine" (ibid. 16).

Amongst the relics of Mesopotamian art there are portrayals of victories in which the captives are shown wriggling in a fish-net. There was thus a pictorial equivalent of Habakkuk's fishing simile, as illustrated by the above reproduction of a fragment of a relief on a victory stele from the end of the third millennium B.C., found at Susa, the capital of Elam. Though the identity of the king who is holding the net full of captives cannot be known for certain, he was probably Sargon the ruler of Akkad (24th cent. B.C.) whose stele was carried off to Susa as booty.

A<small>ND</small> the L<small>ORD</small> answered me: "Write the vision; make it plain upon tablets, so he may run who reads it."

(Habakkuk 2 : 2)

Faced with the military successes of sinful Babylon, the prophet is sorely perplexed by the workings of divine providence. God's reply to his anxious questioning is given in the form of an obscure vision, inidcating to the prophet that he must simply hold fast to the faith in the eventual downfall of Babylon: "For still the vision awaits its time; it hastens to the end — it will not lie. If it seem slow, wait for it; it will surely come, it will not delay" (Hab. 2 : 3). At the same time, Habakkuk is commanded to inscribe the vision — which is the apparent meaning here of the Hebrew word *(baer)* translated "make plain" — on a tablet as a testimony for the days to come, when the prophecy about the overthrow of the idolatrous empire has been fulfilled.

Writing on tablets formed of cleaned and smoothed lumps of clay was practised in Mesopotamia from very early times. The marks on the tablet were made by pressing the triangular-shaped end of a wooden stylus into the soft clay. By a further downward pressure of the stylus, with its point still resting on the tablet, wedge-shaped marks were produced in various directions — vertically, diagonally and horizontally. Usually a group of such wedges form a single sign in what is now known as the "cuneiform" script (from the Latin *cuneus* = "a wedge"). When the writing was completed, the tablet was fired in an oven to make it resistant to damp and salinity — how successfully may be judged from the fact that these fired tablets have remained in a good state of preservation right down to the present day. The illustration is a modern imitation of a clay tablet inscribed in Babylonian cuneiform characters and signed with the impression of a cylinder seal. The writing could be dated by its shape as contemporary with the prophet Habakkuk.

A ND plague followed close behind.

(Habakkuk 3 : 5)

Habakkuk's prayer, in which the prophet describes the manifestations of God's might in nature, is similar both in form and content to such ancient Israelite epics as the Song of Moses (Ex. chap. 15) and the Song of Deborah (Judg. chap. 5; cf. Ps. 68 and 77). Like these songs, the language of the prayer contains poetic images of great antiquity, such as are also found in early Canaanite literature, especially in the Ugaritic sagas (cf. pp. 39, 105). Thus, the word *reshef* (here translated "pestilence"), refers in our verse to an all-devouring divine flame, followed by the plague *(deber)* (Hab. 3 : 5); but this image still contains overtones of the ancient Canaanite signification of the word, as found in the Ugaritic sagas where it is used as the name of the god of war who shatters his foes and lays low his rivals. This god was also worshipped in Egypt, as is shown by the stele reproduced above. On this relief, which was found in an Egyptian tomb from the time of the New Kingdom (second half of the second millennium B.C.) the god Reshef is portrayed with a beard, as befits an originally Canaanite deity. He is wearing an ornamented kilt which is held up by crossed shoulder-straps. On his head there is a conical crown with a gazelle emblem protruding over the brow. In his left hand he is holding a shield and spear, while with his right he is brandishing an axe, the symbol of his power and might.

ZEPHANIAH

"ON that day," says the LORD, "a cry will be heard from the
Fish Gate, a wail from the Second Quarter, a loud crash from
the hills. Wail, O inhabitants of the Mortar! ..."

(Zephaniah 1 : 10-11)

The central theme of Zephaniah's prophecy is his proclamation of the coming Day of the Lord, when both the
idolatrous nations and the sinners of Israel will alike be punished. Nor will the extortioners living in the various
quarters of Jerusalem escape the general destruction. The places mentioned in this prophecy of doom were in the
north and north-western parts of ancient Jerusalem, where the city's main commercial centres were located and
where the merchants' caravans from the coast and the mountains of Ephraim unloaded their wares. Since the
routes followed by these caravans were also those taken by invading armies, the inhabitants of these quarters
were the first to suffer from their attacks.

The Fish Gate (see Neh. 3 : 3; 12 : 39) stood in the northern sector of the city-wall and was so called because
through it fish was brought into Jerusalem (ibid. 13 : 16). The site of the gate is marked on the photograph
above by the figure 1. To the west of the Fish Gate lay the *Mishneh* (Second Quarter) (2). As its name implies,
this area was not part of David's city. The "Second Quarter" was a weak spot in Jerusalem's defences and the
wall which was erected around it after David's time had frequently to be reinforced; it was re-fortified by Uzziah
and again by Manasseh (2 Chron. 26 : 9; 33 : 14). The *Makhtesh* ("Mortar") (3), as its name indicates, is a kind of
natural bowl formed at the point where the valley which passes through the city from the north, at the modern
Damascus Gate (4), southwards in the direction of the Dung Gate (5) is joined by a secondary valley coming
down from the Jaffa Gate. The "Mortar" separates the Temple Mount (6) from the Upper City (7).

276

FOR Gaza shall be deserted, and Ashkelon shall become a desolation; Ashdod's people shall be driven out at noon, and Ekron shall be uprooted.
(Zephaniah 2 : 4)

Zephaniah's pronouncement of the coming destruction of the four Philistine cities is inserted into a message of consolation to Judah (Zeph. 2 : 7). The omission of Gath here (cf. Amos 1 : 7-8; Zech. 9 : 5-6) is explained by the fact that it had ceased to exist as an independent kingdom as early as the 9th cent. B.C. The remaining Philistine cities underwent various vicissitudes of fortune at the end of the 8th cent. B.C. Gaza and Ashdod suffered badly at the hands of the Assyrian ruler, Sargon, while Ashkelon and Ekron were punished for their revolt against Sennacherib. However, after Sennacherib's campaign against Judah (701 B.C.), Ekron, which was situated in the north-west of Philistia (and may perhaps be identified with Khirbet el-Muqanna; see map on p. 35), and Gaza were both permitted by the Assyrian monarch to enlarge their respective territories at Judah's expense.

Reproduced above is a relief from the palace of Sargon II (721-705 B.C.) at Dur-Sharruken (Khorsabad) depicting the capture of Ekron. The city's defenders are standing on its towers and firing with their bows at the assaulting Assyrian soldiers. In the centre of the picture two of the Assyrian auxiliary troops are seen crouching on one knee and aiming their arrows at the defenders. On the wall, inscribed in cuneiform characters, is the name of the city: Amqaruna.

WOE to you inhabitants of the sea coast, you nation of the Cherethites . . .
(Zephaniah 2 : 5)

The ancient smouldering enmity between Israelites and Philistines was once more fanned into open hostility in the 7th and 8th centuries B.C., in consequence of renewed Philistine attempts to encroach upon the territory of Judah (see p. 277). Clear traces of this enmity can be found in the pronouncements of doom uttered by the prophets of Israel (Isa. 14 : 28-32; Jer. 47 : 1-7; Amos 1 : 6-9; cf. p. 147), not least Zephaniah, who here calls the Philistines the "inhabitants of the sea-coast", in reference to their occupation of the coastal strip of Palestine. The other appellation used by the prophet, "nation of the Cherethites", is derived from an ancient tradition according to which the Philistines came from the island of Crete (cf. Ezek. 25 : 16). The racial affinities of the Philistines with the Aegean world are also borne out by other passages in the Old Testament and by archaeological finds (cf. p. 243, and Vol. I, p. 252; Vol. II, p. 193). Like the inhabitants of the Aegean islands and the ancient Greeks, the Philistines too appear to have been sailors and shipbuilders.

The reproduction below — which is taken from a painted Attic vase of the 8th cent. B.C. — represents a ship of the type in which the Aegean peoples sailed the waters of the Mediterranean (cf. p. 252). The prow is topped by the figure-head of a snake, and has a spike for ramming enemy vessels at its base. Inside the vessel the oarsmen are seated in two rows, one above the other. The captain's shield can be seen on the stern.

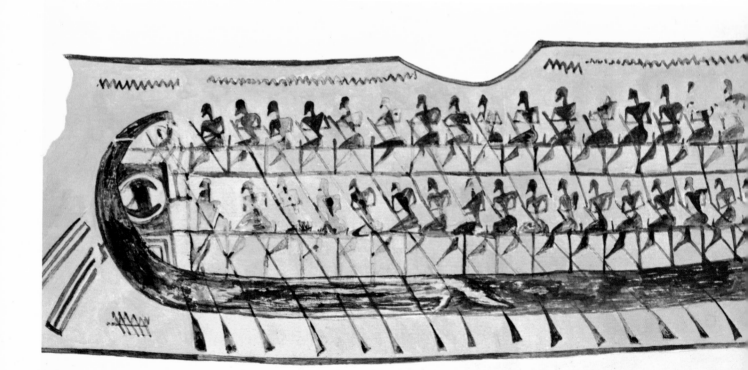

M OAB shall become
like Sodom, and the
Ammonites like Go-
morrah, a land possess-
ed by nettles and salt
pits, and a waste for
ever . . .

(Zephaniah 2 : 9)

Like other prophets (cf. pp. 40, 149), Zephaniah denounces Moab
and Ammon for their arrogance and their hostility to Israel (Zeph.
2 : 8-11) and foresees their utter destruction. So deep-rooted was
their hatred of Israel that it abated none of its ferocity, even in the
presence of the common danger of conquest by Assyria with which
all the peoples of the Fertile Crescent were menaced. This threat did
not deter Moab and Ammon from annexing areas on the eastern side
of the Jordan which were part of the territory of Judah (Zeph. 2 : 8).
For this the day of retribution will come, when they themselves will
be conquered by the remnant of Israel (ibid. 9) and turned, like
Sodom and Gomorrah, into a wilderness of desolation and "a land of
salt pits" (cf. Jer. 49 : 18). This word-picture brings to mind the well
known Mountain of Sodom which, with its huge supplies of salt, is
7 miles long and rises to a height of about 550 ft. above the Dead Sea.
In the above photograph of Mount Sodom, a smooth block of salt
can be seen rising sheer above the cave of Sodom. The upper and
lower strata of the mountain contain a mixture of gypsum, Lisan
marl and salt (cf. Vol. I, p. 61).

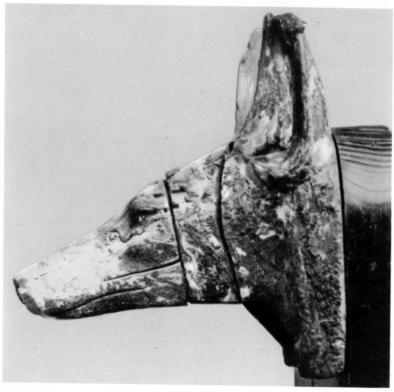

HER officials within her are roaring lions; her judges are evening wolves . . .
(Zephaniah 3 : 3)

Zephaniah castigates the leaders of Jerusalem, her rulers and judges, prophets and priests, for their sins. These notables, on whom devolved the just government of the city, had become brutal oppressors and murderers. The prophet therefore likens them to ravening wolves who devour their prey to the last morsel: "that leave nothing till the morning" (Zeph. 3 : 3; cf. Mic. 3 : 2-3). Ezekiel too compares the rulers of Jerusalem to wolves "tearing the prey, shedding blood, destroying lives" (Ezek. 22 : 27).

The wolf *(Canis lupus)*, which is used in these prophetic passages as a symbol of bloodthirsty cruelty, was common in Palestine in biblical times. To-day it is rarer, being found occasionally in the valleys of the country, in Galilee, in the region of the Dead Sea and in the Negev (see the upper picture). The cunning and agility of the wolf make it a great danger to flocks and herds, whether at pasture or in pens, especially when the beast attacks in packs. The exact meaning of the expression translated "evening wolves" *(zeeve erev)* in our verse here (cf. Hab. 1 : 8) is uncertain. One opinion is that the name refers to the wolf's habit of hunting its prey at dusk. But a more likely view is that the prophet is speaking of wolves that haunt the barren wastes of Palestine, as in the expression "a wolf from the desert" *(zeev aravoth;* Jer. 5 : 6). The lower illustration is a wooden wolf's head from the time of the New Kingdom in Egypt (second half of the second millennium B.C.).

HAGGAI

IN the second year of Darius the king, in the sixth month, on the first day of the month, the word of the LORD came by Haggai the prophet . . .   (Haggai 1 : 1)

Haggai, like his contemporary Zechariah the son of Berechiah, the son of Iddo (see p. 286), prophesied at the time of the return from the Babylonian exile, when the Persian empire, of which Judah was then part, was in the throes of an internal crisis. When Darius I ascended the throne of Persia in the month of Tishri, 522 B.C., revolts broke out in many parts of the empire — in Babylonia, Elam, Iran and Armenia — the repercussions of which were felt also at its western extremities, in Egypt and in Palestine. By 520 B.C. however, Darius had succeeded in consolidating his authority throughout the length and breadth of what eventually became the most far-flung empire ever known in the ancient East, which stretched from India to Nubia (cf. Esth. 1 : 1) and lasted for about two hundred years. According to our verse, Haggai began his prophetic mission on the first of Elul (August 29th), 520 B.C. — i.e. in the second year of Darius' reign. Though the revolts had already been suppressed by then, Haggai was apparently still profoundly affected by the memory of the political upheavals which had marked the beginning of Darius' rule. For the prophet, these dramatic events were a divinely appointed sign that the time had come to resume the work of rebuilding the Temple which had been broken off in the reign of Cyrus (Ezra 4 : 5).

An echo of those fateful years still reaches us from an inscription and relief of Darius' at Behistun, in southern Persia. Reproduced above is the central portion of the relief in which Darius is portrayed as a conqueror in all his glory (for a photograph of the inscription see p. 287). The king, bow in hand, is trampling upon the head of Gaumata, his principal foe in the early days of his reign and the rival contender for the Persian throne. Behind Gaumata stand other rebel leaders awaiting their fate. Above them is a winged sun, the emblem of Ahuramazda, the god of light, who is holding out to Darius a royal ring as a token of his victory and absolute power.

"I AM about to ... overthrow the throne of kingdoms; I am about to destroy the strength of the kingdoms of the nations, and overthrow the chariots and their riders; and the horses and their riders shall go down, everyone by the sword of his fellow."　(Haggai 2 : 21-22)

The convulsions by which the Persian empire was shaken at the beginning of Darius' reign (see p. 283) fired the Messianic expectations of the returned Jewish exiles. Haggai, for example, regarded the political revolutions and the military struggles which accompanied them as harbingers of the Day of the Lord: "Once again, in a little while, I will shake the heavens and the earth and the sea and the dry land; and I will shake all the nations" (Hag. 2 : 6-7). On this day the sovereignty of Israel will be restored in the person of Zerubbabel, the scion of David, the grandson of Jehoiachin, king of Judah who was deported to Babylon (1 Chron. 3 : 16-19), and the power of the gentile empires will be broken. Their downfall is symbolically represented by the overthrow of chariots and their riders in utter confusion (cf. Ex. 15 : 1, 21). Our verse here may contain an allusion to the hoped-for end of the Persian empire, since the kings of Persia, like their predecessors the Assyrian monarchs, were in the habit of making their public appearances in splendid chariots.

In the reproduction above — from the impression of a cylinder seal of Darius I (522-486 B.C.) — the king is seen hunting from his chariot, with his charioteer beside him. As a lion suddenly leaps out at him from the undergrowth, Darius quickly shoots his arrows into it. Another lion, already killed, has fallen under the horse's hooves. The inscription at the side records the king's name and titles.

ZECHARIAH

I SAW in the night, and behold, a man riding upon a red horse ... (Zechariah 1 : 8)

Zechariah the son of Berechiah, son of Iddo, was one of the heads of the priestly families that returned to Jerusalem from the Babylonian exile with Zerubbabel (Neh. 12 : 4). He began his prophetic mission while still young, a short time after his contemporary and fellow-prophet, Haggai (Ezra 5 : 1-2; see p. 283). Like Haggai, Zechariah also expresses his confidence in the restoration of Judah and the annihilation of its enemies, in the rebuilding of Jerusalem and the removal of the wicked nations from its midst (Zech. 1 : 12-17). But unlike the orderly clarity of Haggai's words, Zechariah's prophecy takes the form of a vision which conceals more than it reveals, as is the case with some of Ezekiel's visions. In a dream Zechariah sees a man on horseback with, behind him, other horses which have returned from patrolling the earth (cf. Zech. 6 : 1-8; and see Job 1 : 6-7) and now announce to the angel of the Lord that "all the earth remains at rest" (Zech. 1 : 11). This would appear to be an allusion to the quiet that reigned throughout the Persian empire after the victories of Darius over his foes (see pp. 283, 287); and also to the dashing of the hopes that the restoration of the kingdom of Judah would follow immediately on the decline of Persia's power.

The numerous references to horses and their riders in the prophecies of Zechariah — as in those of Haggai — may perhaps be explained by the prominent part played by these animals in the lives of the Persians, who were great horse-breeders. Representations of horsemen are known in Iranian art from the third millennium B.C. onwards; and the cavalry was the mainstay of the Persian army at all times. The illustration is one of the many terracotta figurines of turbaned horsemen that have been excavated on various Palestinian sites in strata belonging to the Persian period.

A<small>ND</small> they answered the angel of the L<small>ORD</small> who was standing among the myrtle trees,
"We have patrolled the earth and behold, all the earth remains at rest."   (Zechariah 1 : 11)

From Zechariah's vision of the horsemen (see p. 286), it would follow that peace was restored throughout the
Persian empire "on the twenty fourth day of the eleventh month which is the month of Shebat, in the second
year of Darius" (Zech. 1 : 7), i.e., on the 15th of February, 519 B.C. This is corroborated by an inscription and
relief that Darius had incised on a rock at Behistun, 328 ft. above the highway running from Ecbatana to Babylon
(see the photograph). The relief portrays the surrender of those who had revolted against the king (see pp.
282-283); while the inscription, in three parallel versions (in Persian, Elamite and Babylonian), recounts the story
of the political unrest in Persia during the first two years of Darius' reign (see Hag 2 : 6; and cf. p. 283), extolling
the feats of valour wrought by the king. In the course of a detailed chronological record of the events, Darius
boasts that, from the day of his accession, he has waged war against nineteen countries and subdued all his enemies
on every side. Indeed, the empire was virtually quiet again by the year 521 B.C., though after that date there
were still occasional outbreaks of revolt in its western provinces in Asia Minor and Europe. The text of the
Behistun inscription, in the appropriate language and writing, was sent to all the states and peoples of the empire.
A piece of the Babylonian copy survived in Babylon, and a fragment of the Aramaic text was found in the Jewish
military colony at Elephantine (Yeb).

ΑΡΩΝ

So they put a clean tur-
ban on his head and clothed
him with garments . . .
(Zechariah 3 : 5)

In his vision, Zechariah beholds Joshua the son of Jehozadak, the high priest, being tried before the heavenly hosts on an unspecified charge (Zech. 3 : 1-4). From the sequel it may be deduced that there is here an allusion to the quarrel that broke out in the early days of the return from the Babylonian exile between the high priest and Zerubbabel the son of Shealtiel, who as a scion of David (ibid. 4 : 6-10), is called "Branch" by the prophet in reference to his royal descent (ibid. 3 : 8; 6 : 12-13; cf. p. 119). In Zechariah's day Zerubbabel's status, as governor of a Persian province, was still higher than that of the high priest Later, however, after the rebuilding of the Temple, the priesthood took precedence. In Zechariah's vision, Joshua was cleared of guilt. The angel thereupon ordered that his filthy garments, which were the symbol of his sin, should be taken off him and that he should now be clothed in splendid raiment and a clean turban, to fit him for his officiation in the sanctuary (ibid. 3 : 7). Such is the dress in which the high priest Aaron is portrayed in a painting of the Tabernacle on the wall of the synagogue at Dura-Europus (from the middle of the 3rd cent. A.D.). There Aaron is shown standing above the wall of the Tabernacle, his head covered by a rounded turban. Draped over his shoulders is the brown "ephod", and under that is "the robe of blue", with a kind of "girdle" enclosing his waist. He is also wearing trousers, as prescribed for the priests by the Mosaic Law (Ex. 28 : 42). Even the "checker-work" of the coat can be seen in the painting. (For a detailed reconstruction of the garments worn by the high priest see Vol. I, p. 106).

NOW the people of Bethel had sent Sharezer and Regem-Melech and their men, to entreat the favour of the LORD . . . "Should I mourn and fast in the fifth month, as I have done for so many years?"

(Zechariah 7 : 2-3)

In the fourth year of Darius' reign (518 B.C.), when the work of rebuilding the Temple was in full swing, a deputation of Babylonian exiles came to Jerusalem to enquire of the priests and prophets there whether it was still necessary to observe the fasts that had been prescribed for the whole nation after the Temple's destruction, namely "the fast of the fourth month, and the fast of the fifth, and the fast of the seventh, and the fast of the tenth" (Zech. 8 : 19). Counting the beginning of the year from the month of Nisan, the Jewish sages identified these dates as follows (in the Talmudical tractate *Rosh Hashanah* 18b): the fast of the fourth month fell on the ninth of Tammuz, the day when the city walls were breached (2 Kings 25 : 3-4; Jer. 39 : 2); the fast of the fifth month was on the ninth of Ab, when the house of God was destroyed by fire (2 Kings 25 : 8-10); the fast of the seventh month was on the third of Tishri, the anniversary of the assassination of Gedaliah the son of Ahikam (ibid. 25; Jer. 41 : 2); and the fast of the tenth month fell on the tenth of Tebeth, which was the day when the king of Babylon laid siege to Jerusalem (2 Kings 25 : 1; Ezek. 24 : 2). In Zechariah's day, sixty eight years after the destruction, when the rebuilding of the Temple was almost complete, the question naturally arose whether the time had not come to annul these fasts, since Jeremiah's prophecy about the duration of the exile might well be thought to have been fulfilled: "Until the land had enjoyed its sabbaths. All the days that it lay desolate it kept sabbath, to fulfil seventy years" (2 Chron. 36 : 21).

This appeal from the exile to the priests of the Temple at Jerusalem, who were the spiritual leaders of the people in Judah, shows that the Jews of Babylon recognized them as the supreme authority in all religious matters. A similar query with regard to a religious festival is written on a potsherd from about the year 500 B.C., which was found at Elephantine in southern Egypt. The writer of this letter, who was living outside the centre of Jewish settlement in Elephantine, apparently asks one of his fellow-Jews residing actually inside the city about the date of the Passover festival: "Tell me when you are going to celebrate the Passover."

THE LORD of hosts will protect them, and they shall devour and tread down the slingers...
(Zechariah 9 : 15)

When the Messianic age dawns, the Israelites, with the Lord fighting at their side, will wreak vengeance on their foes (cf. Zech. 10 : 3-7). The prophet's description of this apocalyptic war is realistic in detail, the various weapons mentioned by him being amongst the most important used by the armies of the ancient East: the sword, the bow and arrow (ibid. 9 : 13-14), and also "sling-stones" — large pebbles or smooth stones from the bed of a watercourse (1 Sam. 17 : 40) which were shaped to fit into the sling (on the construction and use of this weapon see Vol. II, p. 140). But all these will be of no avail against the Israelites.

The sling was a long-range weapon, like the bow. Hence, in battle the units of slingers and archers were generally positioned side by side. The Dead Sea Scroll of "The War of the Sons of Light Against The Sons of Darkness" also mentions "standards of slingers", each of the soldiers grouped beneath which was armed with seven slingstones (column 5, lines 1-2). The way in which the slinger operated his sling is well illustrated on the reliefs of Sennacherib (704-681 B.C.) portraying the capture of Lachish, a section of which is reproduced here (for the complete relief see Vol. II, p. 286). The artist has drawn the slingers in the act of hurling their slingstones, each with a pile of reserve ammunition at his feet. This weapon was a menace not only to the defenders who fought from the top of the wall of a besieged city, but also to the inhabitants inside, since its high trajectory made it possible for stones to be shot over the wall into the city's streets.

"I WILL bring them home from the land of Egypt, and gather them from Assyria; and I will bring them to the land of Gilead and to Lebanon . . ." (Zechariah 10 : 10)

At the end of the apocalyptic war, the Lord will gather in the widely scattered exiles of His people. The house of Judah and the house of Joseph will be united as of old and they will all be mighty warriors (Zech. 10 : 6-7; cf. Isa. 11 : 11-16). In the prosperity that follows, the rapidly multiplying population will spread till it reaches the Lebanon and Gilead. The Lebanon (see the upper photograph) is referred to in the Old Testament as a symbol of strength, dignity and splendour (e.g., 2 Kings 19 : 23; Isa. 35 : 2), as are the mountains of Gilead. Hence the two are sometimes also mentioned together to denote power and pride: "For thus says the Lord concerning the house of the king of Judah: You are as Gilead to me, as the summit of Lebanon" (Jer. 22 : 6). In our verse too this combination may be intended to demonstrate the future power and glory of the Messianic kingdom of Israel.
The territory of Gilead in Trans-Jordan, with its good soil and abundant crops, was accounted one of the most fertile regions of Palestine, together with the Carmel, Bashan and the hills of Ephraim (Jer. 50 : 19). North of the river Jabbok the soil of Gilead is of the type known as "terra rossa" which is very suitable for agriculture; while the land to the south of the river favours both cultivation and pasture alike (cf. Mic. 7 : 14; Song of Sol. 6 : 5). Seen in the photograph below is the partly wooded northern section of the mountains of Gilead, with the cultivated fields of the Jordan valley at their foot.

ON that day the mourning in Jerusalem will be as great as the mourning for Hadad-Rimmon in the plain of Megiddo.

(Zechariah 12 : 11)

When the people of Israel behold the great salvation wrought for them by the Lord (Zech. 12 : 9), they will undergo a change of heart and be filled with a new spirit, "a spirit of compassion and supplication" (ibid. 10). Then they will return to the Lord their God and every family in Jerusalem will weep and lament (ibid. 12-14) for the past wickedness and idolatry of the land (ibid. 13 : 2). The sound of weeping and wailing that fills the streets of the city will rise to the intensity of the cries of grief uttered for Hadad-Rimmon in the plain of Megiddo. This comparison is sometimes explained as a reference to a public mourning for some notable dignitary. Such, for example, is the rendering of the Targum Jonathan in 2 Chron. 35 : 25. Hieronymus (5th cent. A.D.), on the other hand, interpreted Hadad-Rimmon as the name of "a city close to Jezreel which is to-day called Maximianu-polis," and which modern scholars locate at el-Lajjun near Megiddo. The modern Arabic name is derived from the Latin noun "legio", since it was here that the Sixth Legion *(Legio Ferrata,* the "Iron" Legion) had its camp from the revolt of Bar-Kokhba onwards (see the photograph). Situated on the "Sea Road", the place had great strategic importance as guarding the passage from the valley of Jezreel to the coastal plain. Still a third inter-pretation would refer the words of our verse to Hadad-Rimmon the god of rain and fertility (perhaps to be identified with Baal, the Canaanite-Ugaritic god of fertility), whose death was annually bewailed at the end of the spring, with the coming of the summer's shrivelling heat. A similar ritualistic lament was also uttered for Tammuz (Ezek. 8 : 14). The fertile plain of Megiddo would indeed have made an appropriate setting for the mourning over Hadad-Rimmon, since in Palestine the success of the crops depends on an adequate seasonal rainfall.

ᴀɴᴅ I will put this third into the fire, and refine them as one refines silver, and test them as gold is tested . . .

(Zechariah 13 : 9)

The process of refining metals, especially precious metals such as silver and gold, serves the prophets of Israel as a metaphor of the nation's spiritual purification (cf. Isa. 1 : 25; cf. pp. 101, 178). Thus, in our verse here, the remnant of Israel is compared to the small quantity of pure metal which is left after the smelting and refining: two thirds of the people will be cut off and perish, while the remaining third will be further reduced by being purified in the fire (Zech. 13 : 8-9).

The method of extracting pure gold from the silver and other metals mixed with it by constantly repeated firing was known at an early period in human history, perhaps as early as the first half of the second millennium B.C. A Greek author gives a detailed description of the way in which gold was refined in a porous clay vessel. The vessel, containing lead, salt and zinc in addition to the gold ore, was tightly sealed and then placed in a fired kiln for five days. During this time the dross stuck to the sides of the container, while the pure gold collected in its centre. From many passages in the Old Testament (e.g. Ezek. 22 : 21-23; Ps. 12 : 6) it would seem that this method, or one similar to it, was also the one used in biblical times. The processes of metal-working employed in the classical world are illustrated by a bas-relief decoration on a Greek goblet of the Hellenistic period (4th cent. B.C.), reproduced here. It shows the bearded smith-god, Hephaestos, seated in a smithy beside a kiln (at the left) and holding in his hand the tools of his craft, a pair of tongs and a hammer, which can also be seen hanging on the wall in the centre of the picture. The assistant on the right is carrying away finished articles.

T HEN the LORD will go forth and fight against those nations as when He fights on a day of battle. On that day His feet shall stand on the Mount of Olives which lies before Jerusalem on the east . . .   (Zechariah 14 : 3-4)

The Day of the Lord, the day when God will take vengeance on the nations that have done harm to Israel, is a conception that first occurs in the utterances of the prophets of the Assyrian and Babylonian periods (Isa. 25 : 6-9; cf. p. 259), and is repeated in the visions of their post-destruction counterparts (Ezek. chaps. 38-39). On this day the Lord of Hosts will appear in His glory on the Mount of Olives, the mountain that rises high above Jerusalem, to war against the nations and mete out retribution to them. At this awe-inspiring theophany, the whole mountain will shake (cf. Judg. 5 : 4) and be cloven asunder, as the earth was convulsed in the great earthquake that occurred in the reign of Uzziah, king of Judah (see p. 231).

The Mount of Olives — referred to by this name only here in the Old Testament (though a similar expression, "the Ascent of Olives", occurs in 2 Sam. 15 : 30) — is, in Ezekiel's words, "the mountain which is on the east side of the city" (Ezek. 11 : 23). The aura of sanctity which had enveloped it from the early days of Israelite history was in no way diminished in later times. Thus, in the period of the Geonim (8th-11th cent. A.D.), prayers were regularly offered up on the Mount of Olives, which faced the Temple Mount, and the Scrolls of the Law were carried round in circuit there on the festival of Hoshana Rabba, while its slopes were dotted with the tombs of the pious. The mountain rises to a height of 2710 ft. above sea-level, thus being as much as 330 ft. higher than the Temple Mount. Its soil — grey Rendzina — is well suited to the growth of olive-trees which thrust their roots down into the brittle rock. Hence, in the Mishna and Talmud it is called the Mount of Anointing.

The photograph shows the Mount of Olives, with the Brook Kidron at its foot and the village of Siloam rising up the slope. The Temple Mount and its wall can be seen in the left distance.

MALACHI

BUT I have hated Esau; I have laid waste his hill country and left his heritage to jackals of the desert..

(Malachi 1 : 3)

When Malachi entered on his prophetic mission at the beginning of the 5th cent. B.C., the fortunes of Judah were at a very low ebb. The returned exiles' hopes for the restoration of the kingdom of Judah, to be brought about by the rebuilding of the Temple, (see Hag. 2 : 18-23) had all been dashed, and the general disillusionment and apathy that followed found popular expression in such statements as: "It is vain to serve God. What is the good of our keeping His charge?" (Mal. 3 : 14). Taking issue with this prevalent mood, Malachi endeavours to raise the people's spirit by insisting that the Lord has no more ceased to love Israel than He has ceased to hate Edom. The hostility between Israel and Edom originated in the relations between the brothers Jacob and Esau (ibid. 1 : 2-3). Edom had been the enemy of the Israelites from the first days of their occupation of Palestine and throughout the period of the Monarchy. After the destruction of the Temple, the Edomites expanded northwards, till, at the time of the return from the Babylonian exile, they appear to have been in occupation of southern Judah as far as Beth-Zur and Hebron (which explains why the southern part of the country was called Idumaea by the Greeks and Romans). In the meantime, however, the Edomites had been driven out of their own territory by tribes from the Arabian desert who had invaded the mountains of Edom. Malachi here proclaims God's promise that, whereas Judah will arise from its ruins, Edom's destruction will be everlasting, and its mountains will remain desolate for all time as a memorial of the Lord's anger (ibid. 1 : 4; cf. p. 247).

The mountains of Edom are shown in the photograph above. Formed of multi-coloured sandstone and primeval rock, they rise to a height of 5000-6500 ft. above sea-level and cover an area roughly 120 miles long and 50 miles wide.

WHEN you offer blind animals in sacrifice, is that no evil? And when you offer those that are lame or sick, is that no evil? Present that to your governor; will he be pleased with you or show you favour? . . .
(Malachi 1 : 8)

Bitterly disappointed in the high hopes they had placed in the rebuilding of the Temple, the returned Judeans began to be remiss in their observance of the ritual commandments. The priests accepted from the people animals which had some physical defect and were therefore unfit for sacrifice, and offered "polluted food" on the altar, as if to say "the Lord's table may be despised" (Mal. 1 : 7-8). This gross disrespect for their divine ruler was in glaring contrast to the awe and honour shown by the people to their temporal governor (Heb. *pehah*), the Persian king's representative, for whose "allocation of food" only the best was good enough (cf. Neh. 5 : 14-18). The title *pehah* came into Persian from Assyria where one of the royal ministers was known as Bel-Pahati, i.e. the "possessor" of a province. In the bureaucratic terminology of the Persian empire, the title was applied to the provincial governors directly subordinate to the satrap, who was the military and civil ruler of one of the twenty administrative districts into which the Persian empire had been divided in the reign of Darius. In all probability Malachi is here referring to the *pehah* of the province called "Yehud". A high official of this kind is seen in the illustration above, which is a reproduction of a relief on the sarcophagus of a Persian governor found at Sidon. The Greek influence evident in the dress and facial features indicate that the relief is from the 4th cent. B.C. The governor is seated in royal state on a throne, with his feet resting on a footstool. He is wearing a Persian turban on his head and holding a sceptre.

BEHOLD, I will send you Elijah the prophet before the great and terrible day of the LORD comes.

(Malachi 4 : 5)

The noble vision of consolation, with which the Book of Malachi ends, forms a serene conclusion to the prophetical canon of the Old Testament. Out of the political despondency and spiritual darkness of his own days, Malachi looks confidently forward to the second appearance of the prophet Elijah who will establish peace in Israel, "before the great and terrible day of the Lord comes". Uttered by the last of the divinely inspired prophets of Israel, our verse proclaims that the spirit of the Lord will not depart from His people and that the tradition of revelation and prophecy will be renewed at the coming of the Messiah in the person of Elijah. Malachi, the last in the line of prophets who fought to make the word of God prevail, is thus directly linked to Elijah, the first of that devoted band, who, as the performer of miracles and the great harbinger of the Messianic age, became the hero of later Jewish legend.

The profound influence of Malachi's vision on Jewish thought can be found not only in the numerous allegorical interpretations of it in the Midrash, but also in Jewish art. The wall paintings at Dura-Europus on the Euphrates, from the middle of the 3rd cent. A.D., contain motifs from the Elijah legend. In the picture reproduced here, the prophet is shown in his contest with the priests of Baal on Mount Carmel. In the centre there is a large altar on which a garlanded bull is being devoured by flames descending from the heavens. At the right, conducting the sacrifice, stands Elijah dressed in Hellenistic fashion. Behind him there are three youths carrying jars of water to pour on to the burnt-offering and a fourth carrying wood (cf. 1 Kings 18 : 33). The three figures approaching the altar from the left (also dressed in the manner of the Hellenistic period) represent the people of Israel, who are drawing near to Elijah to witness the revelation of God's might on Mount Carmel (ibid. 18 : 30).

INDEXES

OBJECTS AND MONUMENTS

ISAIAH

REPRODUCTIONS

RECONSTRUCTIONS

by Eva Avi-Yonah: 44 (top), 45 (top), 67, 69, 85, 109 (bottom), 152, 163, 170 (right), 178, 201, 234, 240 (top), 278.

by I. Dunayewsky: 137.

MAPS

drawn by Eng. Pinhas Yoeli: 30, 32, 35, 122, 142, 148, 183, 203.

DRAWINGS

by Ruth Sofer: 200 (according to sketches of Dr. Haran)